National Types of Old Pewter

Cover photo courtesy of Mrs. Wendell W. Forbes

Plate I—An Array of Delights

On the top and bottom shelves are shown eight late seventeenth century, English flat-lidded tankards or measures, the small one on the top shelf and the one with spiked lid below being very unusual.

Behind these tankards, on the top shelf, from left to right, appear a 9½-inch plate salved from the Spanish galleon, sunk in Tobermory Bay in 1588; a 12-inch dish by Thomas Alderson of London, with the royal cypher of King George IV, at whose coronation banquet in Westminster Hall it was used, and in common with many other pieces from the same set, afterwards stolen by the spectators; a 9½-inch plate by Mary Redshaw of London, which bears the badge of Staple Inn, London, and is inscribed "Staple Inn, 1751."

On the second shelf appear two fine narrow-rimmed seventeenth-century plates, 8½ inches diameter; the one on the left being engraved with wriggled-work design, is probably some fifty years earlier than the other which is *c.* 1675. The fine Stuart-type dish in the centre is from Pittenweem Castle, and bears, with the date 1704, the impaled Arms of Durham of Grange, the impaled coat being caused probably by the marriage of cousins. From the general appearance of this dish it would appear to be a generation older than the date engraved upon it.

The centre candlestick is a very fine one, *c.* 1700, and the other two are described in the text of this volume. The small bowl with two handles is one of the very few absolutely genuine Scottish pewter quaichs in existence and is a magnificent example. The other two pieces on this shelf are standing-salts of the late seventeenth century and very fine pieces of their type.

The flagon on left of the bottom row is a fine Charles II example, and the handleless, unlidded pot to the right is engraved "Miles Roe at ye Coach and Horses in ye New Palace, Westminster," and is probably *c.* 1740.

(These pieces are all from the collection of Lewis Clapperton, Esq., C.A., of Glasgow, and the photograph was taken by Messrs. T. & R. Annan of that city, whilst they were on loan at the recent "Provand's Lordship Club Loan Exhibition of Antique Furniture," held at Glasgow in 1924.)

Distributed by Charles Scribner's Sons, New York

National Types
of
Old Pewter

a revised and expanded edition by
Howard Herschel Cotterell,
Adolphe Riff, and
Robert M. Vetter

with a new Introduction by Charles V. Swain,
Pewter Collectors Club of America

THE PYNE PRESS
Princeton

Introduction to the New Edition

Even though frequently looked upon as only a utilitarian metal, American pewter, has since early in this century, been experiencing increased popularity as a collectible. Concurrently, as with any such phenomenon, collectors and students have turned to research and analysis of the form, function, decoration and other such attributes, real or imagined, of the metal.

In time, a body of information is acquired such as pewterers' names, marks, locations and working dates, the value of which should be obvious to any collector. Equally or perhaps more important, a group of principles is developed which, through interpolation, allows insights into the men, their crafts and products beyond the who, where and when of a particular plate or tankard. J. B. Kerfoot's lament, "American pewter has been neglected," is no longer true. Since his pioneer treatise, *American Pewter*, was first published in 1924, the subject of that work has come into its own. Numbers of important public and private collections have been assembled, a superabundance of written material has been published, the sole purpose of which has been to research and document the lives and work of American pewterers from Joseph Copeland to Roswell Gleason and the Pewter Collector's Club of America, incorporated in 1934, is today a large and viable organization.

Untold hours of work have gone into the present state of knowledge about American pewter. Its collectors hold a fascination for the subject to the practical exclusion of its European counterpart but not exceptionally so, for the sentiment is returned by their peers in England and on the Continent. Collecting is after all, by definition, a personal experience and is done best when kept within the confines of a specific interest, one which has not only an intellectual interest but also a highly personal satisfaction.

In light of this, it is not surprising that precious little has been published for the American reading public which deals with pewter made outside this country. This is not to imply there is no information to be had on the subject. Indeed, quite the opposite is true; a number of important works have been published which study the history, development and national character of pewter made in several major European countries. Birger Bruzelli's *Tennjutare I Svrige* and Hans-Ulrich Hadeke's *Zinn* present thorough accounts of the growth and development of Swedish and German pewter, respectively. Hugo Schneider has done a very fine catalogue of Swiss pewter entitled *Zinn*, while Austrian pewter is dealt with by Robert M. Vetter and Georg Wacha in their book *Linzer Zinngiesser* and B. A. Duroff has probably done the best study of French pewter to date in his book *Étains Français*. However, these books are all written in their respective native languages and unless the American collector is multi-lingual, are of limited use to him. Of course, by virtue of our dominant English ancestry, no such language barrier exists with English pewter. Nevertheless, all the major European studies have been addressed to a "restricted," that is to say a Swedish, Dutch, French or English audience and their presentations are therefore necessarily in the nature of an historical treatment of the respective national types; little or no cross referencing exists between the pewter of the various countries.

In 1913 Robert M. Vetter and Howard H. Cotterell, the late dean of English pewter, chanced to meet, resulting in a friendship which was to last until the latter's death in 1936. "Out of a lively exchange of correspondence" between the two, cooperation developed which bore fruit as "a set of articles on European Continental pewter which we started publishing in *Antiques* in 1923. . . ."[1] The focus of their attention, along with that of Adolphe Riff, was to examine and compare Continental pewter with an eye to determining regional characteristics. Separately, Cotterell published a book entitled *National Types of Old Pewter* in 1925 which treats both British and Continental pewter in the same vein. Together, they form the content of this book and enumerate the salient points by which pewter of these various countries can be grouped geographically and temporally.

It might be argued that this has no relevance to American pewter but a critical examination of our pewterers' creations will conclusively disprove such a contention. American pewter did not come to be in a vacuum. In its form and ornament, it is invariably derivative from European prototype, England naturally having provided its greatest stylistic impetus. Comingled with this, however, were a number of important undercurrents which developed as a result of the immigration of Continental pewterers to America.

Such a man is John Will who emigrated from the city of Nieuwied in Germany about 1752 to New York City. Since the details of his life and work were recorded in volume I of Laughlin's *Pewter in America,* a number of new and interesting forms have been ascribed to him, not the least impressive of which are three remarkable flagons recently brought to light.[2] In form they are unlike anything ever known to have been produced in this country, yet their histories and stylistic peculiarities would indicate they could have been produced nowhere else.

An examination of the vessels pictured on page 15, figure 80, and page 57, figure 43a, discloses a more than coincidental relationship with those presently ascribed to Will. This bulbous-bodied type of flagon had been popular in Europe since the 15th century and would naturally have been a familiar form to the pewterer before his emigration to America. When faced with a request for such an important vessel after arriving in the Colonies, he logically recalled that traditional European type which he knew best. Interestingly though, he was apparently not insensitive to the less tradition-oriented English taste to which he most certainly was exposed after arriving in New York, for on all three flagons he used a handle, thumbpiece and lid derivative of English prototype (page 19, fig. 107). The resulting vessel, combining an old-style Continental European body with newer-style English derived embellishments is an important hallmark in the history of American pewter, yet one which would go unnoticed and unappreciated by American collectors without a sound basic knowledge of this flagon's multiple stylistic derivation.

Similarly, with the discovery that the Lancaster pewterer, ICH, was the German immigrant Johann Christoph Heyne, basic problems relating to the style of his pewter were raised. His flagons which incorporated a hollow-cast, bud terminal handle and elevated ball thumbpiece, could not be stylistically explained in light of Heyne's Saxon background or his exposure to and acceptance of the "English" influence when settling in Pennsylvania. The prototype was found when it was discovered that Heyne, after completing his apprenticeship, emigrated from his native Saxony to Stettin, a North German port which had close economic ties with Sweden. This exposure to Swedish influence proved to be the crucial factor which determined Heyne's preference of handle and thumbpiece, a combination unique in American pewter and coveted by collectors today.[3]

These are but two instances of the variety of influences bearing on American pewter. Numbers of additional examples remain unexplored and argue against a "national bigotry" on the part of American pewter collectors. It cannot be denied that American pewter is derivative but, by the same token, it is unique for it exists as a distillation of many influences bearing upon it in varying degrees. Whereas the fascination with English pewter lies in tracing its stylistic development through time, ours is in following the vigor and meld of its stylistic allegances. It cannot be fully understood or appreciated until these sources have been explored, isolated and defined.

The late Percy G. Raymond, who for years was a leading light of The Pewter Collector's Club of America and editor of its *Bulletin*, once remarked disparagingly of "Those monomaniacs who collected only American pewter."[4] This book offers another avenue to the subjects of his barb, collecting European pewter with a view to the exploration, isolation and definition of its national types as they affected our emigrant and native pewterers.

CHARLES V. SWAIN
May, 1972

Notes

[1] Letter, Robert M. Vetter to Alice Winchester, September, 1970. In addition to this series of articles, they also collaborated on similar works published between November, 1928 and April, 1931 in the short-lived magazine, *International Studio*, and a third group was published between March, 1933 and March, 1939 in *Apollo*.

[2] Charles V. Swain, "Three Flagons Attributed to John Will," *Antiques*, vol. CI (May, 1972), pp. 853-857.

[3] Eric de Jonge, "Johann Christoph Heyne: Pewterer, Minister, Teacher," *Winterthur Portfolio*, vol. IV (1966), pp. 168-184.

[4] Carl Jacobs, *Guide to American Pewter* (New York, 1957), "Preface," p. 13.

Contents

Foreword

There exist several excellent works on the pewter of Great Britain. An authoritative and comprehensive work on the pewter of America has recently appeared. For the amateur of soft metal wares who insists upon confining himself to the products either of the British Isles or of America such works are perhaps quite sufficient.

But the true amateur is usually characterized by a wide catholicity of taste; that, indeed, is the trait which distinguishes him from the specializing collector. He is the only genuine internationalist, for he harbors no prejudices. Objects of art appeal to him in the first instance by virtue of intrinsic qualities, which are rendered only the more attractive by a perceptible aura of the exotic. The pleasure which such specimens convey is a double one, compounded of the joy of recognizing merit and the more slowly unfolding satisfaction of distinguishing the subtle attributes which identify nationality and reveal authorship.

Pewterware is in itself peculiarly adapted to the requirements of the amateur. From earliest times to within a generation or two it has been an almost universal product of civilized society. Hence it is, even yet, everywhere to be encountered. Its texture and color are delightful; it appears in a fascinating multiplicity of forms. And lastly, since it is a ware largely of, by, and for the people, it carries with it always a strong savor of nationality.

Curiously enough, however, until Mr. Cotterell began the preparation of this book, it had, apparently, occurred to no one to outline the salient characteristics which distinguish the pewterware of one country from that of another, or the ware of Great Britain as a whole from that of the Continent in general and in particular. The performing of just that service is the purpose of the pages which follow. The treatment will be general, as must needs be where the subject is of such extended scope. For obvious reasons, all discussion of American pewter has been avoided. But the method pursued should enable the fairly ready classification of unmarked pewter according to its probable age, nationality, and relative desirability.

National Types of Old Pewter first appeared as a series of articles in ANTIQUES. The warmth of the reception accorded to its serial appearance fully demonstrated the advisability of preserving the material in permanent form for convenient reference. The text has, therefore, been carefully revised and corrected by the author. A number of illustrations have been added and an indispensable index supplied. As now presented to the public, the book will, it is hoped, constitute the auspicious beginning of a series of brief, authoritative monographs for amateurs and collectors.

HOMER EATON KEYES

Author's Preface

In the following pages I have endeavoured to give a serious and reliable lead to those lovers of old pewter who desire to know something more of the pieces in their possession, or of those which from time to time they may come across in their quest of the beautiful.

From my own experience as a collector, an experience covering nearly a quarter of a century, I know the wants of the genus collector, and these are not accurate analyses of the constituent parts of "fine" pewter, "lay metal" and such like, but some guidance as to the age, provenance, and make of his treasures.

Of course, to the serious collector, a nodding acquaintance with the constituent parts of various alloys is at least necessary; but instead of piling up page after page of these statistical tables, the average collector is better served by having before him such information as shall enable him to become familiar with treasures and able to recognize them when he sees them.

I hope, and sincerely believe, that a careful study of the notes which go to form the pages of the present monograph will prove of real assistance and that the book will fill a great hiatus in the existing literature on the subject of old pewter.

HOWARD H. COTTERELL

Croxley Green,
Herts., England.

Chapter I

IN an early number of the magazine ANTIQUES the Editor vouchsafed the following remark:

"Service is to be rendered by a writer who will summarize and illustrate the major characteristics whereby the nationality of pewter pieces may be determined with reasonable accuracy."

These words are responsible for this book. While much has been written about pewter, particularly about the pewter of the British Isles, no attempt has hitherto been made to assist the general collector in determining the nationality of examples which he finds either quite unmarked or with the mark virtually obliterated by wear and abuse.

In pewter work, as in other handicrafts, national peculiarities have a way of asserting themselves either in design or in tricks of technique. He would, indeed, be a rash critic who would undertake in all cases to distinguish these peculiarities and to assign an unmarked example with unqualified assurance to a specific locality and period. Yet, at the same time, he would hardly deserve to claim authority were he unwilling to state the fundamental considerations upon which, in any instance, he is likely to base his judgment. In the following chapters my endeavor will be to state just such fundamental considerations, which I shall emphasize with illustrative pictures.

Before, however, I proceed to my task, perhaps I may be permitted a word or two in praise of old pewter as a decoration, from the æsthetic point of view and also from its historical side.

Unlike silver and gold, pewter relies on no exterior ornamentation for its claim upon our veneration, yet the quiet, unobtrusive charm of a well-chosen and well-cleaned array, especially if displayed against its natural background, old oak, is one which speaks to us of " our ain fireside " and weaves into the flickering lights of blazing logs, memories of our ancestors and days long since gone by. It was for them their daily environment, and it will ever appeal to us on that account with a call which is well-nigh irresistible.

By way of illustration I give here a few examples of pewter so displayed. Figure 2 was taken in a former home of my own. The delightful little peep in Figure 1 must be nameless for the reason that it came to me without its owner's name, but is, I think, sufficient of itself to persuade the greatest sceptic into becoming a collector forthwith. Figure 3 shows pieces in the collection of Dr. Young of Manchester (England).

* * *

" Is it only nice people who collect pewter; or does collecting pewter make people nice? " So goes the *bon mot*. Be this true or not, the appreciation of pewter makes real

Fig. 1 — AN OAK DRESSER ARRAYED IN PEWTER
From an unnamed English interior.

Fig. 2 — PEWTER AND OLD OAK
" The quiet, unobtrusive charm of a well chosen array." *From the author's collection.*

Fig. 3 — ANOTHER CASE OF AFFINITY
An oaken surface of rich color almost inevitably becomes a place of such a congregation. *From the collection of Dr. Young, Manchester (England).*

Figs. 4, 5, 6, 7, 8 — "Rose and Crown" Marks

Where initials appear *in* the *Crown* or *on* the *Rose*, the piece is Continental. Figure 7 shows a British mark with an initial each side of the *Crown*; Figure 8 shows a British mark with the full name in a device that might suggest a crown. The other marks, *4, 5, 6,* are Continental and exhibit their peculiarities.

Figs. 9, 10, 11, 12 — Angel Marks

The *Angel* as a touch mark almost invariably indicates a Continental piece. *From rubbings.*

demand upon our powers of discrimination, and, when really developed, points to the possession of a truly artistic soul, capable of sensing beauty of form and outline.

Then again it appeals to us, and perhaps this is one of its strongest claims, on account of its antiquity. Before china, earthenware, enamelled-iron and other more or less modern inventions had been conceived in the mind of man, pewter was reigning in the height of its popularity; back through the days of the early Georges and Queen Anne, on through the Stuart dynasty and the troubled Cromwellian period, ever backwards through the reign of the virgin Queen and the days of bluff King Hal, and still we have not tracked it to its source, for is it not yet being found in the excavated sites of Roman towns and camps? And even there its roots are not!

History, aye and plenty of it, and personal association too! What of the dinner service bearing the arms of David Garrick, some specimens of which are in the fine collection of my friend Antonio de Navarro? Could they but speak, what tales those pieces could tell! The Carolean rose-water dishes with the arms of King Charles in enamels in the center . . . have they no tale to tell, no picture to conjure up, of dainty ladies moistening equally dainty fingers in the scented waters? . . . And so one could carry on the story; but space forbids and I must turn to my task.

* * *

Let us, then, consider a few facts which will enable us, at first sight, to recognize the country of origin of several well-known types; for a thorough appreciation of these facts will make many seemingly impossible mysteries vanish into thin air.

Initials in the Rose and Crown

First, then, we will take the mark of the *Tudor Rose and Crown;* and I lay it down as an incontrovertible fact that, where initials appear either *in* the *Crown* (*Fig. 5*), or *on* the *heart of*

the *Rose* (*Fig. 6*), such pieces are either of Belgian, Dutch, French, German, or Swiss origin. The same remarks apply to very small impressions of the *Rose and Crown* mark, similar to that shown in Figure 4.

After something like twenty years of the most careful study, I cannot call to mind a single instance where the initial letters of the maker's name appear either *in* the *Crown,* or *on* the *Rose,* on an American or a British piece. There are a few instances of the full names appearing *in* a crown shaped device (*Fig. 8*), and of initials appearing at the *sides* of the *Crown,* on British pieces (*Fig. 7*), but that is all.

Here then, to begin with, is one all-embracing test by which two very considerable portions of all the pewter still in existence may be separated with certainty and without a trace of anxious questioning.

Three or More Initials: Continental

A second test for European—as opposed to American and British—pewter, is the appearance of *three or more* letters, either in the maker's touch itself, in the *Rose and Crown* mark, or in the imitation silver-marks (or as we call them, for want of a better name, "hall-marks"). I do not think there are three exceptions amongst all the known British marks.

Angel Marks: Continental

A third indication of European origin is the use of an *Angel's* figure for the device in the maker's mark (*Figs. 9, 10, 11, 12*), or the "hall-mark." The *Angel* may be flying, standing with palm branch in hand, typifying Peace, or as Justice with sword and scales, or what not; but, if she is there, the piece is of European origin broadly speaking. There are some half dozen British marks wherein the *Angel* appears, but there is no mistaking her when once the student has become familiar with her Continental sister.

Hammer Marks

Finally—but on this so much reliance cannot be placed as on the foregoing—

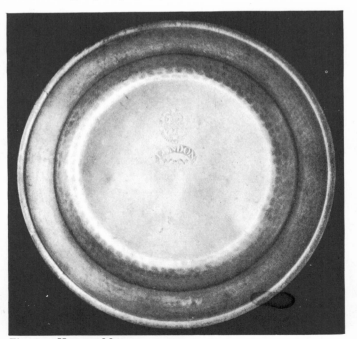

Fig. 13 — Hammer Marks

The clearly visible marks of the hammer on the flanks of this London piece are characteristic of British pewter, and of well made Continental pieces also.

the absence of hammer marks around the underside of the edge of the well of plates and dishes, points to their *not* being British pieces. At the same time it must be remembered that many Continental pieces were likewise hammered: in some French specimens very beautifully, not only around the well, but all over it, and also on the rim.

Eagle and Flag

Thus, even in the types of marking, we are able to discriminate between British and European, whereas most of the known American marks bear, as the device, either the *Eagle*, the *Stars and Stripes*, or both, or the name of the maker in a rectangle, with sometimes his address; but both of these latter are frequently met with on British pieces too. Of course the *Eagle* also appears in many British marks, but here, again, there is no mistaking him for his American cousin, once both have been compared.

The line of demarcation between American and British pewter is perhaps the most difficult of all to draw. Many of the vessels of the two countries are in some ways expressive of their nationality, but this applies more especially to those for holding liquids. Where plates and dishes are concerned, however, it is a different matter; for in both countries the same types were in vogue. Nevertheless, I am bold to say that there are very few instances

Fig. 14 — TANK-ARD AND THUMB-PIECE

The thumbpiece displays characteristics indicative of nationality.

of *British* plates or dishes extant today on which there is *no* sign of a maker's mark, and perhaps the surmise in the editorial note of ANTIQUES (Vol. II., p. 199) is correct, that where these are unmarked, they are of American origin: though, of course, many of the American pieces bore very fine marks. Many European plates are unmarked.

Ornament as a Guide

Let us now turn from the markings to such adornments of pewter as point an unerring finger to the country of origin. In this connection we have many things to guide us.

Of course, type itself is one of the best guides to the connoisseur of experience; but my efforts, at the moment, are directed towards putting before the *would-be* connoisseur, such power of information as shall — by rolling away the stones of doubtfulness and thus clearing the lonely furrow which each of us has trodden or must tread — form the solid basis whereon future self-confidence shall rest.

Let us turn first to the *thumbpieces* of flagons, ewers, lidded tankards and similar vessels.

By *thumbpiece* is meant that upward projection from the lid, which acts as a purchase to the thumb when it is desired to raise the cover either for drinking purposes or for pouring out the contents (*Fig 14*). These thumbpieces take many forms, and several of them are indicative of well-defined localities (large or small as the case may be). We will proceed to consider them individually; with a description and illustration of each distinct type.

Fig. 15

Fig. 17

Fig. 16 — SCOTCH TAPPIT-HEN Compare with Figure 15.

Fig. 15—NORMAN-DY FLAGON

Note the Continental thumbpiece. This type of flagon is sometimes mistaken for the Scotch tappit-hen. See Figures 16 and 17.

Fig. 17 — SCOTCH TAPPIT-HEN

This crested type is later, yet rarer, than the uncrested one above.

Fig. 18 — DOUBLE ACORN THUMBPIECE
The lid of the flagon shown below. The heart shape is characteristic of Continental pewter.

Type 1. The "Double Acorn" Thumbpiece

This type *never* appears on anything but European pewter and it is here shown in two positions; one as a complete flagon, back view, the other displaying the front and the heart-shaped lid (*Figs. 18* and *19*) *which latter also never appears* on any but European pieces.

This thumbpiece and lid are very often, though not invariably, found together. The flagon shown is of the Guernsey (Channel Islands) type, which type strangely enough is sometimes found with English makers' marks, having been made by them for export thence and to Normandy. But the type is a purely Continental one.

I feel that I must here call attention to a widely accepted but very flagrant error of which many young collectors are guilty, and dealers more so; the misdescribing of Normandy Flagons (*Fig. 15*) as Scotch Tappit-hens (*Figs. 16* and *17*). As will be seen from a comparison of the illustrations, the Normandy flagon has a heart-shaped lid with "Double Acorn" thumbpiece, whereas the tappit-hens have domed lids, a deeper upper lip, no spreading base as in the former; and the thumbpiece is

Fig. 19 — DOUBLE ACORN THUMBPIECE
The flagon is of the Channel Islands type, with the distinctive thumbpiece which is never found on anything but European pewter.

entirely different, having more the characteristics of the German types to which reference will be made later.

Moreover, let it be noted that there are two varieties of tappit-hen; the uncrested, or earlier variety, and the crested or later type. The word crested refers to the presence, or otherwise, of the knob on the lid; and strangely enough the crested type, though the later, is far the more difficult of the two to obtain.

One other point in this connection. The true Scots tappit-hen held a Scots pint, which is the equivalent of three English pints and is some eleven inches high. There are many smaller ones and one or two larger sizes of the tappit-hen shape, but the word tappit-hen can only rightly be applied to the Scots pint size. Figures 20 and 21 show the exceptionally fine sets of this type in the collection of my friend, Lewis Clapperton, Esq., C.A., of Glasgow.

The true tappit-hen has, inside the neck and a little way down, what looks like a pimple or blister in the metal, but this is placed there by design and not by accident, and denotes the point of full-measure; it is called the "plouk" or "plouck."

Type 2. The "Ball" Thumbpiece

Of this there are several kinds, but their segregation into their respective localities will be made easy by a careful study of the remarks and illustrations which follow.

We will take first the European types, of which there are the German and the Scandinavian. The German embraces several more or less similar kinds, all of which will be readily recognized by assimilating the details of the two shown in Figures 24 and 26, from which it will be noted that these thumbpieces are very large in size, often too much so for the place they occupy. In Figure 24, for example, the size of the ball gives to the whole almost a top-heavy appearance. The ball is seldom less than three-fourths of an inch in diameter and it is frequently very considerably larger.

The one of which we are speaking shows a very usual type, with narrow fillet around the center and a small projecting finial on the top. The bold outward sweep of the handle in this piece is also characteristically German; whereas that in Figure 26 is more reminiscent of the French types. The ball in the second illustration is, it will be noted, a plain sphere with incised spiral lines radiating down the upper half, from the base of a small decorative upper finial.

In both the illustrations, let it be noted further, the ball does not rest directly on the lid—or rather on the hinge—

Fig. 20 — TAPPIT-HENS
Exceptionally fine sets, crested and uncrested.
From the collection of Lewis Clapperton, Esq.

Fig. 21 — TAPPIT-HENS
The two lidless examples are known as the Aberdeen type of tappit-hens and were made without lids.

Fig. 22 — BALUSTER MEASURES
   The "Ball" thumbpiece is here at its best.

Fig. 23 — ENGLISH STUART TANKARDS
   Amateurs try to glorify the Scandinavian pieces into Stuart tankards such as these.

connection—but is raised from it on a short stem as on footed cups and chalices.

From a study of these two pieces, all others of the same nationality will at once be recognized. One of the chief characteristics of the "Ball" thumbpiece being its "overpowering" presence.

The Scandinavian type, Figure 25, is not a true "Ball" thumbpiece. In fact, although many are more clearly spherical than the one illustrated, they never present a perfect sphere, but one more or less flattened; yet it is difficult to include them in any of the other types. The handle, usually decorated in fashion similar to that of the illustration, is of pleasing design; but compare the acute bend with the full curve of that in Figure 24. This type is often confounded by beginners with the English Stuart tankards illustrated on the left-hand side of Figure 23.

Leaving the Continental European varieties we will now consider the purest of all the "Ball" thumbpieces, illustrated in Figure 22, which shows four fine little Scotch baluster-measures from the collection of Mrs. Carvick Webster of Monkton. Here we have the ball at its best; simple, dignified, restrained; seeking nothing from extraneous adornment, but content to leave its own simplicity and super-evident fitness for its purpose to make its mute appeal to

the imagination. I know of no type of pewter vessel which seems more eminently suited to the metal in which it is fashioned than is this measure; and though at one time such pieces must have been in use in large numbers in certain parts of Scotland, they are by no means easy to acquire.

This ball ranges in diameter from about three-eighths to half an inch, never larger, and, as will be seen, there is not the slightest risk of mistaking it for the European kinds. And, whereas the latter appear on all kinds of flagons, tankards, and ewers, this little Scotch fellow spent all its days in faithful allegiance to its first love, the baluster, as shown in the illustration.

Identification by Style

In considering style as a guide to dating pewter, whether as indicated by thumbpiece or by handle, it is always well to bear in mind that pewterers were often accustomed to follow the designs of contemporary gold- and silver-smiths. It is also well to remember that many pewterers, particularly those of Scotland, were often conservative, and followed the designs originated by their forebears, rather than creating new styles.

Fig. 24 — THE "BALL" THUMBPIECE
   A German example with a top-heavy ball.

Fig. 25 — SCANDINAVIAN THUMBPIECE
   This is **not** a true ball in any sense.

Fig. 26 — A GERMAN EXAMPLE
   Similar type to Figure 24.

Plate II — TANKARDS (*English, seventeenth century*)

Engraved wriggled work design. Compare the thumbpiece of the upper tankard with those shown in Figure 23. The thumb-piece on the tankard to the right consists of two love-birds, respectively, beak to beak. *Owned by Ernest Hunter and John Richardson.*

Chapter II

Type 3 — The "Shell" Thumbpiece

Fig. 32—DETAIL OF FIGURE 33

TWO distinct varieties of this type are known, and one sub-type, which has come to be known as the "Embryo-shell."

Again we will take the European first. But, unfortunately, I measures (on which latter, however, it is more usual to find Type 4). I have never come across it on the pewter of other countries.

Figure 29 shows the Scotch "Shell" thumbpiece, which appears on the pear-shaped measures of that country.

Fig. 27 — SHELL THUMB-
PIECE
The Continental type, detail of which is shown in Figure 28.

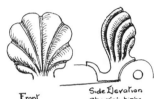

Front
Elevation

Side Elevation
Showing hinge
& lid attachments

Fig. 28

Fig. 33 — EMBRYO-SHELL
Well named, since it displays only the form but not the radiations of the developed shell.

have been unable to get a really good photograph to illustrate it; but Figure 27 will show its main characteristics, and perhaps my sketch (*Fig. 28*) will serve for the details, which, of course, vary somewhat in different specimens; though the main characteristics are the same in all.

Here is a big, bold shell, some seven-eighths of an inch across, and generally of a pleasing and well set-up form, some specimens being very massive and well suited to the hard wear to which they were subjected. This is a very common thumbpiece on Dutch and Flemish pieces, and is met with occasionally on the cylindrical French wine

Fig. 29 — SCOTCH SHELL
Less vigorous than the Continental type.

It is but about half the size of the one just described, much less accurately fashioned and far less adapted to hard wear. It appears on both the Glasgow (*Fig. 30*) and the Edinburgh (*Fig. 31*) types. And here let it be noted that the main difference between these two latter is in the cover; for, whereas the measures of Glasgow origin have a domed lid, either single or double as the case may be, the Edinburgh lids have sloping concave sides.

The "Embryo-shell" is well shown in Figures 32 and 33. It is a most appropriate name, coined by the late L. Ingleby Wood, author of that splendid volume *Scottish Pewterware and Pewterers*. This thumbpiece, which is shell-shaped, as will be seen from the illustrations, is quite plain and displays no such radiating flutes as the others.

Type 4 — The "Bent-back-wedge" Thumbpiece

This is well shown in Figures 34 and 35. It consists of a wedge-shaped piece of pewter with a backward curve, and of rectangular section, "growing" out of the hinge-attachment.

Fig 35

Figs. 30 and 31 — SHELLS OF GLASGOW AND EDINBURGH
Glasgow measures show domed lids; Edinburgh covers have sloping, concave sides.

Fig. 34 — BENT-BACK
WEDGE
Characteristically French.

Figs. 36, 37, 38, 39, 39a — ERECT THUMBPIECE
First two German; last three English. Though similarity of thumbpiece might confuse, there is no mistaking the short German handles for English ones.

This I think one must put down as a purely French type, though isolated examples of Flemish influence one would expect to find where two countries are so closely associated.

Type 5—The "Erect" Thumbpiece

Shall I call it this? I can think of no more fitting name; and the difficulty of an exact description will at once be seen by reference to Figures 36 to 39a, which I have chosen as representative examples, the first two being German and the last three English. It will be seen how very similar these are, yet there are slight points of difference, for in the German pieces one will note that there is a distinct break in the curves at both the back and the front, forming, as it were, a square in the profile, as indicated by the arrow in Figure 37a. This is not so apparent in the English ones. Moreover, the thumbpieces on the latter are very often pierced through with a heart-shaped pattern. This is almost invariably the case in flagons of the kind shown in Figure 39, and is shown fairly clearly in Figure 39a.

However, quite apart from the thumbpiece, the handle will generally give the deciding vote in case of doubt as to nationality; for such short handles as those shown in Figures 36 and 37—reaching barely half way down the drum — are unknown in British pewter.

One occasionally finds a similar, though smaller, thumbpiece of this type on flagons emanating from the Low-Countries; and a comparison with the thumbpieces on the tappit-hens, illustrated in Figures 20 and 21, will show more than a nodding acquaintance with it in Scotland.

Figure 38, examples of which are in existence dating back some three and a quarter centuries (one is known to

Fig. 37a

the writer bearing the date 1601) presents one of the earliest existing types of British pewter flagon. These flagons were always stalwartly made, to which perhaps is attributable the fact of their having come down to us through so long a period of time.

Type 6—The "Embryo Double-Volute" Thumbpiece

One can think of no better name for this type, for, though it does not correspond exactly to the Ionic Volute, it, nevertheless, would seem to be evolved from it. And, as if to confirm the thought that this design was in the minds of the earlier pewterers, we find it more faithfully reproduced in the " Double-Volute " baluster measures which will be described under Type 10.

Both the pieces figured under this type are British. Indeed, this thumbpiece would seem to be confined almost entirely to British pieces, for I have seldom come across it elsewhere. Figure 40 shows a fine example of it on a Stuart English flagon of most pleasing type (*circa 1660*), a type eagerly sought for by collectors. Figures 41 and 42 show the back and front view, respectively, of its Scotch analogue, wherefrom it will be seen that the thumbpiece is more flatly modelled but still carries out the main characteristics of the volute design.

At this point, I feel we must leave the subject of flagons and thumbpieces, and, as a stepping-stone on our way to the wine-measures of various countries, give a passing glance at the national thumbpieces of jugs and tankards, though the word " jug " as applied to pewter sounds as utterly wrong as it does to speak of a china " flagon."

On the continent of Europe one does not find the same allegiance to the *tankard* as is to be met with in England,

Figs. 40, 41, 42 — EMBRYO DOUBLE-VOLUTE
The first and more suave type is English; the more uncompromising, Scotch.

Figs. 43 and 44 — BRITISH THUMBPIECES
The first is William and Mary; the second George III; and the last two George II.

Fig. 45 — GEORGE III

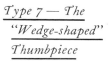

Fig. 49 — LEAF
THUMBPIECE

Fig. 50 —
GEORGE IV

where it seems almost a part of the constitution! Let us, therefore, merely illustrate a few typically British thumbpieces which are to be found on tankards and "jugs." These are given in their order of date, in so far as possible.

Figure 23 shows late Stuart to early Georgian examples from the collection of Richard Davison, Esq.; Figure 43 is William and Mary, from the collection of Walter G. Churcher, Esq.; Figure 44, left, is late George III; right, are two early Georgian, from the author's collection; and the seven pieces in Figure 45 are also in the Churcher collection, and are George III; and Figure 50 is George IV. There are, of course, other types, such as the expanded leaf or flattened shell, whichever title suits it best (*Fig. 49*), from a piece in the collection of Ernest Hunter, Esq., of Chesham-Bois; and others, which, however, space forbids me to describe in detail. So we pass on to a short consideration of the thumbpieces of English measures,

the Scotch and European types having been already reviewed under the preceding ones.

This final group is made up of the English baluster measures, which are four in number, though the last of all displays two varieties.

It will be well to state here that baluster measures *always* have *flat circular* lids, as opposed to the heart-shaped European type, and, with the exception of the Scotch flagon, illustrated in Figures 41 and 42, wherein the lid though round has a very slightly raised centre, they are the only known measures which possess this feature.

Type 7 — The "Wedge-shaped" Thumbpiece

This is found on the earliest-known form of the English baluster, and is extremely rare. Not more than half a dozen of this type are known to exist at the present time. This type is well shown in Figure 48, and, as will be seen, consists of a wedge-shaped piece lying, as it were, on its side on the lid, with a slight projection at its uppermost point to give a purchase to the thumb.

Pieces with this thumbpiece date back at least to the time of Henry VIII and are generally in a more or less battered condition, with traces of what looks like gilding. In reality this is oxidation caused by the action of the air on the surface of the metal.

Type 8 — The "Hammer-head" Thumbpiece (Figs. 46 and 47)

This is another early and rare type, which has the appearance of a double-faced hammer, laid sideways on the preceding type, which it superseded. Specimens are in existence which bear the date 1670, but it came into being at an earlier period.

Type 9 — The "Bud" Thumbpiece

This type followed the preceding one and is distinguished by its being somewhat in the form of an opening bud or fern frond. It is not easy to show well the thumbpiece and lid attachment together, so I have endeavoured to put it before my readers satisfactorily in Figures 51, 52, and 53.

Figure 53 is taken from an unique little measure in the collection of Major John Richardson, D.S.O. It has, around the handle, several narrow bands, each stamped with a crown and the letters G. R. (for Georgius Rex), evidently applied at different times to show that its capacity was up to the standard when tested by the government inspector.

Fig. 46 — HAMMER HEAD
An early and rare type.

Fig. 47 — BALUSTER MEASURE
The appropriateness of the name is evident. All baluster measures have a flat, circular lid.

Fig. 48 — WEDGE SHAPE
Extremely rare.

Figs. 51, 52, 53 — THE BUD

Plate III — Gallon Baluster Measure (*English, c. 1716*)

A fine example of the "Bud" type. *Owned by F. N. Miller.*

Chapter III

Type 10 — The "Double Volute" Thumbpiece

ONCE seen, this type (*Figs. 54* and *55*) will not easily be forgotten, for there is nothing like it elsewhere. It appears on the latest type of English balusters, which came into being about the beginning of the eighteenth century and remained as the prevailing type for upward of a century.

This thumbpiece is *always* attached to the lid by a fleur-de-lys, but whereas, on the larger sizes (gallon down to half pint), this fleur-de-lys is as shown in Figure 54, it appears on the smaller sizes on a diamond-shaped piece of

Figs. 54 and 55 — DOUBLE VOLUTE

metal, as shown in Figure 55, a feature which, as will be seen in Figure 56, is repeated on the body at its junction with the lower sweep of the handle.

Another innovation which came in with this type is the bulbous terminal at the lower end of the handle, which, up to now, had ended in the flattened curve, as in Figure 51.

The foregoing would seem to cover all the recognised types of thumbpiece which it is necessary to consider here; and it will be found that they alone are sufficient to define the nationality of nine out of ten of all the lidded vessels

which the average collector is likely to come across.

Lidless Types

We shall, therefore, now turn to a short consideration of some unlidded types; and, first, we shall speak of what many people describe as " toast and water jugs " (*Figs. 57* and *58*), so called because of the strainer in the lip, which, however, was placed there in order to keep back the hops or other solid material when pouring out the *ale;* for these were ale-jugs and are far too plentiful today to admit of the theory of toast and water — which has never been in great vogue with the healthy Britisher as a form of sustenance.

Figures 49 and 59 show the lidded variety of this vessel, the latter being inserted here merely for a comparison of its shape with that of Figure 60, which is a New York piece, bearing the mark of Boardman & Hart, and which, but for the depressed upper portion of the handle and the overlapping junction therein, seems to bear out much the same main features.

Figure 60a shows a fine series, half-quartern to gallon, of the type which was common in England from the reign of George IV to Victoria and is even in use in many places at the present day.

Figure 61 shows a set of unlidded baluster measures, which, from the bulbous terminals to the handles,

Fig. 62 — BALUSTER MEASURE

Added rim to change capacity.

Fig. 56 — DOUBLE VOLUTE THUMBPIECE

Showing diamond-shaped plate at junction of body and lower sweep of handle.

Figs. 57, 58, 59, 60 — ALE JUGS

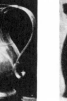

Fig. 60a — LIDLESS MEASURES

A fine series from a half-quartern to a gallon. Common during the nineteenth century.

Fig. 61 — BALUSTER MEASURES

Lidless type; but shape of handle and its terminal betrays double volute period.

Figs. 63, 64, 65 — HANDLE TERMINALS (*Scotch and English*)
First two are Scotch. "Fish-tail" terminal of third shows English make.

Fig. 66 — THISTLE-SHAPED MEASURE (*Scotch*)
The bulb affords a thrifty means of holding back some of the contents of the measure.

will be recognised as of the double-volute period. Figure 62 shows another of this period, but with an attached band around the upper edge of the lip, which has been added to convert it from the old wine capacity to that of the imperial standard.

Figures 63 and 64 show types of handle terminals peculiar to Scotland, wherein the one appears as a blunt end and the other as a rudimentary split end. Had these been English, each would have had a fish-tail terminal, as in Figure 65.

Figure 66 shows a great rarity, the Scotch "thistle-shaped" measures. Though by no means an early type, these are extremely hard to find, very few examples being known to exist at the present time. It is presumed that they were condemned on account of the ease with which a portion of the spirits might be retained from each customer by not tilting them sufficiently to insure the complete emptying of their contents.

Figure 67 shows another very rare series of measures, known as Scotch "pot-bellied" measures, from Mrs. Carvick Webster's collection (as are also those in Figure 61 above). This set is quite unique and I should not know where to look for another set to illustrate. The name is anything but dignified, and, were it not for the fact that it is so generally ac-

Fig. 67 — POT-BELLIED MEASURES (*Scotch*)
A very rare series.

Figs. 68, 69 — ENGLISH AND IRISH MEASURES
The first two are of a type peculiar to the neighborhood of Bristol, England. The third is an Irish "haystack."

cepted, one would attempt to create something a little less grating on one's feelings; but I am afraid it is too late.

Here we must revert to an English type for comparison with an Irish one. Figure 68 shows a very fine gallon measure of a type which, with slight variation, seems to have been confined to Bristol (England) and its district. Figure 69 shows a smaller one compared with an Irish "haystack" measure of which a set of six (half-gallon to half-noggin) are shown in Figure 70. The latter are from Mr. Clapperton's collection and Figures 68 and 69 are from Dr. Young's.

These haystack measures, which lay claim to no very great antiquity, are eagerly sought after, owing to their pleasing form; but they are very hard to obtain, especially in the larger sizes.

Figure 71 shows another type of Irish measure, of which four or five sizes are known. This shows a distinct relation to the baluster family, but is minus the handle and lid. No other use of the baluster shape in Ireland is recorded.

Continental Types

Let us now consider a few European types, and first, those emanating from the Channel Islands. Figure 72 illustrates a series which were in use in Jersey, and Figure 73 the same type without lids. Those shown in Figure 74 emanate from Guernsey, and while similar in shape and detail to the others, have the added feature of bands around the body. These Channel Islands measures are

Fig. 70 — HAYSTACK MEASURES (*Irish*)

Fig. 71 — IRISH MEASURE
Made without lid or handle.

Fig. 72 — CHANNEL ISLANDS TYPES

Fig. 73 — CHANNEL ISLANDS TYPES
These and the measures in Figure 72 are from Jersey.

generally of very pleasing design, well made, and of good metal. Frequently they bear the marks of London makers, though, as has already been stated, they were never used generally in England. They form, as it were, the connecting link between the English and the French types. Figure 72 shows pieces in the collection of Frank Creassey, Esq., Figure 73 in Mrs. Carvick Webster's, and Figure 74 in the collection of W. D. Thomson, Esq., of Birmingham, England.

The next four illustrations show the French cylindrical styles. In Figure 75 the lid, it will be seen, rests *on* the sloping collar. In Figure 76 it falls *inside* the collar; whereas, in Figure 77, the collar has gone en-

Fig. 74 — GUERNSEY TYPES
Similar to Figures 72 and 73 but with bands around the body.

Fig. 75 — FRENCH MEASURES

tirely and a raised lid has taken its place. Figure 78 shows the lidless variety of measure of this latter type. All these types were of quite good metal and well made.

In Figure 79 is shown a lidded measure with a shell thumbpiece from the Netherlands. The variants of this form are, however, so numerous as to forbid anything approaching a detailed dissertation. But the one shown will do for all. Many of these are of exquisitely simple de-

Fig. 79 —
NETHERLANDS MEASURE

Figs. 76, 77 — FRENCH MEASURES

sign and beautiful lines, carrying out precisely one's conception of what an all-round useful, and at the same time beautiful, jug ought to be.

Turning to Swiss pewter, Figure 80 shows two fine wine flagons from the district of Wallis and known as " Walliserkantli." Figure 84 shows one of these latter in actual use by a party of Swiss guides in native setting. Figure 81 shows a circular screw-topped wine can from the Zurich district, and Figure 82, an hexagonal screw-topped wine can from Schaffhausen and a beer mug from Central Switzerland.

Before leaving the subject of Swiss pewter I should like to illustrate a charming little group of that country's wares (*Fig. 83*). This photograph was sent to me before the World War by a very valued correspondent, Mr. Richard Wetter of Winterthur, Switzerland, from pieces in his own collection. From this little group will be seen what a great feature was made in Switzerland of rococo design, which spread even to the chocolate pots in the bottom row.

Fig. 80 — SWISS " WALLISERKANTLI "

Figs. 81, 82 — WINE CANS AND A BEER MUG (*Swiss*)

Fig. 83 — SWISS PEWTER

The flagon, third from the left on the top row, is of the Bernese type and the fifth from the left is a "biberon" for children to drink from. It emanates from the Zurich district. The rest of the pieces would seem to need but little explanation, consisting mainly, as they do, of plates, salts, candlesticks, and soup-tureens of characteristic Swiss rococo patterns.

In Figure 85 is shown an urn of Dutch manufacture, made by G. Hendricks of Alkmaar. This piece is some twenty inches high and has three brass taps and a wooden knob on the lid. These pieces are still to be obtained and are always of Netherland origin: I cannot call to mind ever having seen one of any other nationality. Some of them are quite well made, but often the slender feet seem ill-adapted to carry the great weight of the vessels when full. Many of them have, in fact, collapsed in consequence of being over full.

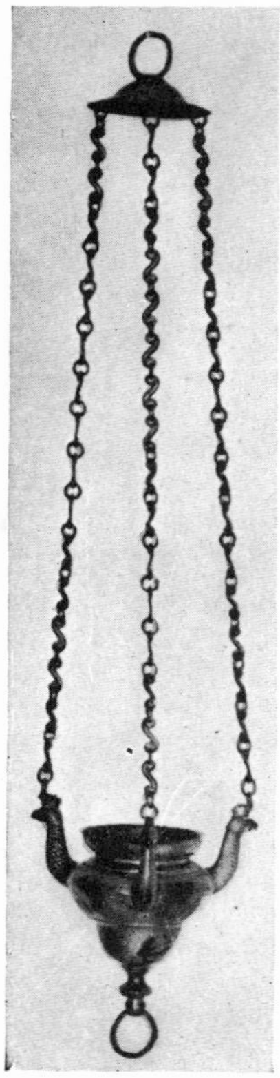

Figures 87, 88 and 89 show three types of altar candlesticks for use in churches of the Roman Catholic faith on the continent of Europe. Figure 89, it will be noted, has images in relief of our Saviour and the Blessed Virgin, and the modelling of the pillar is very pleasing, though the same cannot be said for the base, which would have been improved by a wider spread of the foot, as in Figure 88, where the feeling of top-heaviness is less evident.

Figure 86 shows a very pleasing and graceful Continental shrine lamp, presented to the author by Charles G. J. Port, Esq., F.S.A., of Worthing. Its country of origin is obscure, some connoisseurs saying that it

Fig. 84 — A QUESTION OF TASTE
These Swiss guides seem more concerned with the flavor of the Kantli's content than with the shape of the vessel.

Fig. 85 — DUTCH URN

emanates from Spain, though I have yet to see a piece of Spanish pewter which is thoroughly authenticated.

NOTE—The great number and variety of pewter measures of one kind and another illustrated in these articles serve to emphasize the fact that, until the nineteenth century, pewter was largely used for measuring both dry goods and liquids. Oil, wine, and beer, Massé* tells us, were the fluids most commonly measured in pewter vessels, which, because of their ability to stand rough handling, proved highly convenient. Some of the terms used to denote different measures will bear elucidation. Previous to 1707 one Scotch pint was the equivalent of three English pints. Half a Scotch pint was known as a *chopin*, which, in turn, consisted of two *mutchkins*, each equal to three English *gills*, though four Scotch gills were required to constitute a mutchkin. The English *quartern* is a quarter of a pint, *i.e.*, a gill. A *noggin* is likewise approximately a gill. This is usually associated, in literature at least, with spirituous liquors; the old toper's noggin of rum or gin representing about half an ordinary drinking glass.

*The Pewter Collector, H. L. J. Massé, New York, 1921.

Figs. 87, 88, 89 — CONTINENTAL CANDLESTICKS

Figs. 86 — SHRINE LAMP
Continental, but of uncertain nationality.

Chapter IV

Fig. 89a — BAPTISMAL BASIN
(*Scotch*)
Dating from about 1800. Supported in its original wrought-iron bracket.

Ecclesiastical Pewter

IN the previous chapter I had a word to say concerning altar candlesticks and a shrine lamp. Other types of vessels devoted to sacred usage are the bénitier, or holy-water container; the baptismal basin; the flagon; the chalice; the paten, etc.; and we shall now proceed to consider a few of each type in the order named.

Bénitiers are found in a great variety of forms, but they are always surmounted by some sacred image or emblem. The water-container, as will be seen in Figures 91, 92 and 93, is at the base, above which appears, in some instances, the figure of our crucified Saviour, perhaps with figures of angels or cherubim at either side of the shaft of the cross. In other cases this figure is supplanted by the Blessed Virgin or by a representation of the Last Supper or by other similar motifs, in relief.

Bénitiers are made either to hang or to stand; and, more often than not, they do both. They are invariably of European workmanship, often crudely made; but occasionally are very beautiful in both their design and their workmanship. Owing to the weight of the container when full and to the fragile nature of the backs, they are seldom found unrepaired at the point where the upper-part joins the well.

The baptismal basin was in common use in Scotland, many examples still being in existence, some of them in their original setting. One of these I am fortunate in being able to illustrate here, in Figure 89a, supported in its original swinging wrought-iron bracket, which it was customary to affix either to wall or pulpit. The bowl itself bears the mark of Archibald & William Coats, who were Glasgow pewterers working round about the year 1800.

In Figure 90 are shown two mid-eighteenth century bowls of this type, the smaller one bearing, on the underside, the words "Sutton-Benger, 1761." It is evidently from the church in that village, though an enquiry which I made through the Vicar could elicit no definite information on this point. It is six and five-eighths inches in diameter and two and a quarter inches in depth (an unusually small size for this type), and bears the mark of Ash & Hutton of Bristol. Both these pieces are in the collection of Mrs. Carvick Webster.

The communion flagons used in England have varied considerably in shape from time to time, each type, broadly speaking, having obtained for a time and then been supplanted by what must have been regarded as "an improvement" in design. Looking backward, however, as we are now able to do, over the period of three and a quarter centuries, we are rather tempted to reverse that opinion and to range flagon designs in an ascending scale of ugliness. There are exceptions to this method, it is true, but *who* can prefer the ones shown in the later illustrations to those of earlier type?

In Scotland the shapes have remained more fixed, and deservedly so, for who can cavil at the form of any of the three which I illustrate (*Figs. 94, 96* and *97*)?

Fig. 90 — BAPTISMAL BASINS

Figs. 91, 92, 93 — BÉNITIERS
While occurring in a great variety of forms, these holy-water basins are always surmounted by a sacred emblem.

Figs. 94 and 95 — COMMUNION FLAGONS
The example at the left is Scotch, that to the right is Irish—the only type definitely assignable to that country.

Each makes its own appeal to the imagination, and in none is extraneous ornament "dragged" in to the detriment of beauty of line.

Of Irish flagons but one definite type is known, and I illustrate the example in Figure 95. It has been found both with and without a lid and is of a fine, bold type, reminiscent of the English flagon shown in the centre of Figure 101, but bearin the more modern adornment of the encircling bands around the body. The English one is about a century earlier.

This Irish example bears the mark of Roger Ford, who, in 1752, was in business in Cook Street, Dublin. It is one of a pair which now find sanctuary in the collection of Francis Weston, Esq., F.S.A., of Croydon.

Figure 96 shows an early type of Scottish communion flagon which, as will have been observed in the course of previous chapters, was also in use for domestic purposes. A pair of this exceedingly rare type are in Brechin Cathedral, bearing the date 1680.

Following this, and for some little time coeval with it, came the slightly tapering cylindrical flagon with very slightly domed circular lid shown in Figure 97, a type which remained in general use for at least a century and a half and is by no means obsolete to-day. Mr. Port has one bearing the date 1702 and with the slightly projecting point on the front of the lid, which was a feature of the earlier ones of this type; and I have come across many bearing marks of nineteenth century pewterers.

Fig. 96 — COMMUNION FLAGON
(*Scotch*)
Late seventeenth century type.

Fig. 97 — COMMUNION FLAGON
(*Scotch*)
Eighteenth and nineteenth century type.

Fig. 98 — C O M M U N I O N
FLAGON (*English*)
Unique example. Second half of seventeenth century.

This last variety was to a certain extent supplanted by the elegant flagon illustrated in Figure 94, a vessel full of dignity in every line and comparing more than favourably with the English examples of about the same period. This piece, some thirteen inches in height, is in the collection of Major John Richardson, D. S. O., of Falmouth, and bears the touch of Graham & Wardrop, Glasgow pewterers of about 1790–1800; but it has all the bearing of an early eighteenth century model.

I will now, as briefly as may be, illustrate the characteristic types of English flagons, the earliest of which, *circa* 1600, is shown in Figure 99. This magnificent example is, or was until quite recently, in its original place in Combmartin Church, Devonshire. How beautifully it illustrates the simplicity of the earlier pewter! How eminently suited to withstand hard usage and the ravages of time! Let us hope that it may never be permitted to leave the sacred fane which has sheltered it through these three and a quarter centuries, during which long period of time how many a stalwart son of Devon must have received strength and courage from its life-giving contents!

Next in point of age, *circa* 1650, is the one shown in Figure 100, also from the collection of Major Richardson. This piece resembles the foregoing in its main characteristics, but already displays the pewterer's growing tendency to depart from the simple lines of his forebears.

Figure 101 shows three fine flagons from the Carvick Webster collection, the centre one bearing, on the handle, one of the earliest marks recorded on the existing touch plates of the Pewterers' Company of London, being

Fig 99 — COMMUNION FLAGON
(*English*)
Early seventeenth century.

Fig. 100 —COMMUNION FLAGON
(*English*)
Mid-seventeenth century.

Fig. 101 — COMMUNION FLAGONS (*English*)
Seventeenth century types.

Fig. 102 — "York" Communion Flagon
That to the left is dated 1725 and bears an inscription of which a rubbing is shown in Figure 103.

Fig. 103

Figure 109 (and again I have laid Major Richardson's collection under contribution) illustrates a type in vogue from *c.* 1775–1810. This particular example is one of the earlier ones of its type and of fine metal, but shuns comparison with its Scotch contemporary shown in Figure 94. To close the series, I illustrate two examples which alone are sufficient to demonstrate that decline of artistic feeling in designing these vessels to which reference has already been made. Figure 110 (again from the Richardson collection) and Figure 111, are beyond comment, except to say that the former is of a date *c.* 1800 and the latter, which bears the mark of Watts & Harton of London, is *c.* 1825.

* * *

coeval with the foregoing; whereas the two larger ones must be considered a decade or so later in date.

Another fine flagon from Major Richardson's collection appears in Figure 98. As a type this is quite unique; but, from its general form, we know it to be of the second half of the seventeenth century.

Following this we come to another beautiful and extremely rare type, which has come to be known as the "York" flagon, Figure 102. Of this I do not know of more than ten in existence. Both these examples are in the Carvick Webster collection and, in my opinion, the one on the left-hand side of the illustration, with its fine inscription, dated 1725 (of which a rubbing is given in Figure 103) is one of the finest examples of the pewterer's art which has come down to our time.

The evolution in form through the eighteenth century is well shown in the six illustrations which follow.

Figure 104 displays a type of quite pleasing shape in itself, but it already shows the beginning of that decadence in form which was shortly to dominate this type of vessel. The date of this piece is *c.* 1725, and that of Figures 105 and 106, *c.* 1735 and 1750 respectively. All are from the collection of Mr. Walter Churcher.

The introduction of the double handle about this time should be noted; another step which, even though of utility, is certainly not one of beauty. The alteration of the shape in this way was made to permit of the more convenient handling of the vessel according to the amount of fluid which it contained, the lower half giving a better control over the balance when the vessel was becoming emptied. Figures 107 and 108, both *c.* 1745, show this innovation in its best form, the former piece being in the collection of Major John Thompson, D.S.O., and the latter in the de Navarro collection,—the latter an exceptionally fine and graceful flagon for this type and period.

Figs. 104, 105, 106 — Communion Flagons (English)
Dating respectively, from left to right, 1725, 1735, and 1750 (or thereabouts) these flagons illustrate a changing taste.

Turning our attention to chalices, we are face to face with one of the very rarest of English pewter vessels. Cherished as they have ever been, even in their disuse, on account of their sacred associations, and likely to be the more so in the future in view of the insistent demands of recent years for their retention in their original churches, they will, as the years go by, become, as is only seemly, more difficult of acquisition by collectors.

Figure 112 illustrates one of the rarest of all kinds, a sepulchral chalice, now in the collection of Lewis Clapperton, Esq. In the Middle Ages it was the custom to bury these and other symbols of their office with deceased ecclesiastics; and, very occasionally, when turning up old ground on the site of forgotten burying places, these

Figs. 107 and 108 — Communion Flagons (English)
Both from the mid-eighteenth century, and both excellently exemplifying the use of the double handle.

Figs. 109, 110, 111 — Communion Flagons (English)
From late eighteenth to early nineteenth century, a progressive decline.

Fig. 112 — SEPULCHRAL CHALICE

Fig. 113 — COMMUNION CHALICES
Except for the middle piece in the lower row, these are mainly late eighteenth and early nineteenth century examples.

century. The short-stemmed one in the centre, bottom row, however, is of a considerably earlier date. In Figure 114 is shown a mid-seventeenth century English chalice which bears one of the earliest marks on the existing London touchplates and is in the collection of Dr. Young, of Manchester. An identical example is in the de Navarro collection. One of a pair of fine English chalices in the collection of Major Thompson (*tempus* 1745) is illustrated in Figure 115. Two more Scotch examples of the 1760 period are shown in Figures 116 and 118, the former bearing the date 1762 in the inscription. A late eighteenth century English chalice from the de Navarro collection is illustrated in Figure 120, whilst its Scotch contemporary, from the collection of Dr. Young, appears in Figure 119.

Patens again, and for a similar reason,

relics are unearthed. The one here shown was brought to light in Lincolnshire. Needless to say it is of pewter: but these pieces are usually in such a fragile and crumbling state that they require to be kept in a specially constructed air-tight case after some preservative has been applied to prevent further disintegration.

From the same collection, Figure 117 shows a most interesting little pocket communion set in folding carved wooden case, from Iceland. It is quite unique. Again from this collection is illustrated, Figure 113, a series of chalices mostly Scottish, and of the latter half of the eighteenth or the first quarter of the nineteenth

Fig. 114 — CHALICE
(*English*)
Mid-seventeenth century.

F igs. 115 and 116 — CHALICES
The first English, the second Scotch; both eighteenth century.

are a great rarity. It will be seen that a small one rests on the last-named chalice; and in Figure 123 I give an illustration of a most charming example from the collection of Walter Churcher, Esq. This fine little piece, which has a beautifully cabled moulding around its

Fig. 117 — POCKET COMMUNION SET

Fig. 118 — CHALICE

Figs. 121 and 122 — PATENS
Upper picture illustrates two examples, which below are exhibited in reverse. The more richly decorated of the two is of the William and Mary period.

upper edge, bears the same mark as the chalice referred to under Figure 114. Its total width is but seven and one-eighth inches, whereas it has a rim one and a half inches in width, which gives it a great dignity of proportion and makes it a very desirable possession, a point fully appreciated by its present genial owner.

Figures 121 and 122 show the upper and under sides respectively of two types of paten-plates* or tazza-plates, both of which are from examples in the Churcher collection. The one with the beaded decoration around the rim, foot, and joining of foot and body, is of the William and Mary period; and the plainer one is some twenty to twenty-five years later.

These pieces, which are by no means common and are very eagerly sought for by collectors, seem to be a kind of natural dividing line between ecclesiastical pewter on the one hand, and domestic on the other; and, more often than

Fig. 119 — CHALICE
In this and in Figure 117 observe the decorative effect of handsome lettering well placed. The chalice is here shown surmounted by a small paten.

not, it is extremely difficult to know whether or not a piece should be classed as the one or the other. In case of doubt, however, it is always more honest of purpose to designate it as domestic than to weave around it a false halo of sacred association for the sake of creating an interest which the particular piece has never, and will never, deserve. * * *

Returning to domestic pewter, we will first give a thought or two to the various types of dishes and plates. Here let it be understood that the terms are not

*The paten is an elevated plate upon which is placed the Communion bread. The paten was sometimes made to fit the chalice, as a cover.

synonymous, as so many would seem to believe, from the frequency with which they are confounded. The plate, or trencher, was something less than ten inches in diameter. From it the food was actually consumed. On the larger dishes, or chargers, the various viands were carried to the dining-table. This distinction is worth remembering as I know from personal experience, from a situation in which I once found myself. A friend, who shall be nameless, once asked me if I could obtain for him a few good ordinary *plates* to serve as background for smaller pieces. I procured a few for him only to discover that it was not plates which he required at all, but large dishes!

But the details of domestic pewter I shall have to reserve for another chapter.

Fig. 120 — CHALICE

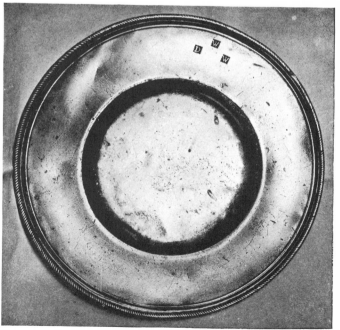

Fig. 123 — PATEN
The wide rim gives this diminutive piece an unusual dignity of proportion. The cabled moulding suggests fine silver work.

Plate IV — PLATE (English, 1661)

One of a pair, the other of which appears on page 41. These are two of the finest plates in existence, and are part of a set of which each was engraved with a different device and initials, but all with the same date. *Owned by S. M. Lennox.*

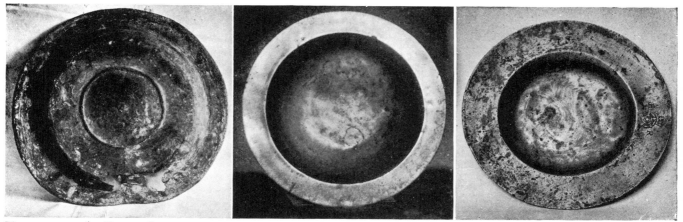

Figs. 124, 125, 126 — ENGLISH PEWTER
The first is the type of Roman pewter used during the occupation of Britain, the second is a Tudor period dish from a sunken Spanish galleon, and the third an English Tudor piece.

Chapter V

Plates and Dishes

To proceed with the story. Commencing at the beginning—and here let it be understood that all the plates and dishes which follow are English unless otherwise stated—the under side of a fine Roman dish, unearthed at Sutton, during excavations, is illustrated in Figure 124, from the Charbonnier collection. As will be seen, it is in a state of very advanced corrosion, which, at the base, has resulted in total disintegration, evidenced by the two large holes which appear there. It is, however, a fine example of the type of pewter dish in use at the time of the Roman occupation of Britain and corroborates, in its main details, similar specimens which have come to light in other parts of the country, from time to time. A noticeable feature is the raised strengthening bead which runs around the under side of the well, roughly midway between the centre point and the bouge.

Between this and Tudor pewter, two specimens of which are illustrated in Figures 125 and 126, there is a great hiatus. Indeed, apart from the records of the Worshipful Company of Pewterers of London and such medieval items as the sepulchral chalice already described under Figure 112, one may say frankly that very little information is available. But a very authentic piece of the Tudor period is shown in the small soup-plate, Figure 125, which was recovered from the Spanish Armada galleon sunk in Tobermory Bay, off the coast of Scotland, and now occupies an honored niche in the pewter room of Antonio de Navarro, Esq. Considering its long immersion—for three and a quarter centuries—it is in a wonderful state of preservation.

Figure 126 shows another fine little plate which, though not so well authenticated as the last, may well be of an even earlier date. This piece bears on the front of the rim, which is quite distinct in the photograph, a Tudor

Figs. 127, 128, 129 — ENGLISH PEWTER
The first two are seventeenth-century plates, the third a rose-water dish of similar period.

Fig. 130 — STUART PERIOD PLATE (*c. 1660*)
Observe the broad rim and the character of the engraving. By William Matthews (*d. 1689*).

Fig. 133 — NARROW RIMMED TYPE

rose beneath a crown between the letters E. R., which may stand for *Elizabeth Regina*; but, although the style of the letters is such as to suggest a later date, the type of the plate itself abundantly warrants the assumption. This plate is in the Carvick Webster collection, as, also, are the two next illustrations. Figure 127 shows a very fine and heavy plate some eight and three-quarters inches in diameter and marked on the rim with an unknown maker's mark, immediately above which, and as part of it, appears the date 1621.

to me, as a memento of my first visit to his beautiful Worcestershire home, by Antonio de Navarro, Esq. It is one of the very rarest types of English pewter plates, a fact which enhances a hundredfold both the generosity of the giver and the pleasure of its present owner. It bears on the back of the rim the touch of William Matthews, who died in 1689. How long it was made before that time it is impossible to say, but probably between 1660 and 1670. Very few authentic examples of English *plates* of this type are known, though its prototypes in the "dish" sizes, whilst still rare, are far easier to obtain.

A fine example of the dish of this type is illustrated in Figure 131, between two plates of a slightly later type of which I shall have occasion to speak immediately, all of which pieces are in the Richardson collection. The dignity of proportion of these two latter types has never been equalled in any of the many

A similar type, but of slightly later date, is illustrated in Figure 128, and this is rendered the more interesting by reason of the wriggled work rose-and-bird design with which it is decorated, a species of ornamentation specially sought for by the collector of discrimination.

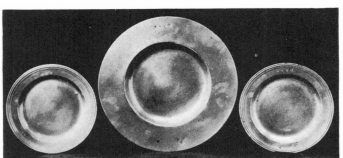

Fig. 131 — BROAD RIMMED DISH AND PLATES
A fine dignity of proportion between bowl and rim of the central piece is here obtained. The other two examples are slightly later.

A rose-water dish, of about the same period, from the collection of Mr. Walter Churcher, is shown in Figure 129. This piece must have spent the better part of its days in a very good home, for it is in a wonderfully well-preserved condition, a condition which one knows will suffer nothing at the hands of its present careful owner.

Figure 130 represents an extremely beautiful plate of the Stuart broad-rimmed type. Some nine and three-eighths of an inch in diameter with a rim one and three-quarters of an inch in width, this fine plate was presented

Fig. 132 — NARROW RIMMED TYPES
Rims reeded and but ¾ inch wide as against 1¾ in the broader type.

Figs. 134, 135 — ENGLISH PEWTER
The first group shows medium rims and reeded edges, the last plate has a single reeded edge, which **was** in full favor until about 1750.

Figs. 136. — PLAIN RIM ABOVE WITH REINFORCING
REED UNDERNEATH
A type which succeeded the piece shown in Figure 135.

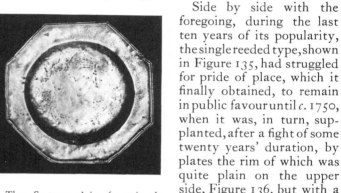

Fig. 137 — OCTAGONAL DISH (*c. 1750*)
By Thos. Chamberlain. The arms are those of David Garrick.

changes which have been rung on the pewter plates and dishes of bygone years. In both the dish and plate sizes these are eagerly sought for by many collectors.

As if to contrast with these beautiful proportions, in the succeeding type the width of the rim had dwindled to a matter of five-eighths or three-quarters of an inch in the plate size, as against the one and three-quarters of its predecessor, and though, in the narrowed type, the rim is by no means displeasing, it fails to impress one as did its predecessor. Two of this narrow-rimmed type, which also is very rare, are shown in Figure 132, wherein it will be seen that the rim is practically devoid of any flatness, but is made up of a series of reedings. A variant of this type is illustrated in Figure 133, bearing the mark of a Bristol maker.

The three last pieces are all in the collection of Mrs. Carvick Webster, as also are those in Figure 134, which shows an unique series of the reeded edge type which was coeval with the last, and which eventually it outlived by a decade. Two others of this type have previously appeared in Figure 131. This fine series shows practically

Figs. 138, 139 — OCTAGONAL PLATES
The first, with a beaded edge, is by Thos. Scattergood (*1736–1775*); the second, whose edge has an inner beading, is by Richard Pitt (*c. 1760*).

every known size, from eight and a half to twenty-five inches, the latter being an exceptionally fine example of craftsmanship and of fine, resonant metal, bearing the same Bristol maker's mark as appears on the narrow-rimmed one in Figure 133 above.

Side by side with the foregoing, during the last ten years of its popularity, the single reeded type, shown in Figure 135, had struggled for pride of place, which it finally obtained, to remain in public favour until *c.* 1750, when it was, in turn, supplanted, after a fight of some twenty years' duration, by plates the rim of which was quite plain on the upper side, Figure 136, but with a strengthening reed some quarter of an inch broad on the under side, which somewhat resembles the preceding type turned upside down.

This plain, narrowish rim maintained its popularity, shared from time to time by the many types of decorated rims of which I shall shortly speak, until the pewterers were forced to bow their heads in admission of defeat, in face of the advancing wave of enthusiasm for the work of

Figs. 140, 141, 142, 143 — FIVE-LOBED PLATES
The first, by Chamberlain; the second, with reeded edge, by Spackman (*c. 1780*); the third, with gadrooned edge, by James Tisoe (*c. 1760*); the last, a gadrooned edge with inner fillets.

25

Figs. 144, 145 — ROUND PLATES (early nineteenth century)
Plain gadrooned edges.

the potters, who, with their more sanitary and more easily cleaned china platters and bowls, caught the public taste and ultimately gave the *coup-de-grace* to an industry which had existed and flourished for century after century

In Figure 140 is shown a plain five-lobed wavy-edged plate of very pleasing proportions, by the same maker as the David Garrick dish referred to above; and a similar plate, but with reeded edge, by Spackman of London (*c. 1780*), is illustrated in Figure 141, this latter a type of very frequent occurrence in Continental pewter plates. The last two pieces illustrated are also in the collection of Mrs. Carvick Webster.

Figure 142, from the W. D. Thomson collection, made by James Tisoe of London (*c. 1760*), shows this same type of five-lobed plate, but with a plain gadrooned border; whilst, in Figure 143, is a similar plate, but with the pleasing addition of the two narrow fillets running around inside the gadrooning. This latter, from the Richardson collection, is another fine example of the pewterer's art.

Of ordinary round plates with plain gadrooned edging, two excellent examples are shown in Figures 144 and 145, each from a set of six in the Carvick Webster collection.

Fig. 146 — OVAL DISHES
These do not appear before the mid-eighteenth century. They are by Samuel Duncomb (*c. 1780*).

as an integral part of the national life—*Sic transit gloria mundi*——!

Of the decorated rims referred to above, Figure 137 shows one of the ovate-octagonal dishes from a service formerly used by, and bearing the arms of, David Garrick, the world-famed actor. This dish, now in the de Navarro collection, bears the mark of Thomas Chamberlain of London (*c. 1750*), and is in a good state of preservation.

In the same collection is a series of octagonal plates with beaded edges, one of which is shown in Figure 138, and upon these plates appears the touch of Thos. Scattergood, junior, of London, who was at work from about 1736–1775.

Another octagonal plate, and the only one of its type which I have ever seen with the very pleasing inner row of small raised beads, and which bears the mark of Richard Pitt of London (*c. 1760*), is illustrated in Figure 139 and is in the Carvick Webster collection. It has the appearance of being considerably older than its mark will permit.

The plain one is some thirty years older than the engraved one, which, as it will be seen, is engraved, *St. Peter's Church, Walworth, Surry, 1827*, where these pieces were formerly in use as offertory plates.

A fine series of plain oval dishes is illustrated from the collection of W. D. Thomson, Esq., in Figure 146. The oval

Figs. 146a, 147 — HOT WATER PLATES
The second is by John Carpenter (*c. 1750*).

Fig. 148 — FRENCH PEWTER PLATES
A beautiful type, not elsewhere produced. The measure is Flemish.

dish did not come into use before the middle of the eighteenth century, and the series illustrated are of the period (*c. 1780*), bearing the mark of Samuel Duncomb of Birmingham.

To round off the series, and the story could not be complete without some reference to them, I illustrate two hot water plates in Figures 146*a* and 147. The former, *en suite* with the plate shown in Figure 138, is in the de Navarro collection; and the latter, of the type familiar to all collectors, is in the collection of Thomas Warburton, Esq., of Manchester, and bears the mark of John Carpenter of London (*c. 1750*).

These hot water dishes and plates would seem to have come into use about the same period as the oval shape in dishes, both being innovations which must at the time have been looked upon as very sensible and most welcome improvements. They were made in almost every conceivable shape and form: with fixed or loose tops; with rigid

Fig. 149 — SWISS PEWTER
These have no counterpart in American or British pewter.

or drop handles; with and without rims; with plain perpendicular sides or those of moulded section and with a hundred variations of mouldings; and all seem still to have a strong attraction for the public taste, for one often finds, even in the houses of non-collectors, a few examples of this type of pewter, for decorative purposes.

We have now glanced at most of the better-known English types, some of which were also in use on the continent of Europe; these latter, however, are usually of softer and much inferior metal, without the hammer marks on the underside, and should cause but little trouble to the beginner if he will but apply the tests enumerated in the first chapter of this book, some of which will, in the

majority of cases, be found to give the deciding word as to the locality of origin.

Turning to these Continental examples, I give in Figure 148 a representation of two very beautiful French plates, of types which have no counterpart in other countries. The larger one of the two, as is also the lidded Bruges measure, is in the Churcher collection. The smaller was in the collection of the late Alban L. G. Distin, but with his other pieces was sold at the time of his death.

Figure 150 shows a type of plate which has been very freely faked to trap the uninitiated who somehow seem to be irresistibly attracted by the French Royal badge of the Salamander beneath a crown in repoussé in the centre, and the field *semée de Lys*. Heraldry and pewter have seemed ever to go hand in hand, both being complemen-

Fig. 150 — FRENCH PEWTER PLATE
A design frequently imitated.

tary to life in the Middle Ages; so perhaps it is not altogether surprising that plates of this kind should stir the imagination and unfold before the mind pictures of the baronial hall, the good old days and scenes of revelry.

In Figures 149 and 151, are illustrated various types of eighteenth century Swiss plates and dishes, the former having no counterpart in American or British pewter, whilst the latter examples closely resemble the one shown in Figure 141.

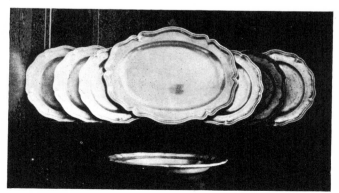

Fig. 151 — SWISS PEWTER
Similar to the plate shown in Figure 141.

Fig. 151a — PEWTER TIME-LAMP

Candlesticks and Lamps

These notes could never claim even a modicum of completeness without some reference to those less showy, but equally indispensable, articles which were of daily utility in the environment of our ancestors. Perhaps one of the next in importance was the candlestick. When we

Fig. 152 — CANDLESTICK
A very handsome early example of the pricket type.

think of the present-day facilities for lighting our homes, it fills us with wonder how our grandparents "existed" after dark! No wonder "early to bed" was the cry instilled into the youthful ears, and had I been fore-doomed to spend my childish winter evenings trying to read, write, or work by the dim, uncertain, flickering light of a rushlight or tallow-candle, I, too, should very willingly and very soon have learned to submit to that slogan, *not* through *force majeure* but of my own untrammelled, free will; for it must have been a *real joy* to go to bed!

Having thus, at any rate to my own satisfaction, laid this spectre of my early days, let us give a moment's thought to such of the lighting devices as come within the purview of our subject; for, with the rush light holder, which was an iron pliers-like device on a tripod or other form of stand, we have nothing to do, since it was never made in pewter. But oil time-lamps were at one time in more or less general use on the continent of Europe, and one of them is illustrated in Figure 151a. The glass container at the top, which screws on, was filled with sperm or similar heavy-bodied oil, the wick lying in the horizontal arm with one end in the oil at the bottom of the glass container, the other end being left free for lighting at the outer end of the arm. When lighted, the oil gradually descended in the container as it was burned away, its descent recording the time on a bar of pewter running down the front, which was graduated in hours. Of course, the lamp had to be lighted at the time shown on this bar when it was freshly filled, an operation which necessitated some little practice in order to fill it exactly to the time desired and which would,

of course, vary according to the time of the year; for, whereas in the winter it would be necessary to light up about four o'clock, in the summer it would not be required until about eight-thirty or nine o'clock, even if at all. These lamps burned with quite passable accuracy, for I once allowed one to burn by my bedside throughout the night and in the morning it was roughly correct. I forget now whether it gained or lost a few minutes, but it matters not, for we shall not be using these contrivances again in this twentieth century!

Of English candlesticks, Figure 152 shows a very beautiful early example which was dug up in Thames Street, London, and was for some time in the collection of the late F. G. Hilton-Price, Director of the Society of Antiquaries of London, but which, at his death, passed into the care of its present owner, Lewis Clapperton, Esq., of Glasgow. As will be seen, it is of the pricket variety, but on account of its being quite unique in design we have nothing to guide us as to its date. It is evidently very early, and is in wonderfully fine condition considering where it was found.

In the same collection is the one illustrated in Figure 153, another extremely fine piece, probably of early seventeenth century workmanship, and again almost unique in type, this bell-shaped base being very eagerly sought for, but very seldom found.

Figure 154 illustrates a type which, to the writer, seems to speak of the severe days of the Commonwealth, but which to other authorities appears a little later; but this is a point which I am afraid will never be finally settled because the marks, when such exist, are generally merely the initials of the maker's name and are not struck upon the touchplates. In the absence of absolute proof to the contrary, I am afraid that these

Fig. 153 — CANDLESTICK — (*Probably seventeenth century*)
A rare type with bell-shaped base.

will continue to suggest to my mind more than a nodding acquaintance with Oliver Cromwell or his times.

In Figures 155 and 156 we have two very fine examples of the extremely rare, later Jacobean candlesticks so eagerly sought by collectors. The former is in the Carvick Webster, and the latter in the Walter Churcher collection. Considering how numerous these candlesticks must have

Fig. 154 — CANDLESTICK
Probably Cromwellian.

Fig. 162 — CANDLESTICKS
Swiss rococo.

Figs. 155, 156 — CANDLESTICKS
Rare late Jacobean types. The former is strongly impregnated with classic feeling.

three and five-eighths inches in height and that in Figure 158, eight and five-eighths inches.

Through the reigns of William and Mary and Queen Anne, the types remained much the same, but gradually evolved into a plainer style of stem until the early mid-Georgian days, when the Adam style of pillar candlestick had a slight vogue. One cannot find that this type ever had great hold on the pewterers, for few examples are known to exist in pewter.

Towards the end of the eighteenth century, the style known as the baluster stem came into fairly general use. It consists of, usually, a rounded base with a stem made up of a series of knops and pear-shaped sections, the assembling of which, in some specimens, is by no means displeasing; but the great majority bear no comparison with the types enumerated above and may but be classed as very ordinary. Figures 159 and 160 show a few of these types, whilst, in Figure 161, is shown a later type in vogue about 1825 to 1850.

been at one time, it is amazing that so few have come down to our time to rejoice the hearts of collectors.

The next stage in progression is shown by the two wonderful examples, from the de Navarro collection, in Figures 157 and 158. This latest type of Jacobean candlestick, which would seem to represent the zenith of the pewterer's art, is also one of extreme rarity, for not more than half a dozen are known to have come down to our time. One of these (I think it was during the month of February, 1923) was sold at auction for £41, and its present owner considered himself fortunate to obtain it at that price, for it is in perfect condition and of somewhat plainer style than those here illustrated. The one shown in Figure 157 is

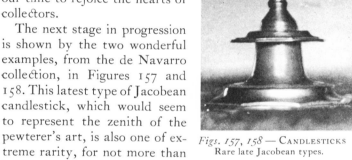

Figs. 157, 158 — CANDLESTICKS
Rare late Jacobean types.

In Figure 162 are shown three Swiss examples, formed in the elaborate, but by no means displeasing, rococo style which one has come instinctively to associate with Switzerland, though to a certain extent it obtained also in certain districts of France.

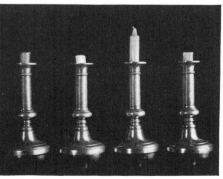

Figs. 159, 160, 161 — BALUSTER STEM CANDLESTICKS
The first five are late eighteenth century; the others a little later (*c. 1825–1850*).

Plate V — Pair of Flagons (*English, 1634*)

    These flagons are engraved "1634. St. Marye, Northgate, Thomas Gilbert and William Wootton, Church Wardens, Decemb. 13th."
Owned by E. W. Turner.

Chapter VI

Footed Cups

A VERY brief résumé of English tankards was given under Figures 44 to 48. I should like to handle it more thoroughly, but space forbids. This is not a treatise on drinking vessels only. Yet these conveyers of refreshment constitute a topic at once so

Fig. 162a — FOOTED CUPS (*early nineteenth century*)

fascinating and so extensive that before leaving it I must illustrate a type of drinking vessel which comes not under the heading of tankards but is known as a footed cup. Very similar to the chalice but, possibly designedly so, shorter in the stem than the majority of these latter vessels, a fine array is shown in Figure 162a, from the Churcher collection. This type of cup was very much *de rigeur* in the early years of the nineteenth century.

Spoons

Of pewter spoons there is a great variety of types, but space again forbids my doing more than lightly touch upon the subject which has been made a distinct branch of collecting by the late Mr. Hilton Price in his charming little monograph *Old Base Metal Spoons*, a book which should be in the hands of every collector of such bijouterie.

In Figure 163 is illustrated an old English rack

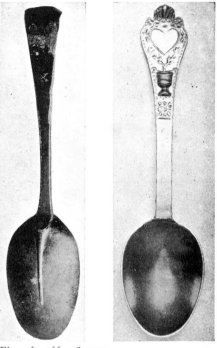

Figs. 165, 166 — SPOONS
The first is a rat-tail, the second a Continental type.

of seventeenth century spoons of the slip-top variety, from the Carvick Webster collection; and, in Figure 164, a corresponding rack of the round-bowled Dutch variety; and here let it be noted that an example of a round-bowled English pewter spoon has, I think, yet to be found, if perhaps one excepts caddy spoons.

Figure 165 gives a very good idea of what is implied by the use of the term *rat-tailed* as applied to spoons. This is of the rounded end, early eighteenth century form. A Continental spoon, of not too desirable type, is seen in Figure 166.

Salts

The salt occupied a very important position in the furnishing of the dining-table of bygone times, when the guests were graded as being "above or below the salt"; and, although the term has passed from usage in its former sense, the spirit still pervades at public banquets, where the guests of honour are ranged on

Figs. 163, 164 — SPOONS
Seventeenth century slip-top and Dutch round-bowled types.

Fig. 170 — SALTS (*see text for dates*)

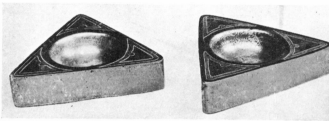

Fig. 169 — TRENCHER SALTS (*late seventeenth century*)

either side of the chairman at the head table, whereas the greater number must perforce submit to sitting amongst the "common herd" at the side tables.

In speaking of containers for salt, by the way, it is worth while to bear in mind that, while perhaps condoned by custom, the use of the term "salt cellar" is really quite incorrect. The French term for a salt container is *salière*, the proper English term is *salt*. It amounts to using the same word twice over, in its French and its English version, for *salière*, from which in this usage cellar is corrupted, is the French for salt. To English ears it suggested the idea of a cavity or depression.

To proceed. In Figures 167 and 168 are illustrated three fine late Stuart spool-shaped or standing salts, those in Figure 167 being in the Clapperton collection, whilst that in Figure 168, which shows delicate tooled designs covering the whole of the body, is in the de Navarro collection—as are also those in the two following illustrations; the pair of flat triangular-shaped trencher salts, Figure 169, being probably of the late seventeenth century and quite unique, whilst the late Stuart example to the left of Figure 170 is similar to one in Figure 167. The cup salt on the right is of the mid-eighteenth century type, as, also, is that shown in Figure 173.

The two centre ones in Figure 170 are Continental, early eighteenth century; and Figure 174 shows a delightful little French salt of sprightly erect type of the same period and with a very small salt container, from my own collection.

Fig. 171 — TRENCHER SALT (*seventeenth or early eighteenth century*)

The fine old trencher salt shown in Figure 171 is in the Walter Churcher collection and is of late seventeenth or early eighteenth century date.

Three salts of the more ordinary type, and of the eighteenth century, are shown in Figure 175; and again I have laid the de Navarro collection under contribution.

All the above examples of salts are English except where otherwise stated.

Tea Caddies and Other Things

A very daintily engraved English tea caddy of late eighteenth century workmanship is illustrated in Figure 172. It has, it will be noted, a small brass handle on the top and is also furnished with a lock and key. The inside of this piece is lined with steel and enamelled, which gives to it a wonderfully solid "reliable" feeling.

Figure 176 shows a bonny little spice box, with loose cover, of the middle of the eighteenth century. Figure 177 is a double ended spirit measure (*c.1820*). One is glad to be able to illustrate one whereon the capacities are plainly marked—¼ gill and ½ gill — for some proof would

Fig. 172 — TEA CADDY (*late eighteenth century*)

seem to be necessary to prove that these are not "double egg cups," a term so often wrongly applied to describe these pieces by many collectors whom one would expect to know better. Presumably the idea is that one end is for a hen's egg and the other for a duck's!! (I have it in mind that I have heard them described in this way.)

Figs. 173, 174, 175 — CUP SALTS (*eighteenth century*). The second is a dainty French example.

Figs. 176, 177 — SPICE BOX AND SPIRIT MEASURE
The latter is by no means an egg cup.

claw feet, made by Thomas Compton of London (*c. 1810*), (*Fig. 181*); and a tundish or funnel made by A. Hincham (*c. 1740*), (*Fig. 182*); both the latter from the Port collection, complete a trio of articles indispensable to the good housewife for the smooth working of her household.

Figure 183 illustrates a delightful little early eighteenth century English sugar bowl, finger bowl or porringer of the handleless variety, whilst examples of porringers with pierced handles are shown in Figures 184–186. The five shown in the former illustration are in the Richardson collection, whilst those in the two latter are in the W. D. Thomson collection.

Fig. 183 — SUGAR BOWL
It may also be called a finger bowl or porringer.

These vessels are found, from time to time, with incised horizontal lines around the inside of the body, each line being numbered from the bottom upwards, which goes to prove that they have been used in surgical work for bleeding-bowls or cupping-dishes, as they are variously termed, in which case the numbers on the inside must be understood to represent fluid ounces, a guide to the surgeon as to the extent of his operation. It is quite a mistake to apply these terms to *all* dishes of this type, whether graduated or not, as is so often done.

The specimens just considered all bear English marks and are of the period *c.* 1690–1720, but the same patterns were in use on the Continent. Examples of these, showing solid handles both plain and embossed, and pierced handles, are given in Figure 187, from pieces in the Charbonnier collection. The Continental examples are usually of much softer metal than their English analogues, whilst an American example by Frederick Bassett was illustrated in the February, 1923, number of *Art in America*. The date of this latter piece is *c.* 1790.

Another indispensable

These two last pieces are from my own collection.

Ink Stands

Two very convincing little inkstands are shown in Figures 178 and 179. Cube-shaped, with two drawers and with removable tops revealing, inside the upper portion, the glass bottle to hold the ink, and with the removable tops having a pen-hole at each corner, these eminently practical little fellows are of Irish manufacture. The latter, which is in the Carvick Webster collection, bears inside the upper drawer the mark of Silvester Savage of Dublin, who was working in 1790. The former piece is in the de Navarro collection and unmarked.

Household Gear

A colander from the Frank Creassey collection, Figure 180; a very finely modelled soup-tureen with ball and

Figs. 178, 179 — IRISH INKSTANDS
The latter is from Dublin and bears the mark of Silvester Savage (*c. 1790*).

Figs. 180, 181, 182 — HOUSEHOLD UTENSILS OF PEWTER
The first is a colander, the second a soup tureen by Thos. Compton (*c. 1810*), and the third a funnel by A. Hincham (*c. 1740*).

Fig. 184 — PORRINGERS

ornaments, a sight familiar to many of us in our childhood days on the kitchen mantelpieces of our grandparents. The latter are from the collection of Dr. Young.

Stills

An English pewter still, dated 1766, twenty-three and a half inches high and twelve inches in diameter, is shown in Figure 193, from the Port collection. These stills, though not of the greatest decorative value, are, nevertheless, very rare and extremely interesting, not more than six or seven of them being known to me. One, with two conical condensers, it has recently been my pleasure to introduce to the Wellcome Historical Medical Museum, London—which now possesses three—very realistically reset in a carefully reconstructed representation

article on the dining-table was the pepper-pot, a fine array of varying forms being shown in Figure 188, from

Figs. 185, 186 — PORRINGERS

specimens formerly in the collection of the late A. L. G. Distin, but now dispersed. This illustration shows well that diversity of form was by no means a monopoly of the silversmiths, but one may as well be quite frank at the outset and admit that it is well nigh impossible to distinguish the Continental from the English examples, for many of the patterns would seem to have been made indiscriminately.

Fig. 187 — CONTINENTAL PORRINGERS

Fig. 188 — PEPPER CASTORS

of an old alchemist's laboratory.

The making of these stills and their complementary "worms" must have provided a considerable volume of work for the early pewterers, and as evidence of this we find, in no less than twenty-two of the London pewterers' touches, that some part of a still has been adopted as one of the chief devices.

A very rare two-handled cup of the William and Mary period is shown in Figure 189, and a similar piece, but with cover and of slightly later date—*tempus* Queen Anne—is given in Figure 190. Both are in the de Navarro collection, whilst another similar example is in the fine collection of Alfred B. Yeates, Esq., F.S.A., F.R.I.B.A., of London.

In Figure 191 is illustrated a late eighteenth or early nineteenth century English water carafe of no very particular charm; and in Figure 192, a pair of chimney

Figs. 189, 190 — TWO-HANDLED CUPS
The first is of the William and Mary period; the second, Queen Anne.

Fig. 191—WATER CARAFE (*late eighteenth or early nineteenth century*)

Snuff Boxes

Figures 194, 195, 196, illustrate a good series of the dainty little snuff boxes which were in use in the latter part of the eighteenth and early part of the nineteenth century. Most of these examples are from the Churcher collection, as are the Scottish, pewter mounted horn snuff mulls shown in Figure 197 and bearing the mark of one Durie, a Scotch maker celebrated for their manufacture.

Fig. 192—CHIMNEY ORNAMENTS

Fig. 193—PEWTER STILL (*1766*)

Measures and Coasters

Figure 198, also Scotch, shows an unusual use for pewter, in the form of a two-handled *standard* measure. Very heavily made, apparently never having been turned or finished on the outer side, so as to leave every ounce of strength in the body to enable it to withstand hard usage, this fine piece, of the time of Queen Anne, bears, on a medallion soldered to the body, the

Figs. 194, 195, 196—SNUFF BOXES

Arms of the Borough of Stirling—a lamb upon a rock. Of gallon capacity, this measure, with four others of the same type, was formerly used by the Borough of Stirling as the standard by which other vessels were tested. It is now in the collection of Mrs. Carvick Webster.

Fig. 197 — SCOTCH SNUFF MULLS
Horn mounted.

An English coaster or wine-slide (*c. 1800*) is illustrated in Figure 199. This piece, as is usual in these coasters, has a turned hardwood bottom.

Figure 200 is included to show the affinity between the English pewter baluster measure and the old leather "Black Jack." The great similarity in shape and general feeling will at once be apparent. Both these fine pieces are in the Walter Churcher collection.

Fig. 198 — SCOTCH STANDARD MEASURE

Miscellaneous Items

Turning to a few European types, Figure 201 illustrates a wine bottle, probably Swiss; and Figure 202 a beaker from the Yeates collection, and of Low Country origin.

Fig. 199 — ENGLISH COASTER

These Continental beakers are by no means uncommon, but I do not think more than half a dozen, even if so many, English ones of undoubted authenticity, are known to exist. Some are in use as chalices in Scotch country churches, but they mostly savour of Continental origin.

The wall-lavabo shown in Figure 203 is but one of many forms of this vessel. As illustrated, it is incomplete, for the underbasin is missing. These underbasins were either fixed to the wall below, on brackets, or rested upon a stand; but they were always present in some form to catch the superfluous water from the container above.

Six delightful little cups, some three and a half inches in height, appear in Figure 204, from the Walter Churcher collection. The odd one in the centre was purchased in Algiers, but they are all of European manufacture and make a fine little set of liqueur cups.

Guild Flagons

Two fine German guild flagons are illustrated in Figures 205 and 206 and represent well this type of vessel, the former being in the Yeates and the latter in the G. E. Davis collection. The shield on the lids of these vessels was used to display the arms of the guild or

Fig. 201 — WINE BOTTLE
Probably Swiss.

Fig. 202 — LOW-COUNTRY BEAKER

Fig. 200 — BLACK JACK AND BALUSTER MEASURE
The former of leather, the latter of pewter.

Fig. 203 — WALL-LAVABO
The underbasin is missing.

of the donor, or the members' names, which also were frequently inscribed around the body of the flagon, as in those illustrated. Another German flagon of very pleasing form, from the Yeates collection, appears in Figure 207.

The standing cups illustrated in Figures 209 and 210, which are in the collections of Charles G. J. Port and Ernest Hunter, respectively, were used on the continent of Europe both for presentation purposes and guild use.

The former, which is German, and twenty-three inches in height, was presented "to the Town Piper, Johannes Weilinger, in recognition of his skill in music, 1729" and bears several German coats of arms. The latter, dated 1760, is an example of a Flemish guild flagon, the names of members being engraved both on the body and on the

Fig. 208 — Pewter Coins

evidenced by those illustrated in Figure 208, which shows, a Charles II farthing, obverse, and a James II farthing, obverse and reverse.

By way of epilogue. When one recalls to mind that *all* the household utensils which now are made in china, pottery, earthenware, glass, galvanized iron, enamelled iron, sheet iron, block tin, aluminium and what not, were formerly made in pewter, one begins to realize what an enormous industry was that of the pewterer; and does it not open up, before the prospecting eye of the collector, a vast field of interests wherein his energies may disport themselves? There need be no monotony; possibly there is more variety than in any other branch of collecting and, withal, as a result, that restful repose which seems to reflect from the mellowed surface of the metal.

Fig. 204 — Continental Liqueur Cups

pendant medallions. This cup formerly belonged to the Guild of St. George, Ostend.

Pewter Coins

My story, for the present at any rate, is nearly told, and I have but to illustrate a few examples of the "Root of all evil," but seemingly one of the most necessary things in the world . . . *money!*

To many it will come as a surprise to know that coins were ever struck in pewter, but that such was the case is

Figs. 205, 206, 207 — German Flagons
The first two are guild flagons.

Figs. 209, 210 — Standing Cups
The first is German (*1729*), the latter Flemish (*1760*).

Plate VI — Communion Chalice (*English, 1762*)

Engraved "For the use of the Associate Congregation of Lesley, A.D. 1762."
Owned by Francis Weston.

Chapter VII

The Composition of Pewter

IN the late Mr. Charles Welch's fascinating *History of the Worshipful Company of Pewterers of the City of London*, there are countless references to the various alloys which from time to time were ordered to be used for various kinds of wares, and also the records of fines and punishments inflicted for breach of the company's regulations; but if I am to avoid allowing myself to run into technicalities, I must endeavour briefly to set down such simple, general formulæ as will do nothing more than remove the first tarnish of ignorance from the mind of the uninstructed in such matters.

The basic metal of all the pewter alloys is tin, and in the early days the quality of English tin was realised to be so far superior to that of other countries that there was a great call for it from abroad, and the London Pewterers' Company made frequent applications to Parliament for laws to be passed prohibiting the export of tin except in the manufactured state, but such applications were doomed to disappointment.

With the tin was mixed, according to the alloy desired or the purpose for which it was intended, lead, copper, brass, antimony or bismuth, and more often than not two or three of these metals were blended together, for, in the heyday of the pewterers' art, several kinds of alloys were enjoined for various kinds of wares; thus "Fine Metal" was ordered to be composed of twenty-six parts of copper to one hundred and twelve parts of tin and this alloy was to be used for plates, saucers, dishes, chargers, salts, square cruets, square chrismatories and "other things which were made square."

The second quality was known as "Tin," wherein the alloy consisted of tin and lead, the proportions of which varied at different times from twenty-six parts of lead to one hundred and twelve parts of tin, to sixteen parts of lead to a hundred and twelve parts of tin, from which alloy was ordered to be made "all other things, such as round pots, &c., &c.," and these vessels were to be called "Vessels of tin (or pewter) for ever."

It is very difficult, nay, almost impossible, to be precise, because the standards were altered from time to time; but the average collector will not desire to go too deeply into the strict analysis of his pieces, which, moreover, would entail the removal from his treasures of fragments of the metal for this purpose! He will be content to know that the main constituent part of any of his pieces is tin, with the admixture of more or less lead, brass, copper, antimony or bismuth.

One pewterer, Richard Going of Bristol, used as one of his marks the device of the Tudor Rose and Crown with the words "Best" and "Bismuth" in labels above and below respectively.

One has often been asked if a certain piece were not made from "Silver-pewter" . . . ! There is no such thing as silver-pewter. It is possible that in the earlier days, with their limited facilities for the segregation of metals, lead of a slightly argentiferous nature was used when mixing the alloy, but anything in the nature of an intentional alloy containing silver is unknown, and the quantity at best which could have crept in through the cause indicated would be so infinitesimally small as to have no appreciable result on the mixture.

On early pewter spoons and other articles there appear, from time to time, signs of what looks unmistakably like gilding, but gilding was strictly forbidden to the pewterers and this apparent trace of it, however convincingly it may appear to be otherwise, is an oxide which has formed on the surface of the metal.

The Fashioning of Pewter

From the beginning it was the custom among the pewterers for various kinds of work to be performed by different classes of craftsmen; thus we find in the early records, that "Sad-ware-men" made sad-ware, by which is meant dishes, plates, chargers and other more or less flat wares; "Hollow-ware-men," as the name implies, made the more bulbous flagons, pots, tankards, etc.; "Spoonmakers" again, made spoons. Another branch was the lidding of stone-pots with pewter lids, and again there were men who specialised in the making of the pewter spiral "worms" for stills, whilst the turn-wheel turned the wheel which operated the lathe.

The methods of manufacture were simple; such things as plates, dishes, spoons, etc., were cast in gun-metal moulds — many of which are still in existence — and afterwards turned, polished and hammered.

Tankards and flagons were cast in several pieces which were afterwards soldered together and the joint turned down in the lathe, the handles being cast hollow, which was effected by pouring the molten metal into the mould and then, when sufficient time had elapsed for the metal next to the mould to cool, the latter was reversed and the unset inner volume of the metal allowed to flow out again. If one examines a flagon around the bulbous portion of the body the junction line will be plainly discerned.

It was enjoined by the London Company that all plates should be hammered around the bouge, as is so well shown in Figure 13. This hammering gives that feeling of great strength which one always experiences when handling a plate or dish which has been subjected to this process by an experienced hand.

Every action of the early pewterer was governed and regulated by his guild; he was not to work at night, first, because of the noise and, secondly, because good work could not be performed in the dim, artificial light of those early days. Every particle of alloy had to be tested by the standards kept at Pewterers' Hall for the purpose before he could put up his wares for sale; no man could work at the trade until he had served his full term of apprenticeship and gained his freedom in the company, and no master was allowed to employ workmen — other than apprentices — who were not freemen of their guilds. "Alien" workmen, by which term is meant workmen from other towns, were not tolerated on any consideration except in the most exceptional circumstances; the weights per dozen and the sizes of the various articles were rigidly fixed and, as has already been shown, the constituent parts of the various alloys for different vessels, and even the quality of the solder to be used, were governed and regulated by the company.

From earliest times the marking of pewter was made compulsory, but in later years, and as the company lost control of its members through the falling off of the trade, through the advent of pottery, enamelled iron, earthenware and the other contributing causes, the enforcement of this became increasingly difficult.

Small wonder is it, then, that during so many centuries, English pewter gained and kept its wonderful reputation for being the best in the world.

Britannia Metal

Britannia metal was first made about 1770, but it was not brought into general commercial use until about seven or ten years later, when James Vickers made a specialty of it.

The difficulty of distinguishing between it and pewter will best be appreciated by the following description of it, culled from my friend Frederick Bradbury's excellent *History of Old Sheffield Plate*, where he gives the following:

"Britannia metal consists mainly of tin with an admixture of antimony and a little copper."

How nearly this approaches to the composition of pewter will at once be appreciated by reference to my notes on that subject above.

An average alloy for Britannia consisted of about one hundred parts of tin to seven of antimony and two of copper.

Thus it will be seen that although there *is* a similarity between the two, the proportion of tin in Britannia metal is *very* much greater than in any of the pewter alloys, and herein some of us believe we *actually see and feel* a difference, for Britannia metal has a harder, whiter, colder look, and a more "dense" surface, due to the entire absence of lead which was *never* used in its composition; it hasn't that wonderful texture which is one of the charms of pewter; moreover, it oxidises in a different way and seems to take on a blackish tarnish "beneath the burnishing", if one may use such an inaccurate description, whereas the tarnish of pewter expresses itself in an exterior oxide which can be felt by its very roughness.

Before me, as I write, stand two lidded tankards, the one marked Dixon & Sons, and the other bearing the marks of Edwards of London, the former a recognised maker of Britannia metal, and the latter of pewter.

To the casual observer these two tankards would seem to be identical in type, and apart from slight variations of the mouldings around the foot they are alike in general outline, shape of handle, plain-drum body, etc., and yet there is *a difference!* The lid of the Britannia metal specimen is either pressed from the flat or spun, and the edge is turned in similar to the folded foot of an old wineglass, whereas the lid of the pewter example is cast and solid. The metal in the former is hard and almost unscratched, whereas, in the pewter example there are those unmistakable little indentations and abrasions which bespeak the softer metal; in short, there is a *very real* difference which, however difficult to explain, is abundantly apparent. The Britannia metal looks clean and cold and almost new, yet, while the pewter example is just as clean and in as fine condition, it tells its own tale of years of use.

Turning from this aspect, however, one finds other and important points of difference. One of the most important is the appearance on many examples of Britannia of the makers' names, names which stamp them immediately as such. It is well for the serious collector to know that the following makers never touched pewter wares in any form: Dixon & Sons; Dixon & Smith; Broadhead & Atkin; I. Vickers; Wolstenholme; Ashberry; Colsman's Improved Compost; Stacey; Holdsworth; Smith, Kirkby & Co., etc.

Then again, so many of the Britannia metal wares are of such different designs from those of the pewterers as to cause one little uneasiness.

Tea-caddies, cream-jugs, sugar-basins, egg-cups, wine-strainers, octagonal and hexagonal tea- and coffee-pots, and those of Queen Anne fluted patterns with ball-feet and decorated finials on the lids, should *all* be treated with suspicion unless bearing the touch of a known pewterer.

The impression of small catalogue numbers on the undersides of salts, peppers, mustards, etc., is a sure indication that the pieces on which they appear are Britannia metal, for the catalogue era is one which has no charm for the pewter-collector, being confined practically to the period *since* about 1800, whereas we seek our treasures as long *before* that date as possible.

We will now pass to a consideration of the fourth item:

Genuine Old Pewter and Its Imitations

Here, again, we are up against one of those things which offers but little trouble to the experienced eye, but which it is *very* difficult to put down into writing.

A general rule which I have so often laid down is worth repeating, — "Pass *anything* which is suspect, no matter *how* enticing it may appear. There is so much that is beyond reproach that it is best to confine yourself to those pieces and to those alone. *Why should you* clog your collection with doubtful pieces which can never be anything but a source of anxiety to you when alone? What if, as will happen from time to time, a discerning fellow-collector pays your collection a visit? His *silence* on your doubtful items will be a more stinging lash than any criticism which he could pass upon your powers of discrimination!"

So much by way of generalization.

It is some source for congratulation that the faker has one great secret yet to learn before the finest of his pieces can become a terror to us, and that is, to imitate the spots and patches of corrosion which in some form, small or great, appear on the great majority of the genuine examples which have come down to our time. So far this has baffled him, but apart from this, some of the faked pieces are extremely clever and most convincing at first sight, blackened apparently with the neglect of years and everything complete to attract the eye of the unwary — *But*, in reality, this blackening is produced by a chemical which, for obvious reasons, were better not named here!

Now let us with a magnifying glass examine this blackening as done by the faker and compare it with the patina on a genuine specimen, and you will note that I use the word *patina* because I am now referring to those pieces which have but the lightest coating or veneer of oxide as opposed to those deeper blister-like incrustations which so often appear and which state is better grasped by the term "corrosion."

What do we gather from this microscopical examination? Just this, that the genuine patina has already set up the first stages of corrosion, giving to the surface of the metal a texture which resembles the beautiful granulation on the shell of an ordinary hen's egg, but the conclusion arrived at by our closer scrutiny of the faked piece is very different, for it reveals none of the granulations, but just what it is, — the "age" is *painted on* and the chemical cannot produce that same delightful surface.

As has already been said, some of the faked pieces are *very* clever and at the first blush have every appearance of being fine and genuine examples, but in the matter just referred to and in the lack of attention to other details, one soon discovers our friend's limitations which eventually enable us to condemn his wares. It would be so easy to put down here a few of these omissions on his part, but did

one do so, one would but take away the whole value of one's tests by giving to the faker that very knowledge, the lack of which is our chief safeguard!

Another way to avoid fakes is to put yourselves in the hands of an acknowledged expert, one to whom reputation counts for more than the mere making of money. The fees which you will pay to him for his advice, or for obtaining pieces for you, will provide you with a first-class, gilt-edged security with each of your treasures, a guaranty which, if at any time you wish to pass on your pieces, will assist materially in the process of doing so.

If you are fortunate enough to have access to the collections of friends of wider experience than yourself, study their pieces and inveigle them into talking over your difficulties with you, and compare notes with them, by which means you will find an added joy in collecting, and many of your greatest stumbling blocks will melt away.

In this connection one might suggest the formation in the United States of America of a "Society of Pewter Collectors." Such a society is now in full and useful operation here in England, and of which I have been a joint-Honourary Secretary since its inception, and if I can assist in any way, by advice, in the founding of a kindred society across the water, I am here to command.

We hold our meetings at one another's houses and discuss the collections piece by piece, and it is impossible to overestimate the good which comes from *frank* but friendly criticism. It will teach you more than anything I can write to you, if you have amongst your number one or two collectors of sufficient knowledge to guide and train your eyes to separate the sheep from the goats.

I am sure that I can vouch for a hearty welcome from our society should anything come of this suggestion, and their whole-hearted co-operation with you in any step which you may take for the furtherance of the cult of old pewter.

European Continental Pewter
and
Other Articles

A EUROPEAN PEWTER COLLECTION

Readers of ANTIQUES will be interested in this Swiss dining room and its arrangement of an exceptional collection of pewter. Immediately at the left of the door hangs, from an iron bracket, a *biberon*, concerning which ANTIQUES has already published some discussion (Vol. VII, p. 246, and Vol. VIII, p. 217.) To the left of this, again, appears, as part of the general room fitment, a lavabo basin, or *aquamanile*, with dolphin-shaped water container above. Such pieces were a dining room feature in days past. Other items will be discussed in the course of the series of articles on European pewter by H. H. Cotterell which begins in this number.
From the home of Caspar Hirsbrunner, Lucerne, Switzerland.

European Continental Pewter

Part I

By HOWARD HERSCHEL COTTERELL,* F.R. Hist. S.

Author of *National Types of Old Pewter*, etc.

INTRODUCTION

A FIELD honeycombed with pitfalls, obstacles, tangles, and quasi-contradictions — such is the foothold afforded anyone essaying the task of discriminating *absolutely* between the types of pewter wares produced in the various countries of Europe. Indeed, the subject of Continental pewter types is so vast as, by its very immensity, to chill all but the most enthusiastic. Such, one feels, must be the explanation of the fact that, up to now, hardly a *material* word has been written on the subject, in the English tongue.

This amazing fact is nevertheless distressing, for the reasons that a great proportion of the pewter which one sees for sale in antique shops *is* European; and that it is an extremely rare occurrence to find a collection of pewter wherein there are *no* European pieces; and, further, that some of the most beautiful types known to collectors *are to be found nowhere except in European ware*. The collector who consistently restricts his collection so as entirely to exclude European pieces, does so, in my opinion, at far too great a sacrifice of much that is singularly beautiful and interesting.

But, returning to the difficulties referred to in my opening remarks: one of the chief obstacles, as one takes a first step across the threshold of the subject, is that of segregating the types of different countries. There is a natural overlapping, inevitable to close geographical relations. In order that this may be the more evident, I have included here a rough pre-1914 sketch-map (*Fig. 1*). By way of comparison, it will be of interest to know that the total areas of the countries here under observation — Austria, Belgium, France, Germany, Holland, Hungary, Italy, Scandinavia, and Switzerland — amount to but 1,125,400 square miles, as opposed to the 2,970,000 square miles in the United States of America. Yet such a variety of patterns and quantity of wares was produced within this comparatively limited territory as utterly to bewilder the imagination; and this takes no account of Russian and Spanish pewter, of which little is known at the present time.

From even a casual glance at the map, it will at once

be seen that pewter types prevalent, for example, in the northern part of Switzerland must have worked across the frontier into southern Germany, and *vice versa;* other types from northeastern France into Belgium; from eastern France into Germany; from southeastern France into Switzerland and Italy; from Holland into Germany; and *vice versa* in each instance. Some types of Dutch and Belgian pewter seem to offer the most difficult knot of all to untie.

Add to all this the fact that Austria, Belgium, France, Germany, Holland, Hungary, Italy, Scandinavia, Switzerland, and so on, had each its own rules and its own organizations, and that, in every large town in each country, there were pewterers whose numbers varied according to the importance of the place as a pewtering centre; and the utter futility of attempting here to tackle the whole subject in anything like the detail it merits, will be, at once, appreciated.

Many learned works on the pewter of various countries are already available, and others are in course of compila-

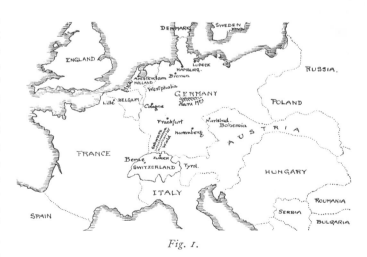

Fig. 1.

tion or of publication; but these works on individual countries, though written by the ablest authorities on the subject, and though replete with local knowledge, are all in the native tongue, and hence — quite apart from the high cost of acquiring them all — they are, except for the multi-linguist, as inaccessible as if they had not been written.

*This is the first of a series of articles on Continental European pewter which Mr. Cotterell, assisted by other notable experts, is preparing for ANTIQUES. The completed work promises to be one of the most important and valuable contributions to the literature of collecting which has appeared. Its eventual publication in book form — amplified very considerably — is promised.— THE EDITOR.

It was to bridge this hiatus in our knowledge that I was urged to take up the subject in its present form.

Consideration of the possibility of one day tackling the subject was not new to me; but, hitherto, the task had been dismissed, if not as impossible, certainly as requiring far more time than I had to give; yet here was a direct call which I felt I could not allow to go unanswered. Spurred on in the idea by my friend Mr. Robert M. Vetter of Amsterdam, himself a great and discerning authority on the subject, and, throughout, aided and assisted by him to such an extent that I can never adequately express my thanks, I responded to the call. These notes, which I trust in part supply the need, are the result.

Of the value, the erudition, and the volume of Mr. Vetter's selfless contributions to this work, I cannot speak too highly. By every law of right, his name should accompany my own as author; but, as he prefers it otherwise, my sole redress lies in the dedication of these notes to him and to Mrs. Vetter, to whom — as also to Mr. P. J. Ducro of Amsterdam — I am immeasurably indebted for much of the fine photographic work for the illustrations which adorn these pages. All the accompanying marks, Figures 2–15, are the photographic work of the latter. Many of them were taken under most difficult conditions from the *inner sides* of the bottoms of flagons and similar vessels. To these, as to many others whose names appear throughout these pages, my sincere thanks are due for allowing me to reproduce their treasures and for help in many other ways.

So much by way of introduction.

The Test of Pewter Marks

One realises that the cry will now at once go up for illustrations—and plenty of fine ones are to follow; but, before that feast is spread, it is essential that some attention be paid to the matter of *mark tests*, which will often be of greater help than illustrations. However, it is *not* my intention either to give lists of pewterers' names, or to delve into the subject of makers' marks; but to see what light may be thrown on the question of *quality* marks, *labels*, and *symbols*, over which various organizations exercised direct control, and which are of consequent service in enabling us, in a limited way, to obtain some knowledge of the country whence came the pieces which such marks identify.

The *labels* referred to above are in the form of labels, or cartouches, of various shapes, and bear certain words referring to the quality of the metal used. They were a guarantee of a certain standard, and, as they differed in various countries, their use for purposes of national identification is obvious.

Let us, however, first learn what clues are available as to the general interpretation of these European pewter marks. Their variety — *quality marks and labels, town and city marks, makers' marks,* and so on—is, at first sight, calculated to bewilder the student; but, as Mr. Vetter so delightfully puts it:

A collector with some practical experience will, if aided by reading and by the study of other collections, acquire a certain flair, enabling him to draw rapid conclusions as to probable age and origin, especially if he keeps his eyes open, *and his ears shut* to the voluble assertions of the dealer. The general style of the mark, its position on the piece, and its depth will all assist him in his diagnosis.

Each Mark Has Meaning

The various devices appearing on individual pieces of pewter are not there for decoration; but each one has its meaning. Like English marks, the older Continental marks were very small, usually of an heraldic character, and, in design, free from ostentation; and they were couched in the language of emblems, as being of greater service to an illiterate public than words. But, from the beginning of the seventeenth century, what is known as the *three-touch system*, with its variants, has obtained; and it is with this system that the average collector — for whom these notes are designed — will mostly be concerned, since pewter of the earlier periods is now become so rare as to be, from the collector's point of view, virtually extinct.

Elements Of The Three-Touch System

The three-touch system originally was made up of:

a. The town or city arms, or other local device, indicative of place of origin.

b. Maker's name, initials, touch or device.

c. Quality marks, the number and variety of which will best be appreciated by a contemplation of the various organizations, guild prescriptions, and trade customs which governed their use in the several countries and towns.

Care should be taken not to confound this grouping of marks with the so-called imitation silver marks, which have been used by *Dutch* pewterers since the eighteenth century, and of which a typical illustration is given here (*Fig. 2*) for comparison with the varying types under the three-touch system, which we shall now consider.

Fig. 2 — Dutch Imitation Silver Mark

The *X, crowned,* which surmounts this device must *not*, of course, be considered as part of the hall mark; but the whole mark was one die and was struck with one blow. It is Dutch, the "floating" angel with trumpet being typically so.

TYPES OF THE THREE TOUCHES

Type I.

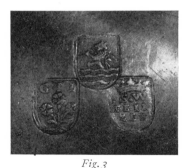

Fig. 3

This type, in its purest form, is shown in Figure 3, and is struck with three blows; i.e., three separate dies. The example is from the *inside* of a teapot of about *1750*.

It is made up of three separate stamps, arranged in accordance with the space available. The *flowers* with the initials constitute the maker's touch; the *lion rampant* emerging from the waves is the *arms* of Karlsbad; and the crowned *S. W. Fein Zin* is the *quality mark*, signifying that only pure tin, obtained from the mines at Schlaggenwald in Bohemia, was used for making the vessel.

Type II.

Fig. 4

Fig. 5

Fig. 6

Figures 4 and 5 (*before 1750*), and Figure 6 (*c. 1750*), show three methods of applying the three-touch system, but grouped differently from the one shown above. In all these cases *the pewterer's name is written out in full.* Figure 4 reveals *I. Wilh Sticker*, residing at *S:Walt* (Schlaggenwald). The *lion with the miner's tools* — hammer and pick — is the arms of that town, with which the official quality label is combined. The maker's private device of *Jonah and the whale* is in the centre, probably punning with his Christian name. Figures 5 and 6 are self-explanatory.

Type III.

Fig. 7

In Figure 7 is shown a variant, in that the town mark is omitted, its name *Augsburg* being introduced *at the bottom of the maker's touch*, which is the middle one, with the quality mark repeated on each side. The one shown in the illustration is one of the touches of the famous Sebald Ruprecht of Augsburg, dated *1712*.

Type IV.

Fig. 8

Figure 8 gives yet another variant, where the maker's touch and the town mark are omitted, the system being complied with by *thrice repeated impression of the quality mark*, a very superficial compliance at best! Where one mark is repeated thrice, as in this case, to the exclusion of the others, it must always be the quality mark which is retained. The touches here contain the maker's initials, *S.P.*, which are those of an eighteenth century Frankfort pewterer.

Type V.

Fig. 9

The omission of a special quality mark is, in itself, a silent admission of *second quality*. Figure 9 shows such a combination, on the left being the arms of the town of Eger, in Bohemia, and on the right the second quality mark of the *tall flagon* and the maker's initials. A date (*16–?7*) is distributed over both marks, which are struck separately. The date refers to the year of establishment of the pewterer's shop.

Fig. 10

In Figure 10, the initials at the top are those of the maker, the shield on the left being the arms of Zurich, and the one on the right, apparently, those of the maker, or his touch. The whole is struck with one die. The touch is that of Hans Heinrich Boshard, a member of a well-known family of pewterers, (*c. 1700*).

QUALITY MARKS

Angels

Having thus briefly reviewed the system of marking, we must now turn to a short consideration of the *quality* marks, of which by far the most frequent is the *angel*, the use of which was strictly reserved, by the most stringent regulations, for metal of the finest quality, free from lead, and carrying just sufficient copper, antimony, or bismuth to give it the requisite hardness. The angel was adopted throughout most of the European countries — Austria, Belgium, Denmark, Germany, Holland, Hungary, and Switzerland — as the sign of the *very best*, from the middle of the seventeenth century.

Embraced with the general term *angel* are all manner of winged female figures, whether seated, standing, flying, resting on an anchor, shield, or what-not, and carrying or holding, all sorts of attributes, such as palm branches, trumpets, swords, scales, and the like, and accompanied sometimes by small animals, deer or lambs.

It has been argued that, where three angels appear, as in Type IV, Figure 8, above, it implies that the metal is of superlatively good alloy; *but this is not the case.* There can be no better than the best, and the metal which bore one angel mark was every whit as good as if it had been covered with angels. The three angels, therefore, have solely to be regarded as a superficial compliance with the three-touch system.

Further, it has been found that the word *Englisch* usually appears on pieces of a style distinctly fashionable, or specially adapted for table use, as opposed to the plainer peasant or older style of wares.

Fig. 11

Fig. 11a

Fig. 12

Figures 11 and 12 show the use of the expressions *Englisch* and *Engli* respectively, both marks being from Frankfort, Germany. Figure 11 is the touch of a Frankfort pewterer named Klingling, the bell being allusive to his musical name. It is of the second half of the eighteenth century, whereas Figure 12 approximates 1780. In Figure *11a* is given another illustration of the *Englisch Zin* mark, that of Andreas Wirz, of Zurich, of the first half of the eighteenth century.

Fig. 13

Sometimes a figure simulating an angel was used, perhaps with the idea of palming off second for first quality.

Figure 13 shows Mercury in place of an angel; but the word *Probzinn* above reveals the true meaning to the more careful observer. The date of this mark is the late eighteenth century. It is an unique mark in that it is a *very* rare instance of the word *Probzinn* on Swiss pewter, probably an attempt by the maker (Johann Widmer of Zurich) to introduce it, an attempt no doubt promptly stopped by the guild authorities.

The Use Of "Englisch"

The use of the words *Engel, Engels, Englisch, Engli, Anglais*, and the like, on European pewter has given rise to the misconception that pewter so marked was imported in the mass from England, which a short consideration of the facts may do much to remove.

First, it does *not* mean that pewter mined in England was used; though this was the case in some instances. *Secondly*, it is a known fact that most of the raw material of Swiss and German pewter was supplied by the tin mines of Saxony and Bohemia, whilst in Holland much of it was imported from the Straits Settlements.

It is, however, an undeniable fact that English pewter enjoyed a tremendous reputation on the Continent, *not so much for the raw material employed as for the manner in which such raw material was blended and treated.*

Such terms as *Engel Zin*, or *Engels Zin*, would seem to have reference merely to the fact that it was of *angel;* i.e., *first* quality; but the words *Englisch Tin* (or Zin), *Engli Tin, Etain Anglais*, and similar phrases, have direct reference, *not* to the fact that English tin was used, *but* that the metal was *treated after the English fashion;* i.e., by the addition of just so much copper or antimony as would harden it, a treatment adopted very widely in later years by European craftsmen, who formerly had alloyed their tin with lead. It is to be remembered, then, that tin inscribed as *Englisch, Engli, Anglais, Engel, Engels*, was *always entirely free from lead.*

In this connection, Mr. Vetter remarks that, by comparison of his London plates with contemporary Continental plate-pewter, which, although white, is soft, he can understand the tendency to make pewter as hard and ringing as the English metal!

THE QUALITY ROSE

Fig. 14

The *rose* was also used as a quality mark, guaranteeing sometimes first, sometimes a slightly inferior quality.

Figure 14 shows a typical example, taken from a Dutch piece of second quality, with the maker's initials inserted in the base of the crown, which is quite characteristic of Holland. This touch is early eighteenth century and differs but slightly from those of the seventeenth century.

MODERN IMITATIONS

The *angel*, being the best quality mark, appears, of course, on most of the imitation pewter which is being put on the market in such enormous quantities today. Where the *marks themselves* are modern imitations, the impression is shallow and of equal depth, and hence not calculated to deceive any but the veriest tyro; but where, as is unfortunately the case, old-established firms are using their *old* angel irons to mark their modern reproductions, the difficulty in detection is far more subtle, and one has to rely on one's own judgment of the metal, methods of manufacture, and so on.

I hope to be able to reproduce a few of the more dangerous of these marks, when treating the subject of Continental frauds.

UNMARKED ITEMS

Again, one comes across pieces bearing no marks at all, and such pieces are by no means to be despised for that reason alone; for, if the metal is good and the piece well-wrought and of pleasing design, the presence or absence of a mark will be a matter of secondary moment to the true connoisseur.

In order to simplify the matter, I propose to give in tabular form, a list of the more familiar quality marks, labels, and symbols, showing in what countries and for which qualities they were used. It is not suggested that the list is complete, but it embraces the better known marks and should prove of much service.

Before giving this table, however, and by way of throwing light upon it, I should like to quote a passage from Jan Wagenaar's work on *Amsterdam*, where he gives certain information concerning the regulations of the Amsterdam Pewterers' Guild. As similar regulations were laid down in other places in Holland, it will be of more than *local* interest. The following is a translation of the passage*:

XLII. *Pewterers' Guild.* The old rules and regulations, dated January 13, 1573, include, Tinnegieters (Pewterers) Kannemakers (Canmakers), Kannedekkers (Makers of potlids), Lepel Makers (Spoonmakers) and such people as lend pewter for hire. Further, the sellers of glass and earthenware vessels were under the jurisdiction of the Guild.

Regarding the composition of the metal used, various rules have been laid down stipulating that no other than the said proportions may be employed in this city. Power is given to the masters of the Guild, to satisfy themselves as to the adherence to these rules in the various shops.

Four sorts of pewter are allowed here, i.e., *blok tin, fyn roostin, keurtin* and *kleine keurtin*. Blok tin is the purest, without any addition whatsoever. It has to be marked with an *angel*. By some makers the arms of the city are added. The common fine pewter is called *roostin* because it must be marked with a rose. It must consist of ninety-four parts of blok tin mixed with eight parts of lead. The lowest grade of pewter must be marked with the city arms, besides which the letters K.K. must appear, meaning Kleine Keur (Small Test). It may be of lesser quality than the *keurtin*, but both sorts of *keur tin* may be used only for such wares as stills, koffee pots, beer and wine cans without spouts, syringes and enemas, funnels, inkstands, spoons, and ornamental work. Every pewterer may add his own mark provided same is known to the Guildmasters.

From the above it will be seen that, if a pewterer, in addition to the quality mark of the *angel*, struck his own private touch and the city arms too, the three-touch system was accomplished.

The above simple rules were flagrantly broken in the late eighteenth century, so much so that Mr. Vetter informs me that he has seen a piece marked with an *angel* and *K.K.*, or *best* and *worst* qualities in one piece! Needless to say, it was in reality *K.K.*

Also, one finds such marks as an *angel* and a *rose* on the same piece in the eighteenth century, which may point to an intermediate quality. This combination, which is Dutch, is well shown in Figure 15, which I am able to give through the courtesy of M. C. Brandes, Esq., of Amsterdam.

Fig. 15

*Amsterdam, 1766 edition, by Isaak Tirion, Tome IX, p. 204.

Quality (or "Control") Marks, Labels & Symbols

ALL PRE-1914 TERRITORIES →	AUSTRIA			BELGIUM			FRANCE			GERMANY			HOLLAND			HUNGARY			ITALY			SWITZER-LAND			SCANDI-NAVIA			RUSSIA=R POLAND=P		
	Quality			*Quality*			*Quality*			*Quality*			*Quality*			*Quality*			*Quality*			*Quality*			*Quality*			*Quality*		
	1st	2nd	3rd	1st	2nd	3rd	1st	2nd	3rd	1st	2nd	3rd	1st	2nd	3rd	1st	2nd	3rd	1st	2nd	3rd	1st	2nd	3rd	1st	2nd	3rd	1st	2nd	3rd
ANGEL MARK	X			X						X			X			X						X						XP		
*AMSTERDAM, ARMS OF — If alone, is the mark for use on KEURTIN, or 3rd quality														Amsterdam only X															
If with letters KK it is the mark of KLEINE KEUR, q.v.														Fourth Quality X															
If with Angel mark, it is the symbol of BLOCK TIN, or first quality													X																	
?BELL, may be as a symbol for *Etain Sonnant*																														
BERGZINN, a Saxon and Bohemian expression meaning mountain tin, or pure tin	X									X																				
BLOC TIN (These signify 1st quality & that no scrap metal is used in the alloy.)										X						X														
BLOCK TIN										X			?X																	
BLOCK ZIN(N)										X						X						X								
BLOK TIN													X																	
†C.=Compo	X																		X											
C, Crowned=Does not mean *clair* or *control* but third quality or *Commun*; i.e., common					X			X																						
ƆC, Crowned								X																						
₵ Crowned—CLAAR UND LAUTER, i.e., clear & pure. An old Saxon quality mark										Saxony X																				
†COMPO		X																		X										
†COMPOS		X																		X										
CRISTALIN							X															X								
CRISTAL ZIN										X																				
CROWN=KRONZINN, i.e., Crown tin											X																			
DEMI-FLEUR-DE-LYS							X																							
EAGLE, with human face										Nuremberg X																				
EAGLE, with Crown										Nuremberg X																				
EAGLE, with Crown & Rose										Nuremberg X																				
ENGELI TIN										X												X								
ENGELS TIN													X																	
ENGELS BLOCK ZIEN *or Tin*				X						X												X								
ENGELS GEPOLYST HART TIN													X																	
ENGELS HARD TIN													X																	
ENGELS PLOCK TIN										X												X								
ENGELS ZIN										X												X								
ENGELSK TIN=Angel Tin																									Danish					
ENGLI BLOCK ZINN										X						X						X								
ENGLISCH AUGSPURG										X																				
ENGLISCH TIN										X																				
ENGLISCH ZIN(N)										X																				
ENGL ZINN										X						X						X								
ENG ZIN										X						X						X								
ESTAIN ANGLAIS							X															X								
ESTAIN FIN							X															X								
ESTAING FIN							X															X								
ETAIN ANGLAIS							X															X								
ETAIN ARGENTIN=Silvery tin							X																							
ETAIN BLANC=White tin							X																							
ETAIN CLAIR=Clear tin							X																							
ÉTAIN CRISTALIN							X																							
ETAIN FIN							X															X								
ETAIN D'ANGLETERRE				Liege X																										
ETAIN FIN D'ANGLETERRE							X																							
ETAIN FIN CRISTALIN							X																							
ETAIN RAFINE							X																							
ETAIN SONNANT							X																							
ETIN CRISTALIN							X																							
ETIN DANGLETERRE (*sic*)							X																							
ETIN FIN							X									X			X			X								
F, Crowned or uncrowned=Fein, Fin or fine				X									X									X								
F. C.=Fine Compo		X																												
F. E.=Fine Etain				X						X												X								
FEIN BLOCK ZIN										X																				
FEIN BLOCK ZING										X																				
FEIN COMPO		X																												
FEIN ZIN or F. Z.	X									X						X						X								
FEIN ZINK	X									X												X								
FEIN ZINN	X									X												X								
FEINZINK	X									X												X								
FESTES BLOCK ZINN	X															?X														
F. F. Crowned							X																							
¶F. Crowned							X																							
FIN								x														X								
FIN ETAIN																						X								
FIN ETEIN																						X								
FIN ETIN																						X								

Quality (or "Control") Marks, Labels & Symbols (*Cont'd*)

ALL PRE-1914 TERRITORIES →	AUSTRIA			BELGIUM			FRANCE			GERMANY			HOLLAND			HUNGARY			ITALY			SWITZERLAND			SCANDINAVIA			RUSSIA=R POLAND=P		
	Quality			*Quality*			*Quality*			*Quality*			*Quality*			*Quality*			*Quality*			*Quality*			*Quality*			*Quality*		
	1st	2nd	3rd	1st	2nd	3rd	1st	2nd	3rd	1st	2nd	3rd	1st	2nd	3rd	1st	2nd	3rd	1st	2nd	3rd	1st	2nd	3rd	1st	2nd	3rd	1st	2nd	3rd
Fin Zin	X									X						X						X								
Fino	X																		X			X								
Flagon		X	X								X	X																		
Fleur-de-Lys							X																							
Fleur-de-lys with palm branches										Saxony X																				
Fyn	X												X									X								
Fyn Engels Hart Tin													X																	
Fyn Engels Gereinigd = Fine English purified													X																	
Griffin with Flagon	X																													
Hammer, A Pewterer's, Crowned or uncrowned				Small X			X	X		Early Nuremberg X												Western X	X							
Hard Tin													X	X																
I.P.Z = ? . . Prob Zinn	?X																													
K.= Kannenzinn										Konigsberg X	X																			
Keur Tin													X																	
K.K.= Kleine Keur — See "Amsterdam" above														X																
Kleine Keur =														X																
K.T.= Keur Tin													X																	
Kron Tin = Crown Tin																									Danish					
Kronzin = Crown Tin										Bremen X																				
Lion with Flagon	X	X																												
Lion with Hammer & Flagon	X																													
London										X						X														
L.Z.= Lauter Zinn, i.e., pure tin										Saxony X																				
Mang(g)ods = Mixed, Good																													Danish	
M.E.= Maintzisch Englisch										Maiance X																				
Mercury, & similar figures simulating Angels, are 2nd quality marks																									X					
Metal Argentin							X															X								
Metal du Prince = Prince's metal							X																							
Nuremburg, Arms of										X																				
Plock Zin	X									X						X						?X								
P.M.E.= Pur Maintzisch Englisch										Maiance X																				
Prob		X								X							X						X							
Probezin										X	X																			
Prob Tin										X																				
Prob Zin(n)		X								X							X						X							
Prob Zuinn										Saxony X																				
Prosin		X																												
P.Z.= Prob Zin		X								X																				
Rafine							X																							
Rose, Crowned or uncrowned. In Holland, it implied 6 parts lead to 94 of tin and was called Fine Roos Tin. In Nuremberg, 1st quality in 16th, 17th & 18th centuries. Appears in Austria sometimes in the maker's touch, when using the three touch system.	X (If with Angel or S.W.)				X			X		X (If with Angel flanked by Palm branches, Westphalia, Cologne, Rhineland)	X		?X (Sometimes with Angel)	X		X (If with Angel and palm branches)										X				
Rosenzin										Saxony X																				
Salzburger Prob Z	Salzberg X																													
Sonnant de Saxe										Saxony X																				
Stolberg Fein Zin										Saxony X																				
S. W.= Tin from the Schlaggenwald Mines, near Carlsbad, Bohemia	X															X														
S. W. FEIN	X															X														
S. W. Fein Zin (n)	X															X														
S. W. Fin Zin	X															X														
S. W. F. Z.	X															X														
Vermischtes Zinn		X																												
V. Z.= Vermischtes Zinn		X																												
V. Zinn = Vermischtes Zinn		X																												
X										Saxony X																				
X Crowned — Tin & Lead in the proportion of ten and one	Vienna X				X					Saxony X			With Angel X	X		With Angel X	X													
X / 10										Saxony X																				

*Amsterdam is inserted not as being unique, but as being typical of the custom in vogue in many of the continental pewtering centres, where the town Arms were very often used to designate a particular quality.

†Vermischtes Zinn has the same meaning as Compo and Compos; i.e., "Mixed Tin." The former had to be stamped on Austrian wares made from scrap pewter, in conformity with a regulation of 1770, which also prescribes Schlakenwaldter Fein Zinn for wares made from new block tin, which must be absolutely free from lead.

NOTES

Arms of a city, accompanied by a maker's private touch may be read as indicative of second quality pewter, or *Probzinn*.

It is probable that the *angel*, as a quality mark, originated in Holland. It was used in a limited way, on French pewter.

An *anchor* flanked by palm branches *may* mean *Feinzinn*.

The *miner's tools*, a crossed hammer and pick, appear in Saxon and Bohemian marks very frequently, but have no reference to quality.

A *lion with two tails*, working the rock with hammer and pick, is the arms of Schlaggenwald, Bohemia.

A *deer, or stag, beside the angel* is found in Frankfort touches.

It is not definitely known yet whether, in early times, the city arms or quality marks were impressed by a guild official — as a *hall mark* — or not. It is, however, certain that, in the majority of cases, the master himself saw to the marking of all his pewter. It would seem from old guild and government regulations that, in early times, *hall marking* was customary; but it is obvious that, with the expansion of the trade, such a custom was bound to disappear and that the guildmasters would have to content themselves with making occasional surprise visits of inspection.

To Jorgen Olrik, Esq., Managing Inspector of the Dansk Folke-Museum at Copenhagen, Denmark, I am indebted for the following and much further information concerning Danish pewter and its markings, most of which he has courteously permitted me to cull from his *Gammelt Tintoj*, published in *Tidsskrift For Industri*, Copenhagen, 1906, and for several fine photographs, many of them especially taken to illustrate my future notes on Danish pewter.

The foundation of the first Danish pewterers' guilds cannot be easily traced, but there is a well-known Charter of King Kristian V, which, in 1685, apparently confirms existing guild regulations.

These regulations would seem to have been adhered to fairly closely until the time of the pewter decline (*c. 1800*), and the marking done in accordance therewith permits of an easy distinction between the various qualities and from the types of other nations.

The regulations lay down the following, with regard to marking:

The standards of quality are to be as follows:

1. *Engelsk tin* (English tin) has to be marked with an *angel* in addition to a separate second touch of a *crowned rose* bearing the town arms *on the rose*. The second touch must bear also the name or initials of the maker and the year of his admission to membership of the guild; i.e., leave to start in business on his own account. If he was a member already in 1685, this date was to be added.

This combination is shown in Figure 16, where the quality mark of the *angel*, the arms of Copenhagen (three pinnacles) — are on the rose — and the maker's initials *E.L.B.*, and the date of his admission all appear.

2. *Kron tin* (crown tin), the second quality mark. This consists of the town arms surmounted by a shamrock or clover leaf, in which latter the name or initials of the maker were to appear, with the date also in the mark. Two differing examples of this type of quality mark are shown in Figures 17 and 18.

In the former the arms are again those of Copenhagen, whilst in the latter they are those of the town of Odense (the double lily).

Fig. 16

Fig. 17   *Fig. 18*

3. *Mang (g)ods* (mixed good) was the name of the third quality, and was to be marked twice with the maker's touch bearing his name. Unfortunately, owing to its rarity, I am unable to give an illustration of this form of marking.

Mr. Olrik says that Danish labels bearing such indication of quality are rarely found.

These simple rules, confirmed in 1685 by King Kristian, were found sufficient and practicable, and were followed with singular fidelity as compared with other countries, where a certain degree of anarchy would seem to have obtained from time to time.

Krontin agrees roughly with Nuremberg *probzinn* and is slightly below the standard of Dutch *keurtin*.

In Figure 19 is given a permissible form of compromise for *Engelsk tin*, where there is not sufficient space to admit of both the marks as shown in Figure 16.

Fig. 19

It is hoped that the foregoing remarks may have the desirable effect of simplifying the reading of the preceding table.

(To be continued)

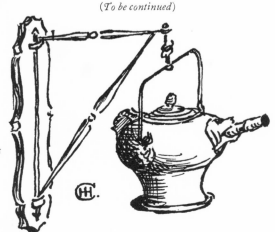

PEWTER BIBERON

European Continental Pewter

Part II

Distinguishing National Features, Other Than Marks

By HOWARD HERSCHEL COTTERELL,* F.R. Hist. S.

Fig. 20 — THE PLAIN BALL
The Ball is Germanic in origin. Common to Germany and German-speaking countries. Shows many variations.

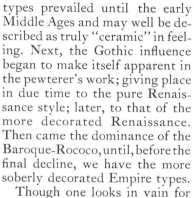

Fig. 21 — STRAIGHT-LOBED BALL

ALTHOUGH the greatest of all tests of the nationality of a piece of pewter is to be looked for in the maker's marks, there are other and very unmistakable features which, in some cases, point an unerring finger either to the *actual country* or to the *general region* of origin. Specific features, or characteristics, often remained constant to, and confined by, the boundaries of their native countries. But often, again, they have unassumingly overstepped such limits to find an adoptive welcome awaiting them in lands contiguous to their own. In any such latter case, however, more often than not one finds native features more or less modified so as to conform to the traditions of the country of adoption.

To those whose acquaintance with Continental pewter types is limited to such items as they may encounter in curiosity and junk shops, many of the illustrations which accompany these articles of mine will be something of a revelation, as indeed they have been to me, whose life, for upwards of a quarter of a century, has been devoted to pewter research.

EVOLUTION OF PEWTER FORMS

From the enlightenment so gained one can now begin to understand the steady but inexorable process of evolution which has governed and guided — albeit unwittingly — the pewterer's mind and hand throughout the ages.

We may, for our purposes, assume the influence derived from the Romans, whose designs are replete with the suggestion that they were based upon the work of the pottery vessels of clay made upon the potter's wheel. Simple, devoid of anything but the slightest ornament — and that but sparsely used — such

types prevailed until the early Middle Ages and may well be described as truly "ceramic" in feeling. Next, the Gothic influence began to make itself apparent in the pewterer's work; giving place in due time to the pure Renaissance style; later, to that of the more decorated Renaissance. Then came the dominance of the Baroque-Rococo, until, before the final decline, we have the more soberly decorated Empire types.

Though one looks in vain for evidences of a similar evolution in the pewter work of Great Britain, each successive "wave of influence" left its indelible mark upon the craft throughout the Continent of Europe.

These remarks, though a digression here, *are essential* to an intelligent appreciation of our subject.

THE THUMBPIECE AS A GUIDE

Let us now, however, turn to such definite national characteristics as it may be possible to review in the space at our disposal. I think I cannot do better than to observe the same procedure which I adopted in my *National Types of Old Pewter,** and, first of all, give consideration to some of the European Continental thumbpieces. I shall have occasion frequently henceforth to refer to them, and, for brevity's sake, must do so by name.

The ones which I propose to mention here are: the *Ball*, the *Brambleberry*, the *Bent-back Wedge*, the *Cleft*, the *Erect*, the *Leaf*, the *Lens*, the *Linked*, the *Mascaron*, the *Plume*, the *Rams' Heads*, the *Shell* (or *Palmette*), the *Twin Acorn*, and the *Twin Pomegranate*.

We shall consider these in the alphabetical order named, beginning with:

THE BALL

This would seem to be essentially *Germanic*, by which word — where-

Fig. 22 — THE STRAIGHT-LOBED BALL

*Continued from the January number of AN-TIQUES. Copyright, 1927, by Howard Herschel Cotterell. All rights reserved.

*Published by ANTIQUES, *Inc.*, Boston, 1925.

Fig. 23 — Horizontal Fillet Ball

Fig. 24 — Vertically Filleted Ball

the collection of A. J. G. Verster, of the Hague; Figure 26 shows the cupped finial on a fine *Thuringian Pechkrug,* also in the collection of Mr. Verster.*

The Ball thumbpiece would seem to have come into existence during the seventeenth century; but its great popularity to have been reached during the eighteenth.

Before leaving the Ball, I feel I must make my apologies to the correspondent who, in the issue of ANTIQUES for May, 1925, called attention to this thumbpiece as a receptacle for holding nutmeg, a statement which I queried in a reply published in the same magazine for October, 1925. I was wrong in casting doubt on "G. A. R. Goyle's" statement; and, if this should catch his eye, I hope that he will accept my humble cry of "peccavi!"† *These Balls were, at times, made to unscrew* for the purpose stated. A similar feature is occasionally found on the *inner* sides of the bases of the short, stumpy Austrian tankards, where a ferrule, or nipple, holds the nutmeg in position by the operation of a thumbscrew, as indicated in the accompanying sketch (*Fig. 27*). Thus the nutmeg apparently was immersed until the tankard was emptied.

The use of the Ball as a foot will be noted, as a point of interest, by referring back to Figure 21.

The Bent-Back Wedge

This may, possibly, be a modification of the erect type, but its introduction, or evolution, so far as known, is comparatively recent. I do not remember having seen it on pieces earlier than the eighteenth century, or of other than French nationality, and then principally on Normandy flagons and cylindrical measures. (See Figures 28 and 29, respectively.)

ever I may use it — I mean to convey the thought that, while the Ball was a product of Germany, it was also used in the German-speaking parts of Austria, Hungary, Switzerland, and so on. The Ball is believed to be thoroughly German in its origin; and its appearance elsewhere must be considered merely sporadic. It takes many forms, from that of a plain sphere, to that of a sphere with perpendicular lobes, spiral flutes, horizontal and vertical fillets, which sometimes cover its whole surface, sometimes but the upper half.

In certain cases the sphere has a somewhat flattened or crushed appearance, and again we find it with a small cup, or chalice or a spool-like protrusion on the top. Early in the nineteenth century the ball developed, at times, into an urn shape, though the sphere persisted, and still persists on students' beer-mugs and so forth.

Figure 20, picturing an example from the collection of Alfred B. Yeates, F.S.A., of London, shows the plain Ball on a Hanseatic flagon. The straight-lobed Ball — side and top views — is shown in Figures 21 and 22 on a guild flagon in the collection of my collaborator, Robert M. Vetter of Amsterdam.

The horizontal fillet occurs in Figure 23, and the vertical — covering the entire sides — in Figure 24, from an example in the collection of Charles G. J. Port, F.S.A., of Worthing. The flattened Ball is well exemplified in Figure 25, from

Figs. 25, 26, 27 —
Flattened Ball, (*Left*)
Cupped Ball, (*Right*)
Nutmeg Clamp, (*Below*)

*A point worth noting *en passant* is that the Ball is sometimes placed immediately over the hinge, and at other times on the lid, or between the hinge and lid.

†This was, of course, written considerably before the publication of G. A. R. Goyle's article *The Nutmeg Vindicated* in ANTIQUES for December, 1926.

Fig. 29 — The Bent-Back Wedge
Characteristically French: on cylindrical measures.

Fig. 28 — The Bent-Back Wedge

Fig. 30 — THE BRAMBLEBERRY
French. The example is of *1706*.

THE BRAMBLE-
BERRY

This, too, would seem to be an evolution, but, in this instance, from the Twin Pomegranate or Twin Acorn. The Brambleberry is quite an uncommon type, and the fine illustration here given, in Figure 30, is

above the lid hinge; *never* over the lid itself.

Distribution of the Erect thumbpiece covers Austria, Bohemia, Germany, Eastern Hungary, and Switzerland and — in slightly modified form — Belgium, France, and Holland.

In the last named country it became more crude and had a little raised square pad, or eminence, on the end, presumably to give a better purchase to the pressing thumb.

Fig. 31 — THE CLEFT
North German or Danish.

from a small French flagon in the possession of Etienne Delaunoy, of Amsterdam. It bears the date *1706*.

THE CLEFT

This would seem to have been inspired by the work of Augsburg silversmiths. The illustrative example, chosen from Mr. Vetter's collection, is dated *1778*. It is a North German or Danish piece (*Fig. 31*).

THE ERECT

The chief claim which one can put forward for the inclusion of this type here is that it *is* a thumbpiece! Certainly it has *no* national individuality. Quite the reverse, for I believe it to have been one of the most widely distributed of them all. And yet it must be admitted here to give completeness to the series.

There seems little doubt as to the Gothic origin of the

Figs. 32, 33 — THE ERECT
Composed of two C curves in opposition. Of mediaeval origin, but of wide distribution in Austria, Bohemia, Germany, Eastern Hungary, and Switzerland, and, in slightly modified form, in Belgium, France, and Holland.

Erect thumbpiece; but the type had a very long run from that period until well into the late eighteenth or early nineteenth century. In construction it consists of two opposed circular sweeps, and, like all Gothic creations, it is admirably adapted to its purpose, and fits the grip perfectly. It is always poised

Bertram, of Chemnitz. A later example, from another fine

In Belgium and France, the upper circular sweep gives place to a straight section, the terminal of which finishes in a sort of baluster motif and a kind of double wedge lid attachment, reminding one of the wavelets running over one another across a flat sandy shore.

A very beautiful and early example of the general type is shown in Figure 32, from a magnificent flagon, dated *1589*, in the famous collection of Fritz

piece in the Yeates collection, appears in Figure 33. The Dutch, Flemish, and French types are shown in Figures 34, 35, and 36, respectively, the former from the collection of Mrs. L. Payne, of Amstelveen; and the latter from that of Mrs. J. Denys, of Amsterdam.

THE LEAF

This type, as will be seen from

Figs. 34, 35, 36 — THE ERECT
Here, in the order shown, are Dutch, Flemish, and French expressions of the Erect thumbpiece.

Fig. 37 — THE LEAF
This example is from a sixteenth century French flagon.

Fig. 38 — THE LEAF
From a *burette* of 1700.

the beautiful flagon illustrated in Figure 37, from the collection of H. C. Gallois, of the Hague, has its roots buried in the early period. This example, probably dating back to the sixteenth century and emanating from France, shows the Leaf in its early form; while the little burette in Figure 38 — from the Yeates collection — shows the thumbpiece development in the year 1700.

THE LENS

Here one must remove one's shoes in reverence; for one stands before a type the origin of which is lost in remote antiquity. The Lens type is shown in the centre of the three primitive pieces illustrated in Figure 39, the photograph of which was kindly supplied by Jørgen Olrik from certain pieces in the Dansk Folkemuseum at Copenhagen, of which institution Mr. Olrik is managing Inspector.

These examples were found at Assen, on the Island of Fünen. They demonstrate, with more force than can any words, the evolution of the pewter vessel from its forerunner in clay; and they give point to the remark made on an earlier page that such early pewter is "ceramic" in feeling. I shall have occasion to revert to this photograph and this subject in a later article.

In this Lens type of thumbpiece, which crosses the connecting bar at right angles, there occur on both back and front, two convex, lens-like protrusions, or bosses, which give to the whole a very severe appearance. It is probably of North German Hanseatic origin.

THE LINKED

The Linked thumbpiece is well shown in the extremely good example of Figure 40, from the lid of a stone pot in the collection of Mr. Vetter. Here is another rather early

Fig. 39 — THE LENS
Probably of North German origin. These three superb examples, found on the Island of Fünen, illustrate an old form of this thumbpiece.

type, and Mr. Vetter assures me that none of the examples he has seen may be dated later than 1600. It is believed to be a purely Dutch type.

THE MASCARON

The Mascaron may be considered a variety of the Erect, and usually has slanting or bevelled flanks. It mostly appears on German, Alsatian, Austrian, and Eastern Hungarian work, from about 1550 onwards. The Mascaron itself represents Medusa, and is intended to symbolize the frightening of evil spirits. The same device is sometimes repeated on the finial of the handle, as on the handsome flagon in Figure 42. Figure 41 is from a Heidelberg flagon — somewhat indistinct from wear.

If laid flat against the body of the vessel, the Mascaron is a reliable indication of Austrian origin. Figure 42 illustrates both this and our next type:

THE PLUME

The Plume, which is illustrated in Figure 43, stands straight up from the hinge part and is very popular in Alpine districts. It is probably a seventeenth century development.

THE RAMS' HEADS

This type takes the form of two rams' heads, back to back, set at right angles to the strengthening bar of the lid, at the front end of which a third head is sometimes found, *affronté;* i.e., looking out toward the front of the lid. This type is exclusively found on Swiss flagons from the canton of Wallis. An example will be seen in the

Fig. 40 — THE LINKED
A Dutch type not observed after the year 1600.

centre of the fine row of these flagons, in the Vetter collection, which I illustrate in Figure 43*a*.

THE SHELL (OR PALMETTE)

In point of popularity this would seem to be the Dutch analogue of the contemporary German ball; but it is by no means exclusively Dutch, for it is found on Flemish pewter, too, and, occasionally, on pewter of other nationalities. But the low Countries were *very* fond of it (*Fig. 44*).

THE TWIN ACORN AND THE TWIN POMEGRANATE

Here again, we are contemplating types so old, so inextricably interwoven with the early "ceramic" types of pewter that they, too, have thus far evaded our efforts to confine them within given dates. Like the Lens type, in their early expression they are objects of our veneration.

Figure 45 shows an extremely rare and beautiful early example of the Pomegranate, once more from the Verster collection. Figure 46 shows its later development on a Wallis flagon; whilst, in Figure 47, a fine example of the early Acorn is given on a small sixteenth century ointment jar from the Rijksmuseum at Amsterdam.

In Figure 48, appear three eighteenth century Wallis examples of the type,

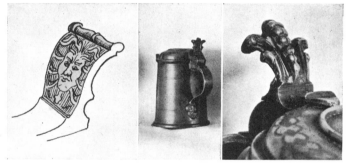

Figs. 41, 42 — THE MASCARON; *Fig. 43 (right)* — THE PLUME
The Mascaron appears in Alsatian, Austrian, and Eastern Hungarian pewter from 1550 onward. Figure 41 is from a Heidelberg flagon; Figure 42 shows the Mascaron as the terminal of the handle.
The Plume, a seventeenth century development, is very popular in Alpine districts.

Fig. 43a — RAMS' HEADS AND TWIN ACORNS
Exclusively Swiss. The Rams' Head thumbpiece appears on the middle member of this group of flagons from the Wallis Canton.

Fig. 44 — THE SHELL
Chiefly of the Low Countries.

Fig. 45 — TWIN POMEGRANATE
A thumbpiece type of very early origin. Here shown on a Dutch tankard.

standing, as was their custom when not in use, upside down on the shelf with their lids hanging down. This picture gives a very good idea of the heart-shaped lid and the varying lengths of the strengthening bars. Likewise it demonstrates the position of the acorns immediately on the flap-hinge.

OTHER TYPES

It must not be assumed that the above enumeration by any tive terminology, which conveys some fair idea as to their general form and outline, and thus, by suggesting a mental picture, provides a readily understood means of reference for connoisseurs.

Many types not thus far referred to will be found illustrated on succeeding pages; but few, if any, of these may be viewed as representative of the steady progress of pewter evolution. Rather they must

means exhausts all the types which were in use, the design of which, after all, was obviously subject to any passing caprice of the individual pewterer. In the present article, it is to be remembered, reference is permissible only to such standard types as give some measure of indication regarding the country of their origin, and are, solely on that account, eligible for inclusion in a dissertation on *distinguishing national features*. All of the types enumerated, further, may be classified according to a distinctively descrip-

Figs. 46, 47 — TWIN POMEGRANATE AND TWIN ACORN
The first is a later Swiss development of the Pomegranate shown in Figure 45. The second, the Acorn, appears on a sixteenth century ointment box.

be regarded as possibly culled from the art of the silversmith, or as illustrating the personal predilections of individual craftsmen.

It is hoped that the classification here presented may be adopted universally by connoisseurs, collectors, and dealers alike, and that it may become the standard method of reference to the various types of European pewter. This result, already accomplished in Great Britain with reference to British types, has, in every way, proved itself of the greatest help to all concerned.

(*To be continued*)

Fig. 48 — TWIN ACORNS
These Wallis Canton flagons, standing on their heads on a shelf, show the acorn thumbpiece. The beauty of the turning is emphasized by the position.

"Rembrandt" Flagon (*Seventeenth Century*)
    A Dutch example with tall base. Referred to as Figure 55 in Part III
of the series *European Continental Pewter*, which appears on page 382.

European Continental Pewter

Part III

By HOWARD HERSCHEL COTTERELL,* F.R. Hist S.

IN some earlier articles on European pewter, I have discussed methods of determining the nationality of specimens which may be encountered. First, of course, we have the guidance of the marks which the pewterers impressed upon their pieces. Second, as I pointed out in my article in ANTIQUES for March, we may look to the thumbpiece of lidded items as an index of nationality.

Turning now from thumbpieces, we must look for other distinguishing features, either in specific details or in completed types. And first let us see what we can learn from handles, handle-finials, lids, bases, and so on.

I have already written about the German handle in my *National Types;* but one might write much more about it had one the space. Here, however, I must condense my remarks and leave my readers to draw their own conclusions from the illustrations which I shall give when I come to write my notes on the pewter story of Germany. Suffice it to say here that, unlike the Dutch, who seem to have viewed both handle and thumbpiece as of secondary importance, devoting to them but little thought or finish, the Germans have treated these details as important parts of a thing of beauty, and have developed them to a degree of excellence never surpassed in the manufacture of any country.

*Continued from the March number of ANTIQUES. Copyright, 1927, by Howard Herschel Cotterell. All rights reserved.

HANDLES

Take, for example, the very fine types shown in Figures 32 and 33; and there are many much finer than these.* The beautiful handle shown on the Swiss *Stitzen* in Figure 49, and Mr. Vetter's vigorous sketch accompanying it (*Fig. 50*) wherein the detail is more plainly shown, with its pleasing baluster motif thrice repeated, is of distinct German inspiration, and may serve to enforce the point.

A little shield affixed to the lower end of a handle (*Fig. 50a*), points to Eastern Hungarian or Hanseatic (Bremen, Hamburg, Lubeck) origin; and handles with relief decoration appear in examples from Eastern Hungary, Wallis (Switzerland), and on the oldest flagons known at present.

From a glance at the primitive examples illustrated in Figures 39 and 45, it will be seen that, in the earliest days, the terminals were quite plain and were stuck flat against the body of the vessel after the manner of pottery, nothing being left to chance so far as strength was concerned.

Flagons with chain handles or "stirrup" handles (*Fig. 52*), appear in Switzerland, the latter also in Eastern France. Such handles are seen also on certain small soup tureens from Lubeck (the local name is *Seeltopf*), and on all sorts of aquamaniles, bénitiers, etc. The ones shown are on flagons

Figs. *49, 50* — SWISS STITZEN — DETAIL OF HANDLE
The baluster-turned volute is an attractive feature here.

*The illustrations accompanying this series of articles are numbered consecutively. References to figures not appearing in the immediate text apply to earlier parts of the series.

Fig. *50a* — SHIELD FINIAL OF HANDLE
Indicates Eastern Hungarian or Hanseatic origin.

Fig. *51* — BLACKAMOOR KNOB
This appears on Bernese flagons and Dutch tobacco jars of the eighteenth century.

Fig. *52* — STIRRUP AND CHAIN HANDLES
Both examples here are Swiss.

Fig. 53 — Stitzen
(*Left to right*) — Austrian, South German, Swiss.

from the collection of Professor Calame of Winterthur, Switzerland.

On older German flagons, the ends of the hinge-pins are visible. In the late seventeenth century they disappear, after which, generally speaking, visible pin-ends were not popular in Germany, a flush side being shown on the hinge portion of the handle. Brass, copper, and iron pins are products of the eighteenth and nineteenth centuries.

Fig. 54 (*Left*) — Stitzen (*eighteenth century*)
Probably of Alsatian origin.
Fig. 56 (*Right*) — "Frans Hals" Flagon (*seventeenth century*)
Another Dutch type which finds an analogue in Switzerland.

Lids and Lid Figures

A modeled figure, either animal or human, supporting a shield on the lid of a flagon points to guild use, and usually, though not exclusively, to Germanic origin.

A Blackamoor's head *as a knob on the centre of the lid* appears on Bernese flagons and Dutch tobacco jars of the eighteenth century (*Fig. 51*).

Of Continental lids, the ones seated perfectly flat on the lip are the oldest type. After these follow lids, the rims of which overlap the neck of the body (*Fig. 33*). The lids with a shallow inner collar fitting inside the lip are the most recent type. National preferences for one or the other will be pointed out on a later page.

Bases

I have already used the word *Stitzen*, which is the name given to the type of flagon shown in Figures 53 and 54. The former shows, from left to right, Austrian, South German, and Swiss (Zurich) examples, from the Vetter collection; the latter, a magnificent specimen, some seventeen inches high, from the collection of Théodore Fisher of Lucerne, is probably of Alsatian origin.

Stitzen means stumpy, and, though it may be appropriate to the ~~shorter~~ specimens shown in Figure 53, it

would be hard to find a flagon to which the name was less appropriate than the graceful example in Figure 54.

This type was a very great favorite throughout Central Europe. In Swiss examples the bottom is usually hollow from the inside, or, in other words, the bottom is flush with the table on which it stands; whereas the German equivalent is often raised on a hollow base which increases the aspect of importance without adding to capacity.

Another type of base which gives a clue to the country of origin is to be found in Figures 55 (*Frontispiece*) and 56, which illustrate the two types of seventeenth century Dutch flagons known to collectors by the names of *Rembrandt* and *Frans Hals* (or *Jan Steen*) respectively. As will be seen, this base in each is very wide, with very little concavity of the sides, and wherever this type is encountered, it may be taken as an almost sure sign of Dutch origin or influence.

The two types shown are purely Dutch, and are from the collections of Mr. Vetter and the Rijks Museum, Amsterdam, respectively.

Another purely local base is that of the Hanseatic flagons — called locally *Roerken* — illustrated in Figures 57 and 58. The former, dated *1768*, is from the collection of Miss Chichester of Arlington Court, and the latter, a seventeenth century piece, is from the Verster collection. Other examples of this type have already been shown in Figures 20 and 25.

There is no mistaking this Hanseatic type which, in reality, is a tall slender beaker plus a cover and a handle. Its slenderness is one of

Figs. 57, 58 — Hanseatic Flagons (*eighteenth century*)
Locally known as Roerken, these flagons are narrow-waisted to allow for a hand grip at the middle, the handle serving as a kind of brace.

the characteristics by which it is known; for, in use, it may easily be grasped round the body with one hand. There are, in South Germany and Switzerland, certain beer-mugs which resemble this Hanseatic type of flagon, in that they taper towards the base; but here the similarity ends, for the circumference of the mug is too great to admit of a comfortable single-handed embrace. An example of the tapered mug is shown in Figure 59.

In many of these Hanseatic flagons, a die is found, caged within a grille in the hollow of the raised base. This ancient gambling implement was used in determining who should pay for filling the flagon.

Fig. 59 — SWISS BEER MUG Tapering after the Hanseatic manner, but less slender.

SPOUTED FLAGONS

Reverting to the spouted *Frans Hals* flagon, or *Kan*, to apply the local name: there were, in Switzerland, four flagons which made use of this long spout; and each bears the name of the district, or town, where it was made. They are the Aargau, Bernese, Fribourg, and Lausanne (or Vaud).

It is more than probable that these

Figs. 60, 61, 62 — SWISS SPOUTED FLAGONS
60, Aargau; 61 and 62, Bernese.

Swiss forms were inspired by Dutch examples which reached Switzerland *via* Basle and that great natural highway of commerce, the River Rhine. Evidence in favor of this theory may be discovered in the fact that at Basle occurs a variant of the *Frans Hals* flagon, though smaller

and with a more erect spout, and, on the whole, of less vigor in general design.

Each Swiss type displays peculiarities expressive of local ideas; and we find that, with the exception of the Fribourg type, which retains to a great extent the contour of the *Frans Hals* body, all these types changed their shape entirely from northern forms, taking on a slender waist; whilst all of them, including the Fribourg type, add a crest to the lid and a very practical and necessary connecting-bar between the upper end of the spout and the lip of the body. This bar, which gives to the flagon a much more serviceable look than is displayed by its Dutch progenitor, moreover, took many forms: sometimes simulating the human arm, sometimes showing the baluster shape; and in the later examples, displaying Baroque design.

Another interesting metamorphosis may be seen in the contour of the handle, which is changed from a loop to the hooked form with an upper and outward circular sweep, which terminates in a straight vertical line at the bottom. This shape of handle is very old, since it appears on many early Nuremberg flagons. It is suitable to flagons whose body swells at the bottom into a large bulbous form. Such vessels were operated by being grasped round the narrow waist. The loop of the handle

Fig. 63 — SWISS SPOUTED FLAGON
Of Dutch importation. From Fribourg.

Fig. 64 — SWISS SPOUTED FLAGON
From Lausanne.

Fig. 65 — Danish Spouted Flagon

Fig. 67 (Above) — Swiss Wine-Cans
The first two are bell cans from Zurich; the third, a peasant's wine-can, carried by a strap over the shoulder.

Fig. 68 (Below) — Swiss Wine-Cans
The first two are rare examples from southern Switzerland; the third, a later example from Grisons (*c. 1800*).

Fig. 66 — French Spouted Flagon

afforded wrist room, and the under side of the connecting-bar provided a comfortable and practical rest for the thumb and prevented the long spout from bending. The section of the spout on these flagons, and on flagons of the *Frans Hals* type, was always hexagonal.

Analysis of Spouted Flagons

In order that the work of distinguishing these types may be facilitated, I give below a classified comparison, which, with the illustrations on page 383, should make the task an easy one.

	Base	Lip Profile	Thumbpiece (*Usually*)	Handle
Aargau	Domed*	Truncated cone	Erect	{Germanic hooked‡ " "
Bernese	"	" "	{Plume or Erect	Plain "
Fribourg	Dutch†	Flattened semi-spherical	Erect	" "
Lausanne	Domed	Semi-spherical	{Erect or Twin Acorn	" "

Figures 60, 61, 62, 63, and 64 show these various types. The Aargau appearing in Figure 60 is from the collection of C. Hirsbrunner of Lucerne. The Bernese types, one showing a Plume thumbpiece (from the Calame collection); another the Erect thumbpiece (of strong French feeling) are shown in Figures 61 and 62. The Fribourg flagon, from the Verster collection, appears in Figure 63; and

*The word *Domed* means inverted, deep-saucer shaped, and hollow underneath.
†*Dutch* means flush-bottomed.
‡*Germanic* means more ornate; for this handle is decorated with an elaborated finial, and there is a peculiar little curved finial inserted on the inner side of the handle — at the junction of the curved and the straight sections — branching inwards towards the body of the flagon.

the Lausanne form, from the Hirsbrunner collection, in Figure 64.

A Danish spouted flagon is illustrated in Figure 65, from the Dansk Folkemuseum, Cophenhagen; and a French example, from the collection of E. E. Kleiner, of Winterthur, in Figure 66. The Danish example bears the date *1617* in the mark, and the Arms of Rensburg (Holstein). It has, in addition, the engraved date of *1656* with an inscription. The local name is *Pibekande*, or pipe-can. The French flagon is from Avignon and has the French Erect thumbpiece, curved and straight sections, with the curious addition of the rounded end-section of baluster form both here and as a handle finial.

Wine-Cans

Before leaving the subject of spouted flagons, mention must, of course, be made of the wonderfully well-known series of wine-cans which were in everyday use in Switzerland, the Tyrol, Eastern France, South Germany, and the vine growing districts of Upper Italy.

Figures 67 and 68 show examples from the collection of Professor Calame of Winterthur. The former shows the familiar Zurich bell cans, large and small; and, on the right, a peasant's wine-can, which was carried by means of a strap over the shoulder. Figure 68 shows, on the left, two very uncommon and rare types from southern Switzerland, and, on the right, a modernized version (*c. 1800*) from Grisons. Another type from the same Canton is shown in Figure 69, and a South German example in Figure 70.

The lids of these wine-cans were fixed either by a screw-on cap or the device known as a *bayonet catch*.

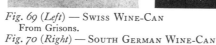

Fig. 69 (Left) — Swiss Wine-Can
From Grisons.
Fig. 70 (Right) — South German Wine-Can

Figs. 71 and 71a — BIBERONS

BIBERONS

We now turn to the last of our spouted vessels, a type concerning which, perhaps, more nonsense has been written than about any other. I hasten to state at once that this is *not* a teapot, *nor yet* is it an oil lamp! It is essential that these statements be made, because the questions have so often been raised. The vessel under discussion is a *biberon*, or drinking fountain, and of a type almost entirely confined to Switzerland and its borderlands.

The beautiful photographs (*Figs. 71 and 71a*) from pieces in the Vetter collection, serves to illustrate the type and the method of suspending it. The smallest specimen in the group is a child's toy. A further example may be observed, *in situ*, in the picture of Mr. Hirsbrunner's dining room, which appeared with the first of this series of articles.*

The local name for this vessel is *Brunnkessi*, or fountain kettle, a name which at once sets at rest all doubt as to the

Fig. 72 — COLOGNE FLAGON

use of the piece. It appeared in every farmhouse, hung on an iron bracket, of varying design, at a convenient height for people to apply the drinking pipe to their mouths. In short, though the idea may not appeal to our modern conception of hygiene, the biberon was the container of drinking water for the family, and though it *might* serve a convalescent invalid, it must in no way be regarded — as has been stated — as an invalid's feeding bottle! These pieces mostly date from the eighteenth century.

COLOGNE FLAGONS

In Figure 72 is shown another purely local type, the *Cologne* flagon, from the collection of P. J. Ducro of Amsterdam, and a very bonny and pleasing little fellow, too. Its unique raised centre to the heart-shaped lid and Dutch type erect thumbpiece, are departures from what one has been accustomed to expect, for the heart-shaped lid is almost invariably flat or *very slightly* raised, and its usual thumbpiece is the Twin Acorn or a similar twin device.

Fig. 73 — FRATZENKANNE
(*seventeenth century*)
Face flagon from Solothurn or Basle, Switzerland.

*See ANTIQUES for January, 1927 (Vol. XI, p. 33).

Fig. 74 — FACE FLAGON OR
FRATZENKANNE
From Solothurn or Basle, Switzerland (*seventeenth century*).

Here, again, is a local type known as the *Fratzenkanne*, or face-can, which converts the characteristic lip projection into an old man's face. Figure 73 shows a decorated example, of seventeenth-century workmanship, with erect thumbpiece. It is from Solothurn or Basle. Figure 74 gives a plainer type from Solothurn with a wonderful illustration of the Plume thumbpiece. This latter is *circa 1700;* both are from the Hirsbrunner collection.

And now I think we must close these notes on distinguishing features, and pass on to a consideration of the more general types which were in use in a broader way throughout the European continent.

Fig. 101 — WALLIS FLAGONS
Tallest, 16″ high.

European Continental Pewter

Part IV   *The Pewter of Switzerland*   *By* HOWARD HERSCHEL COTTERELL,* F. R. Hist. S.

IDENTIFICATION of pewter by distinctive features of form or decoration, and by marks — official or otherwise — has provided the theme for preceding chapters. Our attention must now be given to a more specialized consideration of the pewter of individual countries, commencing at the "Heart of Europe."

It will be readily understood that, from their very geographical position, the pewterers of the ancient political union of Switzerland have drawn their inspiration from types produced in surrounding countries. Hence, it is hardly going too far to say that none of the Swiss pewter types, as we know them today, are truly indigenous; all must be regarded as happy modifications of the types of other countries, so reshaped and improved, however, as fully to subscribe to national desire and sentiment, and thus to have become essentially Swiss. Nowhere else, therefore, is such a diversity of type to be found as among the twenty-three cantons of Switzerland, each of which has evolved its own particular forms. Yet there is unity even in this variety, for all these different Swiss types lend themselves to very exact classification within a grand, national family.

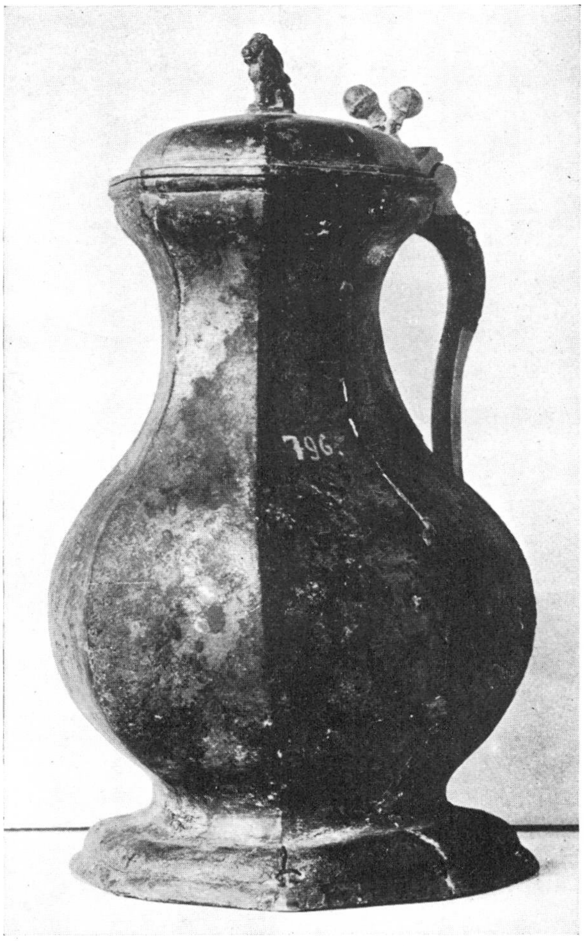

Gay and picturesque, they are yet a powerful rendering of the fundamental types adopted. Distinct and well-defined in all their details, heavily but well proportioned, and never gaudily decorated, they show the love of thoroughness and efficiency lodged in the minds of the proud Swiss mountaineers.

The accompanying *Pewter-map* of Switzerland, studiously prepared by Mr. Vetter specially for these notes, and based on the pre-war status, offers a ready key to the distribution to the various cantonal types, and, further, discloses the nature of the influences which surrounding countries must have exercised. On the west, we find modified French forms; whilst, in the east and north, German taste has prevailed; and Dutch ideas, possibly continuing the course of the Rhine, have provided the inspiration for several spouted flagons. The existence of this Dutch influence in Switzerland seems beyond all trace of doubt; it still lives in the popular names for certain furniture types. One also finds, as is but natural, certain hybrid styles wherein French and German ideas cross.

Fig. 75 — SWISS FLAGON *(fourteenth century)*
True Gothic type. Built of strips of pewter.

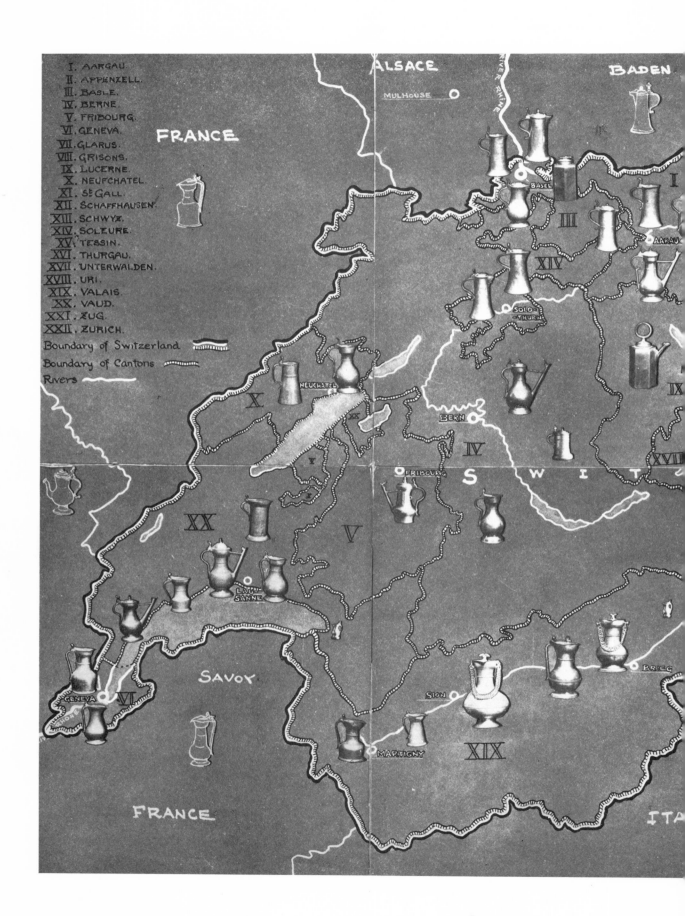

I. AARGAU.
II. APPENZELL.
III. BASLE.
IV. BERNE.
V. FRIBOURG.
VI. GENEVA.
VII. GLARUS.
VIII. GRISONS.
IX. LUCERNE.
X. NEUFCHATEL.
XI. S? GALL.
XII. SCHAFFHAUSEN.
XIII. SCHWYZ.
XIV. SOLEURE.
XV. TESSIN.
XVI. THURGAU.
XVII. UNTERWALDEN.
XVIII. URI.
XIX. VALAIS.
XX. VAUD.
XXI. ZUG.
XXII. ZURICH.
Boundary of Switzerland
Boundary of Cantons
Rivers

FRANCE

ALSACE

MULHOUSE

RIVER RHINE

BADEN

BASEL

AARAU

SOLO THURN

BERN

FRIBURG

NEUCHATEL

SWITZ

SAVOY

LAUSANNE

GENEVA

FRANCE

SION

MARTIGNY

BRIEG

ITA

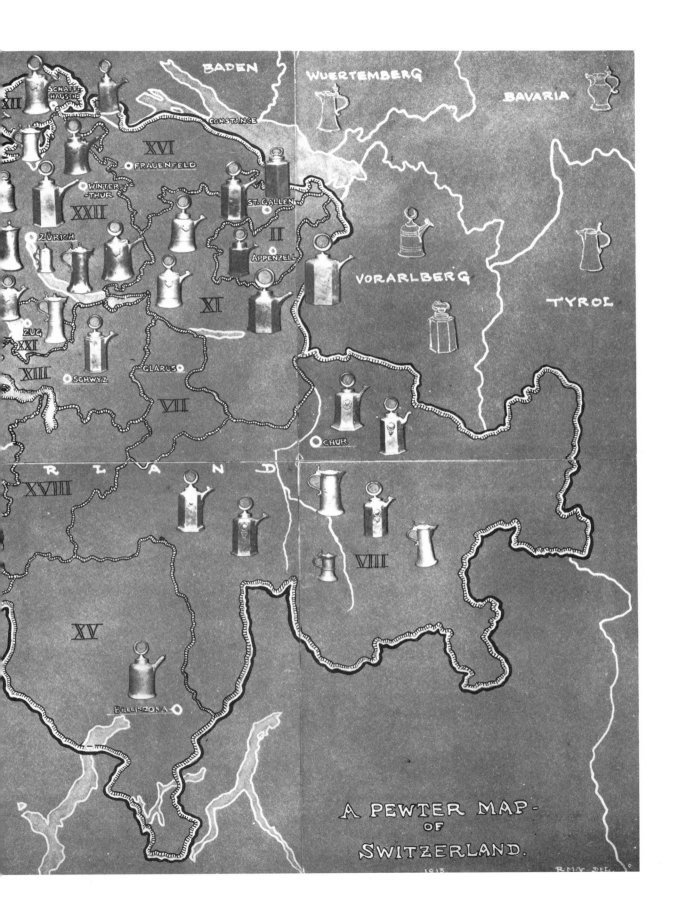

A PEWTER MAP OF SWITZERLAND.

Fig. 76 — COUNCIL FLAGON (*c. 1500*)

Fig. 77 — COUNCIL FLAGON (*sixteenth century*)
Somewhat later than Figure 76.

The pen-and-ink decorations on this page are taken from Chinese porcelain wine-pots of the late sixteenth century, with contemporary silver mountings of English workmanship.

Fig. 78 — FLAGONS (*c. 1600*)

The scarcity of pewter types in Ticino would seem to be accounted for by the preference of the Italian speaking inhabitants for earthenware vessels for storing and dispensing various liquids.

EVOLUTION OF THE FLAGON

Probably one of the earliest known pieces of pewter with a Swiss connection is the pure Gothic flagon illustrated in Figure 75. This wonderful piece, of polyhedrous construction, and with rudimentary Twin Acorn thumbpiece and Lion sejant knop on the lid, is now at the Aarau museum. It was found among the ruins of the Homburg castle (Aargau) destroyed by earthquake in 1356. It dates, therefore, in all probability from not later than the early fourteenth century.

Following this are shown, in Figures 76–79 five extremely interesting flagons known as *Cimaises*, *Stubenkannen* (hall flagons) or *Ratskannen* (council flagons). These pieces resemble nothing so much as early Chinese bronzes in their mighty, vigorous outlines. Partly primitive and partly Gothic, they are more wildly uncouth than contemporary German and French examples.

The flagon of Figure 76, some twenty-four inches in height, is, with that of Figure 79, in the Schweizerisches Landesmuseum at Zurich, by the courtesy of whose officials both are here reproduced. This first example, dating from about 1500, is quite primitive in every detail, with strong bell-shaped foot and simple domed lid. The arms are those of the Bubenberg family, whose ruined castle still stands in the neighborhood of Berne. The flagon emanates from Spiez on the lake of Thun, and may well be a progeni-

Fig. 79 — COUNCIL FLAGON (*1655*)
From Stein am Rhein.

tor of the later spouted Bernese flagons illustrated in the preceding chapter, modified by Dutch-Flemish influence. The iron stirrup handle is provided with a stop to prevent its falling against and denting the side of the flagon. These early workmen left *nothing* to chance!

The flagon of Figure 77, which is from the Hirsbrunner collection, shows a somewhat later development. It is of the sixteenth century, and the arms are those of the town of Frauenfeld, the capital of Thurgau. It was the property of the Gesellschaft der Constabler, or Constaffel; i.e., the Club of the Constables, to which were admitted the clergy, nobility, and citizens of importance, and whose hall, or *stube*, was the hub of the city's social life — banquets, weddings, and general festivities being held there.

Figure 78 shows two similar flagons (*c. 1600*), from Payerne, in northern Vaud. One is not greatly surprised to find adherence to western Swiss detail, for the body and handle roughly agree with those of a Wallis flagon (*Figs. 46 and 48*). The rectangular section of the spout is exceptional, and it will be noted that, on account of the weight of these flagons when full, and probably also from none too careful usage, the feet have become crushed down into a reverse, or saucer, form — evidence, if such be needed, of less solid construction than that indicated in the previous illustrations. These two examples are in the Payerne Museum.

The latest of the series (*Fig. 79*) is dated *1655* on the escutcheon. This example is from Stein, a town that still exists in all its mediaeval splendor near the spot where the Rhine leaves Lake Constance. Gothic feeling still lurks in the wrought-iron stirrup handle and in the

Fig. 80 — SPOUTED BERNESE FLAGON (*seventeenth century*)

Fig. 81 — SPOUTED BERNESE FLAGON (*standard type*)

Fig. 82—WINTERTHUR BULGENKANNE
(1667)
Made by A. Graf.

sistence of earlier ideas in this country.

To round off this outline of evolution, we may add Figures 80 and 81, showing two spouted Bernese flagons from the collection of Dr. Kurt Ruhmann of Vienna. Figure 80 represents a very rare seventeenth century specimen of that desirable type, whereas Figure 81 represents the ultimate rendering, which became nearly standard during the eighteenth century and the first half of the nineteenth.

BULGENKANNE

A typical and exclusively Swiss modification of the mediaeval canteen flask is the *Bulgenkanne, Ferriere,* or bulging can, a famous specimen of which adorns the remarkable pewter collection of the Schweizerisches Landesmuseum at Zurich (*Fig. 82*). To the body, which seems to be made of two porringer-shaped bowls soldered together, a foot is added; the chain, once intended for carrying during the march, is retained as an ornamental feature; and the cylindrical nozzle, with hinged lid and its thumbpiece in the shape of a mermaid is, where it joins the body, strengthened by the addition of a concave fillet, or collar, which gives to this member a helmet-like appearance, very effective in carrying out the armorial character of the whole. The height of this flagon is about eleven inches; and the arms, painted in bright colors on both sides and bearing the date 1667, are those of two Winterthur families probably united by a marriage.

Another treasure of this famous collection is a rare example of Swiss guild trophy in the form of a mediaeval jester's shoe (*Fig. 83*). This piece was made for the Boot-

bronze-like, angular ears of this flagon. The height, with stirrup extended, is some eighteen inches. On the escutcheon appears a rough relief of St. George slaying the dragon. The date, *1655,* is late for a piece of this character, and is evidence of the late per-

makers of Zofingen in Aargau. The decoration is pure Renaissance in type, and the shoe rests on three dolphin feet. It is some twelve inches in length, and probably dates from the early seventeenth century.

POLYHEDROUS WALLIS FLAGONS

We turn now to another beautiful type, the polyhedrous, quasi-Gothic variety of the Wallis flagons. A magnificent example from the fine collection of Fritz Bertram, of Chemnitz, is shown in Figure 84. This glorious piece, some seventeen inches in height, has a gargoyle-like dog's head on the lid, a chain handle, and Twin Pomegranate thumbpiece. Its date is c. 1650. It belonged to a Cooper's guild at Sion in Wallis (Valais).

Another example of this quaint variety of flagon is shown in Figure 85. It is nineteen inches high, with businesslike stirrup of pewter, double Ram's head thumbpiece and Ram's head crest. This piece is from the Landesmuseum at Zurich. We must observe the strong handle on both these latter pieces, for it is a sign that both were originally made thus extra capacious, and are not fraudulent combinations of the upper portion of an ordinary Wallis flagon and a newly-made lower one. And here I take the opportunity to warn my readers to beware of Wallis cans of

Fig. 83 — GUILD TROPHY (*early seventeenth century*)
Made for the Bootmakers of Zofingen in Aargau.

these types, which are frequently spurious.

Before leaving the subject of flagons, it will be well to turn back for a moment to the spouted examples illustrated in Figures 60–64. With the exception of that of Figure 60 (the Aargau type) each of these has its prototype *without* spout. But curiously enough, *always* with the *spout-*

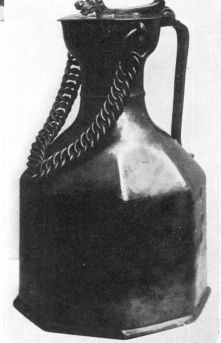

Fig. 84 — POLYHEDROUS WALLIS FLAGON
(*c. 1650*)

Fig. 85 — POLYHEDROUS WALLIS FLAGON (*seventeenth century*)

IN RESUMÉ

In the last article I spoke, in connection with Figures 67–70, of the well-known Swiss wine-cans, but only in so far as they completed the series of spouted flagons.

These wine-cans are found both with fixed circular handles and with fall-down, decorated, bow-shaped handles, but — and I think I am correct in saying so — the latter always appear with a screw-on lid, never with what is known as the bayonet-catch type of lid. The latter, by the way, are sometimes provided with a locking device to insure against the catch's becoming disengaged at inopportune moments!

The spouts of these vessels were closed at the end, either by a little shield-shaped flap, which gives to them quite an ostrich-like appearance, or by a screw-cap attached, at times, to the spout by a chain. We also find these cans without spouts, both in the hexagonal and the *Glocken* or Bell shapes, both of which, either in the spouted or spoutless style, are found in Lucerne, St. Gall, Schaffhausen, and Zurich. In the Ticino, the Bell shape takes on a much plainer form.

The ones illustrated in the tail-piece to the present article are from Grisons, and show a beautiful modern adaptation of an old form; or, in the words of Mr. Vetter, "a neo-classical decoration on a quasi-Gothic body." The ones with the broad, spreading bases are of the early nineteenth century.

The varieties of these wine-cans are so many that an enormous collection could be formed without a semblance of duplication. A reference to the pewter-map will give some idea as to their distribution and as to the various cantonal types. In this map, also, it will be seen — from the skeleton sketches beyond the border-lines — that such types were not confined to Switzerland alone, but tended to spread into adjoining lands.

Fig. 86 — ZURICH TANKARD (*1813*)

less variety, a *flat heart-shaped lid is substituted* for *the domed one which appears on its spouted confrère.*

The head-piece to this chapter (*Fig. 101*) shows a unique and quite wonderful series of chained Wallis flagons, the tallest some sixteen inches high. Figure 102 which forms the tail-piece shows a fine series of the Grisons type of wine-cans. For both pictures I have again levied on the Hirsbrunner Collection.

A BEER TANKARD

A Zurich beer tankard is illustrated in Figure 86. It bears the date *1813*, but the style suggests an earlier period, a further instance of the persistence of type in Switzerland.

(*To be continued*)

Fig. 102 — GRISONS WINE-CANS

European Continental Pewter

Part V

The Pewter of Switzerland

By Howard Herschel Cotterell,* F.R. Hist. S.

Wall Fountains

NO account of Swiss pewter could be satisfactory without some mention of the vessels variously known as *lavabos, aquamaniles,* or fountains. These took many forms, but all were operated in the same way and for the same purpose. When complete, they consisted of an upper part, or reservoir, to which a tap was attached. Below this stood a basin for the actual washing of hands; and frequently, behind all this, a pewter-lined recess acted as a "splash-back." The whole affair was let into the sideboard. An example is pictured *in situ* in the Frontispiece of Antiques for January.

Figure 87 shows a box-shaped cistern of the seventeenth century — from the collection of A. J. G. Verster of The Hague — which is of the type usual in peasants' dwellings. Figure 88 shows one of the dolphin type from the Landesmuseum, Zurich. These sea monsters sometimes had brass fins and tails, whilst the eyes were fashioned from colored glass. A complete dolphin set, of the seventeenth century, some thirty-four inches in height, is shown in

illustrated in Figure 90, the work of the Lucerne pewterer J. F. Gloggner (*c. 1700*). Such sets were used for ablutions after meals as well as for baptismal and other church purposes. The ewer shown here is a beautiful example, skilfully engraved, of the type known as *helmet-shaped.* It is one more item from the Hirsbrunner collection.

Covered Porringers or Broth Bowls

We now turn to a type of vessel of which the many examples still preserved bespeak its great popularity. This is the *Grellet, Écuelle à bouillon,* or *Kindbettschuesseli* — a broth bowl, or covered porringer, chiefly used as a gift for young mothers at the birth of a child. Figure 91 shows a specimen from the Zurich Landesmuseum, and Figure 92, an exceptionally fine one from the Chichester collection. Both represent the early eighteenth century. The former is of Zurich make and the latter bears the mark of Nicolas Ubelin of Basle. The covers of these vessels, turned over, form plates or shallow dishes on three feet. Figure 93 presents the bottom of another

Fig. 89 — Wall Niche with Cistern (*seventeenth century*)

Figure 89, from the Hirsbrunner collection. These cisterns were made in many other forms, but the ones illustrated must suffice for the present.

A lavabo set of the ewer-and-basin type is

type, from the Yeates collection, bearing a Basle mark; and Figure 94, from the Vetter collection, pictures the Rococo, or Louis XV, version as made in eastern Switzer-

Fig. 87 — Wall Cistern (*seventeenth century*)

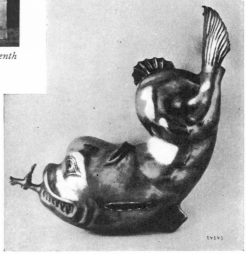

Fig. 88 — Wall Cistern
From Beckenried.

Fig. 91 — BROTH BOWL (*early eighteenth century*)
Zurich make.

Fig. 90 — EWER AND BASIN (*c. 1700*)
By J. F. Gloggner, Lucerne.

Fig. 92 — BROTH BOWL (*early eighteenth century*)
By Nicolas Ubelin of Basle.

land during the second half of the eighteenth century.

DECORATIVE PEWTER

Some very fine examples of decorative pewter, known in Germany as *Edelzinn,* and in France as *Orfèvrerie d'Étain,* were made at St. Gall, Basle, and in the Wallis district. Figure 95 shows a very vigorously designed, ornamental plate, some eight and one quarter inches in diameter, from the Vetter collection. Its thirteen lobes contain the arms of the thirteen (old) cantons; and the centre shows the taking of the oath of the Ruetli in 1308, the year signalized by the foundation of the Swiss Republic. The mold for this plate was the property of two St. Gall pewterers, whose initials are cast in the rim beside the *G* for St. Gall.

Fig. 93 — BROTH BOWL
Basle mark.

TABLE WARE

Swiss dishes and plates adopted the forms common to most other countries; the plain narrow rim in the sixteenth and early seventeenth centuries; the broad, flat rim during the greater part of the seventeenth century; and the variously molded and reeded, medium-width rims following the differing styles of Baroque and Rococo, in due sequence.

Figure 96 illustrates some Baroque (Louis XIV) plates and one oblong dish, from the Vetter collection, the latter of a type very popular in western Switzerland. Figure 97 shows a broad-rimmed plate, from the Yeates collection, which bears the touch of Pierre Roze of Geneva (*1609*). In Figure 98, from the same collection, may be seen, in addition to three characteristic Zurich Rococo plates, some analogous spoon-stands and salts made by various Zurich pewterers during the latter half of the eighteenth century.

Likewise from the Vetter collection is the cruet shown in Figure 99, made by the Zurich pewterer Johann Caspar Manz. It is exceptional inasmuch as the rich Rococo design was rarely adopted by Swiss pewterers, who preferred solidity and simplicity to the frivolous lightness of the coquettish Rococo patterns.

STITZEN AGAIN

In Figure 100 is illustrated a very elegant *Stitzen* by a Basle maker, from the Hirsbrunner collection. This piece, which is of the early eighteenth century, is of standard outline with gracefully engraved detail, a fine example of the Basle ideal of combining French ease with German utility.

Other examples of Stitzen will be found in Figures 49, 53, and 54.

CONCLUSION

In the compass of a maga-

Fig. 95 — DECORATIVE PLATE
From St. Gall. The thirteen lobes carry the arms of the thirteen original cantons.

Fig. 94 — BROTH BOWL (*second half eighteenth century*)
Eastern Switzerland.

zine article it is out of the question to dilate upon the many types shown in the pewter-map, for space does not permit; but several of these have been discussed in the previous chapters, and their more complete treatment will be undertaken when these notes appear in book form. The fine illustrations will, in themselves, enable the student to become familiar with the various local distinctions.

Swiss pewter is in great demand, not only by many devoted Swiss collectors, but in every European country. So much is this the case that, in nearly every European collection of importance, some examples are included.

This wide demand, of course, gives occasion for countless reproductions; and when, as is the case in many instances, these are made from the old molds, a special note of warning is necessary to prevent one's readers

Fig. 96 — DISH AND TWO PLATES
The former of a type popular in western Switzerland.

Fig. 98 — PLATES, SPOON-STANDS, AND SALTS (*second half eighteenth century*)
By various Zurich pewterers.

Fig. 100 — STITZEN (*early eighteenth century*)
From Basle.

Fig. 97 — BROAD-RIMMED PLATE (*1609*)
By Pierre Roze of Geneva.

Fig. 99 — CRUET (*second half eighteenth century*)
By Johann Caspar Manz, Zurich.

from accepting them as antique examples.

Bernese and Wallis flagons are especial favorites, and countless reproductions of them are on the market, many of the latter being stamped on the lid with the initials *L. D. B.* (for Lorenzo della Bianca, of Visp), in addition to the quality mark of the crowned *F*, and the Wallis shield of stars. *All chains* on Wallis flagons must be considered as suspect, unless accompanied by a written guarantee of genuineness or the opinion of an expert.

In closing this chapter, I give an excellent sketch by Robert M. Vetter, of a type of vessel which has puzzled the majority of collectors who have come across it either in Swiss antique shops or elsewhere, and I am further indebted to

SWISS BULB JAR
A convenient device for growing onions indoors. As their inquiring green tops were thrust through the holes they were cut off for cooking purposes.

Mr. Vetter for the following explanation as to its use:

"Colloquially termed *Böllekessi* (or Bulb Kettle), this vessel was made in pewter *only*, and exclusively in eastern Switzerland, where it may still be found in remote villages, suspended from the kitchen ceiling. Its purpose is to hold onions, which, in the warm kitchen air, develop shoots which, emerging through the circular holes, are, when sufficiently long, snipped off by the housewife and put into the soup.

"Many of these Böllekessi have found their way into collections beyond the confines of their native country, and it is quite the exception to find them correctly described."

European Continental Pewter

Part VI

*The Pewter of France from the Sixteenth to the Nineteenth Century**

By Adolphe Riff

Conservator of the Museums of Strasbourg, France

With a Foreword by Howard H. Cotterell, F. R. Hist. S.

Foreword

It has been, and will be my endeavor, and that of my able colleague Robert M. Vetter, to put before readers of this series of articles only such information as is entirely reliable and authoritative. In furtherance of that aim we had collected many beautiful and useful photographs to illustrate our French notes. We felt, however, that neither these nor our own knowledge of France would fully satisfy the high standard we had set out to achieve. We therefore decided to invite the greatest authority on French pewter to undertake this task for us; and the accompanying notes by Conservator Adolphe Riff are the outcome of that invitation.

M. Riff is the author of several standard monographs on various aspects of French pewter, several of which are referred to in his article. He is at present engaged upon extensive researches in connection with his great work on French pewter in general, which he hopes to publish within the next few years.

Upon his consenting to undertake this task for us, we gladly placed at his disposal such photographs and information as we had accumulated. Some of this material he has adopted, supplementing it with much more from his own rich collections. The resulting article is one which it gives me genuine pleasure to submit for the edification of readers of Antiques.

To Mr. Vetter are due thanks for the preliminary rendering into English of M. Riff's notes, and for many helpful suggestions, both to him and to myself. M. Riff informs me that, his investigations not having extended as yet to a consideration of Channel Islands' pewter, he prefers to leave its discussion to me. I have, therefore, added a few notes on this subject, immediately at the end of his article. H. H. C.

ALTHOUGH old pewter stands at present in the focus of so much attention with many general and specializing collectors, and in spite of the fact that, by many, the work of the French pewterers is considered the most desirable, up to the present no comprehensive and practical treatise on the subject has existed. Many of the works which have already appeared deal only, for the most part, with certain aspects of the pewter of the Middle Ages and the Renaissance period, such as the work of the celebrated craftsman, François Briot;† yet, besides these exceptional masterpieces of the pewterer's art, numerous types of best quality pewter were made in all the French provinces; and, though not connected with so celebrated a name as that of Briot, they are, nevertheless, well worthy of our attention.

When compiling our monograph on the pewter of Strasbourg,‡ we were struck by the complete absence of French pewter literature available for purposes of comparison, with the result that we were compelled to start on a comprehensive study of French pewter in general. The first fruits of our research were laid down in two papers on *l'Orfèvrerie d'Étain en France:* (1) *Les Écuelles à bouillon* (1925), and (2) *Les Aiguières en Casque* (1926). These treated of the more ornamental types of the well-known French porringers and the so-called helmet-shaped ewers. Nevertheless the subject still remains as unilluminated as it is vast, and we expect that at least another two years of study and research will be necessary before we shall be able to complete our detailed and extensive work on French pewter.

We gladly answered the call to contribute to this series now appearing in Antiques a concise and entirely original treatise,

derived from our research up to the present, and touching all the principal aspects of the topic. It is certainly the first practical paper on French pewter such as the average collector may thus far reasonably hope to acquire.

We have decided to omit entirely the customary but somewhat arid quotations from archives, and to follow the general trend of the work of which ours is to form a part: *i.e.*, to show the student of European pewter how to recognize French types, how to allot them to the different provinces of France, how to understand the evolution of their shapes and decorations, and last, but not least, how to distinguish the marks or "touches" which we find upon them.

For the convenience of readers not entirely familiar with European geography, we have drawn up a little chart in Figure 103, whereon we have marked the places and districts referred to in these notes.

French Pewter Marks

Let us commence with the French pewter marks, upon some recognition of which the decision as to nationality may often rest, and about which, up to the present, nothing of importance has been available.

It had been duly ordained that the pewterer strike upon his wares his private or personal touch (*poinçon de maître*), as a means of identification in case of fraud in the matter of the permissible proportion of lead used in the alloy — a proportion which was prescribed strictly by the rules of the guilds. Generally speaking, three qualities of metal were permitted, *viz:* superior, medium, and common, each of them indicated by a differing quality touch (*poinçon de contrôle*). Therefore French pewter generally shows two marks, that of the maker and that of the grade; and very frequently a combination of the two was used.

We also find the touches of individual assayers or searchers (*contrôleurs*), gauging marks (*poinçon de jaugeage*), and owners' marks (*poinçon de propriétaire*).

Makers' Marks

The pewterer's marks mostly take the shape of circular or oval labels or escutcheons, wherein, besides certain emblems, such as pewterer's tools, we find also the pewterer's initials; and, since the beginning of the eighteenth century — though at first infrequently — the pewterer's name in full, and sometimes, also, the name of the town in which he worked.

Quality Marks

The quality touch takes a shape similar to that of the maker's mark, and usually shows the town arms and a letter or emblem, crowned or uncrowned, indicating the quality of the metal. Thus, the finest quality is indicated by an *F* (*fin*) or two *F*'s back to back, crowned, and circumscribed by the name of the town, and, in addition, a date indicative of the introduction of some new rule regulating the composition of the metal (*Figs. 104 d and e*). *C*, or two *C*'s back to back, is indicative of common quality

*Continued from the September number of Antiques. Copyright, 1927, by Howard Herschel Cotterell. All rights reserved.

†Germain Bapst, *L'Étain*, 1884.

‡*Les Étains strasbourgeois du 16e au 19e siècle* 1925.

These two marks are the ones most frequently met with on French pewter (*Figs. 104 a, b, and c*).

The ordinance of 1691 referred to above was not valid for the whole country, the Franche-Comté, Alsace, and French Flanders retaining their own system of marking. There the pewterer's hammer, the fleur-de-lys, and the crowned rose, respectively, were used, as well as the following words: ** fin, étain fin, étain cristalin, étain d'Angleterre (Fig. 104 k), étain de Cornouailles* (Cornish tin. *sic*), and *antimoine* (antimony), referring to a component part of the alloy.

RECORDED MARKS

Touch plates of lead, upon which these touches had to be recorded, were kept at the various guild headquarters, and, did they still exist, would furnish an enormous amount of most valuable information; but, unfortunately, the only ones now known are those at Lille and Nancy. The former is reproduced in our *Écuelles à bouillon.* On this plate we find, besides the pewterer's name, the rose, the fleur-de-lys, and the hammer — all symbols used to mark different qualities of metal. It must also be noted that the pewterer's private touches were used in different sizes, and we have counted as many as seven of these for one pewterer!

These leaden documents eloquently demonstrate to us the great number and variety of touches. Considering that the same state of affairs may be assumed to have existed in all towns of importance, we may easily realize the great difficulty of identification, especially if we bear in mind that production was in full swing in hundreds of places during several centuries.

HINTS FOR IDENTIFICATION

The following hints will afford further assistance in arriving at a classification of marks:

The *crowned rose* was in use chiefly in northern and north-eastern France, within the regions covering the towns of Lille, Nancy, and Metz. The initials of the pewterer are generally found *in* the crown, whilst the arms of the town are often found in the centre of the rose. The arms of Lorraine are the double cross, so characteristic of the district.

The *crowned fleur-de-lys (Fig. 104 f)* is the mark really most frequently met with. It was popular in nearly every part of France; but subtle differences exist, characteristic of the various regions, and sometimes difficult to identify. These differences are to be found either in the shape of the lily itself, or in its framing. For instance, at Lille, we find a lily in full blossom, surrounded by a wreath of leaves; whilst at Paris we get a very small one beneath the letter *P.* At Strasbourg we find a *demi-fleur-de-lys;* whereas in Lorraine we find in vogue a stiff, archaic, quasi-Gothic

variety (*Fig. 104 f*). It should be noted, in this connection, that the fleur-de-lys occurs also on Swiss and German pewter, but in the maker's touch, and *not* as a quality mark.

The *crowned pewterer's hammer* is also a frequently used quality symbol, sometimes alone and at other times grasped in a hand. The assumption that the hammer was used to denote beaten ware may have held good in the sixteenth and seventeenth centuries so far as pewter is concerned; but certainly not for later periods, when we find it on all grades of metal, even down to the commonest. The region north of the Loire may be considered its true home. It is usually flanked by the initials of the pewterer (*Fig. 104 g*), and in Paris it surmounts the letter *P.*

The three preceding quality marks were but little used in southeastern France, where town arms on cartouches and escutcheons played the leading role.

The *angel with sword and scales* rarely occurs on French pewter, a fact which should be well kept in mind. Only a few pewterers at Lyons use it, in combination with the word *fin (Fig. 104 j)*; and, further, the Alsatian pewterers of Strasbourg, Colmar, and Mulhouse employ it after the manner of their German and Swiss confrères, with whom this symbol played so important a part.

A Parisian mark which was shown to us by Mr. Vetter (*Fig. 105*) displays two angels supporting a crown over a hammer, but in this case the angels are not so much symbolic as ornamental.*

A *Phrygian cap* was the symbol introduced during the great revolution by certain towns, *e.g.,* Montbard. Dates in such marks refer to the new revolutionary calendar: thus, *An 6* corresponds with the year 1798.

Fig. 103.

Fig. 103 — MAP OF FRANCE

Showing positions of departments and of places mentioned in the text.

TOWN ARMS

Of marks containing town emblems one may mention Besançon (*an eagle supporting two columns*), Carpentras (*the bit of a horse*), Colmar (*a mace*), Mulhouse (*a mill wheel*), Strasbourg (*a shield with "bars"*) (*Fig. 104 h*), and Nancy (*the double cross of Lorraine*).

DATES OF MARKS

Dates on French pewter marks may be interpreted as follows. They have a twofold significance: in quality marks they refer either to the adoption of a new rule or to some modification of an existing regulation; in the pewterer's touch they usually have reference to the year in which he became a *master.*

From this one may draw the important conclusion that dates on such marks do not, by any means, tally with the actual date of the piece on which they appear.

Very great deviations are possible in this respect; for instance, a piece bearing a quality mark with the date *1691* may quite well

---

*See Label Table, ANTIQUES for January, 1927 (Vol. XI, pp. 38 and 39).

*A remark which may also be applied to the few English marks which adopt this device. H. H. C.

have been made as late as 1730, or even later, for this marked date merely guarantees that the metal conforms to certain rules laid down in 1691. On the other hand, a date in a pewterer's touch, say, *1740*, refers back to the date of the maker's acceptance into the guild as a master pewterer, and not the actual year in which the piece was fashioned, which may well have been some thirty or forty years later, since he was not permitted to alter the date in his touch from year to year.*

It is, therefore, by no means uncommon or surprising to find a piece showing marks with apparently conflicting dates, as, for example, the Joinville measure from the collection of Étienne Delanoy of Amsterdam (*Figs. 137 a and b*, to be published later).† On the lid of this piece appears the quality mark of the crowned *C*, with date *1691*, whereas in the pewterer's touch of the crowned hammer occurs the date *1706!* The piece itself may well have been made even some years after this latter date.

GAUGING MARKS AND OWNER'S MARKS

Totally different in character and meaning are the gauging marks which one finds struck on measures and so are the marks of ownership which from time to time appear.

Gauging marks indicate nothing more than that the capacity of the measure has been tested officially by an authorized inspector of the Government. At Strasbourg these marks took the form of escutcheons bearing the town arms over a barrel and accompanied by the letters *K — Z*.

Owners' marks were sometimes struck on pewter belonging to households of the nobility, or belonging to institutions using large quantities of the ware, such as hospitals, monasteries, corporations, taverns, and the like. They are but rarely found on the possessions of private individuals, who were content to have their initials punched or engraved upon their pieces. But methods of distinguishing private property do not fall within the scope of a treatise on pewter marks.

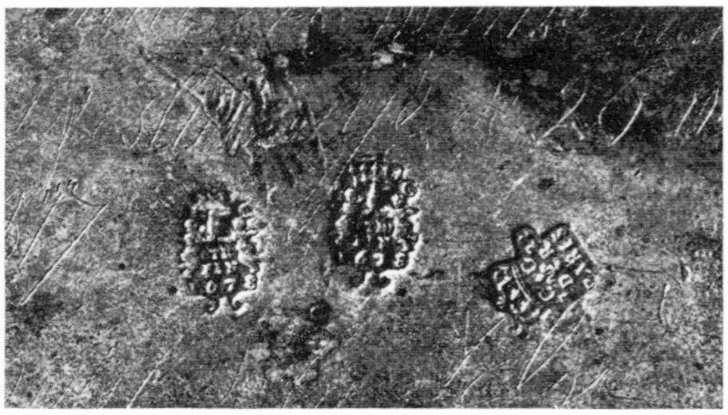

SHAPE AND DECORATION

The production of pewter in France varied in the different departments of the country, not only in quantity, but in quality as well. The less flourishing districts, where the populations made their living out of agriculture or fishing, produced pewter in smaller quantities and of simpler character than that of places where a well-to-do bourgeoisie — as in the prosperous wine growing departments — called for abundant and beautiful pewter. So the whole eastern region of France, including Lyons, Dijon, Besançon, up to the Alsatian towns of Mulhouse, Colmar, and Strasbourg (*Fig. 103*), may be

Fig. 104 — CHARACTERISTIC MARKS ON FRENCH PEWTER

regarded as the veritable home of the choicest French pewter pieces, though many towns outside this district — otherwise famous for the high artistic development of their crafts, such as Bordeaux, Orléans, Paris, Rouen, and Lille — shine also in the light of their pewterware.

Generally speaking, French pewter was made from excellent metal of silver-like brilliance. It is further distinguished by its great purity of form and style of decoration. Hence the high appreciation extended to it by all collectors is fully justified. Good balance of outline and pleasing proportions characterize even the most simple objects, and the exaggeration and clumsiness of decoration so frequently met with in German and Dutch pewter are avoided.

As in other countries, most of the pieces which have escaped destruction up to the present date from the second half of the seventeenth, but still more from the eighteenth century, which is the period of elegant pewter. Objects of earlier times have become very rare on account of the habit of melting down old pieces and recasting them into new shapes.*

From about the middle of the eighteenth century, the quiet charm of pewter seems to have been less appreciated. The severe competition of earthenware and china manifests itself, backed by the pottery dictates of fashion; and in France the rise in popularity of the wares of Rouen, Moustiers, Nevers, Strasbourg, and several other manufactories of less importance, are coeval with the rapid decline of French pewter.

A FAMILY TRADE

In France, as in other European countries, we see the pewterer's trade pass from father to son, and we meet the same name for several generations. The following few names of such pewtering families will assist in identifying French pieces: *Fabreguette* and *Soulignac* at Bordeaux; *Archimbaud, Morand,* and *Laubreaux* of Lyons; *Buffard* of Dijon; *Varin, Cornet,* and *Ledoux* of Besançon; *Koechlin* of Mulhouse; *Waldner* and *Doll* of Colmar; *Faust, Isenheim, Wehrlen, Bergmann,* and *Borst* of Strasbourg; *Darras* of Metz; *Henault* of Nancy; *Barry, Laumesnier, Gevrey,* and *Perrin* of Paris; *Lefèvre* and *Oudart* of Lille; *Gaillard* of Rouen; *Dorey* and *Leseigneur* at Caen; and *Salmon* of Chartres.

As will be seen from their names, most of the pewterers working in France were Frenchmen, but, in some instances, immigration took place, especially from Switzerland and Italy. The beautiful Louis XVI cruet to be illustrated later in Figure 142, from the Riff collection, emanates from southern France, as proved by the word *fin* in the touch, but the latter also bears the name *Battista Sartori*, who was probably an Italian craftsman who had settled in France.

Fig. 105 — PARISIAN PEWTER TOUCHES
Showing two dates (*1678 and 1722*) on one and the same piece.

---

*This same remark refers also to English pewter. H. H. C.

·†The thumbpiece of this was the one chosen to illustrate the Brambleberry thumbpiece in a preceding article of this series. See ANTIQUES, Vol. XI, p. 197, *Fig. 30.* H. H. C.

*The same procedure would seem to have obtained in all countries. H. H. C.

(To be continued)

European Continental Pewter

By Howard Herschel Cotterell, F. R. Hist. S.

Part VII

*The Pewter of France from the Sixteenth to the Nineteenth Century**

By Adolphe Riff

Conservator of the Museums of Strasbourg, France

DECORATIVE METHODS

CASTING in relief, graving by means of the burin, and punching were the techniques chiefly employed for the decoration of French pewter.

Relief decoration was invariably accomplished by casting into dies, or molds, carrying the desired design in the negative. The richest pewter examples were made by this method, such as the wonderful dishes of Briot and the splendid French porringers.

Relief casting also furnishes certain details or constructional elements in the form of mascarons, angel heads, shells, and the like, which were applied to otherwise plain articles. So, the heads of the pins to which stirrup handles are affixed, are finished off with mascarons; and angel heads mask the points where the two links are fixed to the sides of *gourdes*, or flasks. We refer our readers in this connection to Figures 107, 108, and 111. Figures 112 to 115 are examples of Renaissance relief

Fig. 107 — CIMARE: CHAMPAGNE DEPARTMENT

ures 126 to 129 (the last three to be shown later) furnish a few examples. It has the effect of enlivening plain surfaces, and, in a more practical way, is used for adding inscriptions, arms, or names for identification or embellishment.

Punched ornament. As its name implies, this method is accomplished by the use of small punches, wherewith small motifs such as fleurs-de-lys and rosettes are struck into the metal. By arranging these impressions in rows or festoons, pleasing effects may be obtained, as in Figure 128 (to be shown later).

Repoussé work. True repoussé work, as applied to other metals, would seem never to have been used to any extent on pewter, the metal being but little suited for such work.*

PEWTER TYPES

The Middle Ages have left us but few pewter objects of any importance, but we may safely assume that great simplicity of style prevailed during this period, and that highly ornamented

Fig. 106 — CHRISMATORY (*sixteenth century*)
The gothic prototype of the Louis XIV example shown in Figure 124.

pewter, whereas Figures 116 and 117 show the development of eighteenth-century relief decoration on two porringers. Let us add that the tastefully designed handles, thumb-pieces, and finials on French pewter must also be ranged under this heading.

Graving by burin. Of this style of decoration, Fig-

pieces were the exception. Some ecclesiastical pieces such as chrismatories and chalices have survived. Figure 106, from the Museum of Applied Arts, Strasbourg, pictures a chris-

*In this connection, it is well to point out that much pewter which seems to be repoussé is really cast into the desired shape, but the effect of repoussé work is consciously aimed at. This remark applies to all sorts of European pewter of the eighteenth century, following in its design the lead of the silversmiths. R. M. VETTER.

Fig. 108 — CIMARE (*c. 1700*)

Fig. 109 — CHALICE (pure Gothic)

Fig. 110 — CHALICE (seventeenth century)

matory. Two fine chalices are illustrated in Figures 109 and 110. Both are in the Verster collection. The one with lobed base clearly represents Gothic design and proportions, and is probably of the sixteenth century. The other one may be some hundred years later. Under the influence of the Renaissance movement, the taste for richly ornamented pewter increased considerably, such wares becoming to the wealthier middle classes what silver was to the rich.

the date *1651* in the touch.

PORRINGERS

To the Renaissance decorated pewter movement must also be attributed the beautiful and characteristic ornamental porringers (*écuelles à bouillon*), of which the most charming ones date from the reigns of Louis XIV and XV. These vary from about six inches to six and three-fourths inches in diameter, exclusive of the ears. Their covers, as also their flat, ear-like handles, are richly and variously decorated.

Decorations were either engraved or cast in relief, and it is this latter technique which has made French pewter so famous and which has found so many imitators. It was employed on the rarest and most valuable pieces, such as the incomparable works of the great French pewterer François Briot, who worked chiefly at Montbéliard, between *c.* 1575 and *c.* 1616. His *Temperantia* and *Mars* dishes, with their companion ewers, all covered with the most beautiful and perfect relief work, are already universally known, since international pewter literature contains many detailed descriptions of these highly artistic productions. Briot's splendid *Mars* dish, now in the Museum of Applied Arts at Strasbourg, is shown in Figure 112.

The example of Briot was followed by Isaac Faust at Strasbourg,* and by the Swiss Caspar Enderlein, who established himself at Nuremberg. Briot's works have been described so frequently and exactly that we may omit further comment on them here, and give a moment's thought to others of his school who are less known.

TANKARDS

In Figure 113 is reproduced a very beautiful relief-decorated tankard (*chope*), also from the Museum of Applied Arts at Strasbourg. This piece was made by Isaac Faust of Strasbourg (*1606-1669*), and was for a long time regarded as the work of Briot, on account of its grace of proportion and fine workmanship. It well demonstrates the high standard of the Strasbourg pewter of those days (*See also Les Étains Strasbourgeois*). Figure 114, from the Verster collection, and Figure 115, from the Bertram collection, give further examples of Renaissance relief pewter. The latter, about eight inches in diameter, is a product of Lyons and bears

Strasbourg, Bordeaux, Lyons, and Rouen were amongst the towns in which the best specimens were wrought; and pieces emanating from these places have become very rare. The finest examples of this class of ware were produced by Isenheim at Strasbourg, the Fabreguettes at Bordeaux, and Laubreaux at Lyons.

The decoration varies according to the district of origin and the period when the pattern was conceived. The relief of the best ones is deeply cut and vigorous in design. The two here reproduced are illustrated for the first time, and many other examples will be found in our work, already referred to, *Les Écuelles à Bouillon*. Of the two illustrated here, Figure 116 is the more ancient, its cover being fitted with three feet, in the form of griffin heads, to keep it from touching the table top when reversed and used as a plate. The cover also shows three medallions with allegorical designs, the space between them being filled with beautiful scrollwork, which, with shells, forms also the decoration on the ears. It is of strong French influence and of Strasbourg origin. Both this and Figure 117 are in the Riff collection.

The porringer illustrated in Figure 117 hails from Bordeaux, and is conceived in a very bold Louis XV style, the swelling cover terminating in a bud-like knop, the ears being of rich Rocaille design. It is but one of several Louis XV patterns of Bordeaux porringers, and we draw our readers' attention to the fact that this type is frequently imitated.

In addition to these richly decorated porringers, there were other types more simple, but not less interesting. On some of these, linear designs in shallow relief appear, mostly from the districts of Paris and Rouen. Others show engraved ornament, which gives them a

*Adolphe Riff, *Les Étains Strasbourgeois.*

Fig. III — TRAVELING FLASK, OR GOURDE (sixteenth century)

rustic character; whilst some remain quite plain, with the exception of relief decoration or piercing of the flat ears. An example, from the Yeates collection, is shown in Figure 118. It bears the date *1702* in the crowned *C* quality mark, but 1750 in the maker's mark; and it was made in Tours.

HELMET-SHAPED EWERS

Another important group of French pewter is that which comprises the helmet-shaped ewers (*aiguières en casque*), deriving their name from the fact that, when inverted, they bear a strong resemblance to an antique helmet. Here again the type is subject to the laws of stylistic evolution. The older ones, dating from the seventeenth century, are heavy in build and pour through a tube-like spout, somewhat detached from the body and ending in a little bill; whereas the point where this spout touches the body is accentuated by a mascaron or shell-like ornament, and the handles are of the volute type, beautifully curved.

In the more recent ewers of this series, such as that shown in Figure 119, which dates from the early part of the eighteenth century, the horizontal upper rim of the older types is retained, but the spout joins the body over its whole length. Figure 120 shows quite the latest development, a distinct spout being absent and the upper rim being curved. It is but little later than the one shown in Figure 119. Both are from the Lyons district, the former from a photo supplied by A. E. Kimbell of London, and the latter from the Strasbourg Museum of Applied Arts. The feet, handles, and body moldings are similar in both pieces. Examples occur also in the region of Besançon, where sometimes they were beautifully engraved. Lorraine is also rich in these ewers, some of the most beautiful examples emanating from there.*

WALL FOUNTAINS

Another very attractive group is found in the French wall fountains (*fontaines murales*), the

*The characteristics and evolution of these types are thoroughly considered and richly illustrated in *Les Aiguières en Casque*, Adolphe Riff, 1926.

Fig. 112 — DISH WITH CAST RELIEFS

One of François Briot's creations. Full of the genius of the Renaissance. Diameter, 19 inches.

set always consisting of two pieces: the water container — or fountain proper — which was fixed to the wall, being suspended by the two lateral ears, and from which a tap serves to regulate the flow of water; below this appears the bowl which was actually used for ablution purposes.

The most beautiful sets were made at Lyons and Besançon, from which latter place came the one shown in Figure 121. The extreme height of the reservoir is twelve and one half inches, and the measurements of the basin are eleven and one half inches by eight inches by three and one quarter inches. It is box-shaped with rounded handles and domed lid, and differs from those made at Lyons, which, since their fronts sometimes imitate architecture, present the semblance of small edifices.

In the Alsace district, the wall fountain simply resembles a pear-shaped flagon, minus its foot. The lid is domed, and to the lower portion is fitted a tube, ending in a tap with its outlet in the form of a dolphin's head.

OTHER TYPES

Of other pewter objects, more or less decorated, we may mention flasks (*gourdes*), the purpose of which is not so much the storage as the transportation of various liquids. Sometimes these are of large capacity and are provided with long necks, such as the one shown in Figure 122, from the Port collection. This piece is some fifteen inches high, and of the eighteenth century. It is closed by a substantial screw cap, and fitted with a convenient stirrup handle of most businesslike appearance.

Sometimes the attachments of the *eyes* to the body, are masked by mascarons, as on the rare sixteenth-century traveling flask (*gourde de voyage*) from the Riff collection, shown in Figure 111. This is some eighteen centimeters high. It is one of the smaller kinds, and has a more flattened belly to make it less cumbersome when slung at the traveler's side.

The ornamental motif of an angel's head is used in a similar manner on the pail-like food con-

Fig. 113 — TANKARD WITH CAST RELIEFS (*c. 1646*)

Ascribed by Demiani to Briot, but now definitely recognized as the work of his clever disciple, Isaac Faust of Strasbourg. Height, 7¼″.

tainers which are frequently met with in France. Figure 123 shows one such. These pieces usually bear the mark of one Bouvier of Clamecy, who seems to have specialized in the manufacture of such practical articles, which were used to carry soup to the people working in distant fields.

PARISIAN PEWTER

Our readers may perhaps be expecting to see more about the product of Parisian pewterers, whose activity seems to have been great and important — as far as artistic merit is concerned — owing to their position in the centre of a big community and their obligation to satisfy the most fastidious clients; but Parisian pewter has become extremely rare.*

The only interesting piece of Parisian pewter which we are able to show is a small chrismatory dating from the reign of Louis XIV, of which we reproduced the mark in Figure 105. This piece is in the Verster collection, but since it has lost the surmounting cross, we illustrate, in Figure 124, an almost identical piece from the Strasbourg Museum of Applied Arts. Mr. Vetter of Amsterdam assures us that the Verster example is of very good metal and tastefully proportioned and decorated.

The rarity of Parisian pewter is further explained by the fact that old metal was easily bought up in Paris during the nineteenth century and was consumed by various industries, at a time when collectors paid practically no attention to modest pewter. This scrapping went on in the provinces as well, but it will be readily understood that, in the capital, metal was much more liable to be snapped up by the ubiquitous junk collector than in the more conservative countryside.

ECCLESIASTICAL TYPES

We have already spoken of the ecclesiastical uses of pewter during the Middle Ages, and we have shown, in Figure 124, the Louis XIV version of the Gothic, box-shaped chrismatory, illustrated in Figure 106, from the same Museum. While the latter example, which is some fourteen and one half cen-

Fig. 114 — EWER (c. 1600; pure Renaissance)

Fig. 115 — DISH WITH CAST RELIEFS
From Lyons, dated in the touch 1651, showing the vigorous scrollwork of the late Renaissance.

timeters in height, is quite plain; the former has a gadrooned foot and a frieze of scrollwork running around the upper edge. The interiors contain two phials for holy oils.

Bénitiers and candlesticks, sometimes decorated with angel heads, chalices, pyxes, and so on, offered further opportunities for the pewterer to compete successfully with the workers in other crafts.

Later, for the Protestant services, baptismal ewers and communion flagons were in demand. Of these latter we show, in Figure 125, a very graceful Alsatian specimen from the latter part of the eighteenth century, fashioned by one of the famous Isenheims of Strasbourg. This piece is from the Hirsbrunner collection, and the handle, with the angel head, deserves special attention.

In Alsace, also, we find pewter for the rites of the Jewish community, such as engraved Seder dishes, Khanukha lamps, and the like.

LATE EIGHTEENTH-CENTURY DECADENCE

The end of the eighteenth century brings with it the decadence of decorated pewter. Relief decoration disappears completely; and the art of engraving passes into coarser hands, approaching more and more the level of the popular peasant craft. Many plates and goblets were decorated in that crude and somewhat dilettantish fashion, and the regions of Lille and Paris, as well as of the Alsace, seem to have been very prolific in this respect.

From the Lille district we find the so-called "marriage dishes," showing two hearts surrounded by an inscription; whereas in Alsace we find, from time to time, plates decorated with one big star, male or female saints, or other religious subjects and symbols, and patriotic emblems such as eagles (Fig. 129, from the Riff collection — to be shown later), fleurs-de-lys, or cocks.

Some of these plates are merely flat circular discs of pewter without rim or reeding around their edges. The use of such pieces was in the presentation of cakes at village feasts.*

Figure 126 shows a Parisian goblet, from the Riff collection, of the popularly decorated

Fig. 116 — PORRINGER (*Louis XIV*)
Strasbourg workmanship.

Fig. 117 — PORRINGER (*Louis XV*)
Rococo design; by Fabreguette of Bordeaux.

kind, with gadrooned foot. It is some twelve centimeters in height and is attributable to *c.* 1740. Such goblets are sometimes engraved with scroll-work, rustic scenes, or shepherds in pastoral surroundings.

SIMPLE HOUSEHOLD TYPES

So much for decorated pewter. We now turn our attention to some of the plainer varieties of French household pewter, often of such striking simplicity and good structural quality as to win the hearts of many collectors. In reviewing these pieces, we must pass over

Fig. 118 — PLAIN PORRINGER: TOURS

such objects as candlesticks, oil lamps, inkpots, tobacco jars, warming pans, and so on; and must confine ourselves to a consideration of plates and dishes and, in our next installment, to flagons.

PLATES

With the former, the shape remained circular until the end of the seventeenth century, when broad rims were the fashion. Hammering was also very much practised at this period, and one finds the hammer marks placed with skilful regularity on the backs of plates and dishes. Some-

Fig. 119 — HELMET EWER: LYONS

Fig. 120 — HELMET EWER: LYONS. Height, 10″.

Figure 122

Figure 121

Figure 125

Figure 123

Fig. 121 — Lavabo Set (*c. 1750*)
From Besançon.

Fig. 122 — Vessel for Carrying Wine

Fig. 123 — Vessel for Carrying Soup

Fig. 124 — Chrismatory (*Louis XIV*)
Height, 5 inches.

Fig. 125 — Protestant Church Flagon
(*late eighteenth century*)
The work of Isenheim of Strasbourg.

Fig. 126 — Goblet (*c. 1750*)
Decorated in the popular style, as made
in the Paris district.

Figure 126

times the rims are beaded or gadrooned, or, much more rarely, punched, as in Figure 128 (to be shown later).

At a later period, the influence of the stylistic movements of the reign of Louis XIV manifests itself in the adoption of oval dishes, as well as by the narrowing of the rim, the outer contour of which resolves itself into many curves. Variations of these curves are interesting to distinguish; sometimes they are interrupted by short, straight bars on four

Figure 124

sides.* The number of lobes also varies considerably, and each variety may be attributed to a particular period or reign. These wavy edged plates and dishes remained in vogue during the whole of the eighteenth century.

(To be continued)

___
*The oval dish shown in Figure 96, Antiques, Vol. XII, p. 218, though of western Swiss make, illustrates this type of contour, which shows a typically French idea. H. H. C.

Fig. *127* (*centre*) — Broad Rimmed Dish (*seventeenth century*)
Fig. *128* (*left*) Dish with Punched Decoration
Fig. *129* (*right*) Strasbourg Plate (Diameter 11½ inches)

European Continental Pewter

By Howard Herschel Cotterell, F. R. Hist. S.

Part VIII

The Pewter of France from the Sixteenth to the Nineteenth Century*

By Adolphe Riff

Conservator of the Museums of Strasbourg, France

Fig. *130* — A Lorraine Flagon
Height 10¾ inches.

FLAGONS, measures, and tankards, used for serving drinks, are the pieces most frequently met with, and are by no means the least interesting for the collector; for each of the many quaint types belongs to a certain reign, so that variations in outline of body and neck, shape of feet, lids, thumbpieces, and handles convey a very definite meaning. These regional types remained in vogue, with but slight modifications, for many centuries; and the shapes and details of many are akin to the oldest types conceived in pewter, and on that account are most worthy of our respect and attention.

Unable here to go into all the subtle differences which the careful reader and col-lector will discover from a comparison of our illustrations, we may, however, sum up a number of common features of many of these truly French vessels, from whose universal constructional plan only a few Alsatian types deviate. These features are: a spherical, or pear-shaped, belly, a distinct neck of varying width, with pinched-in lip, and a heart-shaped lid with thumbpiece of the Twin Acorn, or similar, design. As a matter of fact, the Twin Acorn is the most popular type of thumbpiece, such rather exceptional ones as the Bramble-berry, the Bent-back

Fig. *131* — A Besançon Flagon
Height 10½ inches.

Fig. 132 — A Le Mans Flagon
Height 10½ inches.

Wedge, and the French Erect having been described previously in these articles and illustrated in Figures 28, 29, 30, and 36.*

The flagon illustrated in Figures 137 *a* and *b*, which served previously as the illustration of the Bram-

bleberry type (*Fig. 30*), is now shown as

their touches as follows: Figure 130, from Lorraine; Figure 131, with more slender neck, from Besançon; Figure 132, a typical piece from Le Mans, with large spherical body and Norman lip; Figure 133, from Carpentras. All the foregoing strongly resemble western Swiss types and may possibly have served as models to the Swiss pewterers.*

Figure 134, which is from Lille, betrays abundant evidence of Flemish influence; Figure 135 and the plainer example of

Fig. 133 — A Carpentras Flagon
Height 8½ inches.

a whole with the interesting markings already referred to. A further variety of thumbpiece from the Besançon district is shown in the accompanying sketch. It may be designated by a name already adopted by Mr. Cotterell for the same type, which appears on English pewter, as the Embryo Double-volute.

The handles of French flagons are, for the most part, of a flattened bar section, somewhat crudely fashioned, and the touches, if any, are usually found on top of the flat heart - shaped lid, which, on

Fig. 134 — A Lille Flagon
Height 9¼ inches.

Figure 136 show Alsatian flagons from Strasbourg, and are strongly akin to the German and Swiss stitzen. The circular bands, however, on the level of the lower handle finial, and the heavy lid crest in Figure 135 are quite characteristic of this Alsatian variety. Figures 137 *a* and *b* have already been mentioned as coming from Joinville (Champagne). Figure 138 pictures the well-known Norman flagon. Figure 139 shows the seventeenth-century rendering of this same type, with Hammer-head thumb-pieces.†

Fig. 135 — A Strasbourg Flagon
Height 10¼ inches.

its hinges, is strengthened by a bar. On the Alsatian variety, alone, is the mark found upon the handle; but far better than any words, the accompanying Figures (130–141) will serve to illustrate the principal varieties of these vessels, which can be allocated to the places of origin by

*Antiques, Vol. XI, pp. 196, 197

*It is, of course, merely a hypothesis that the French types were established prior to the Swiss ones, but it seems likely that the shape followed the course of domestic civilization, which is from the plains to the mountains and not vice versa. R. M. Vetter.

†Referring back to the cylindrical measures illustrated in Figure 29, Vol. XI, p. 196, we have come across a set of these bearing the marks shown in Figure 139 *a*, five of which, it will be noted, bear the marks of Caen pewterers.

Fig. 136 — A Strasbourg Flagon

Fig. 137a — JOINVILLE (CHAMPAGNE) FLAGON

Fig. 137b — THE LID OF FIGURE 137a

Fig. 138 — NORMAN FLAGON (*eighteenth century*) Height 10 inches

In Figure 66* was shown a French spouted flagon from the south of France (Avignon). We now give two further examples in Figures 140 and 141, the former a milk can from Lyons, eighteenth century and sixteen inches high. So far as our knowledge goes, it differs from anything else in the way of pewter flagons or cans. The semicircular handle is fixed, as is the front part of the circular lid, to which the other half is hinged. The spout is in the form of the neck and head of a bird, making altogether a picturesque and practical combination.

The flagon illustrated in Figure 141 is another very interesting spouted fellow,

*See ANTIQUES, Vol. XI, p. 384.

Fig. 139—NORMAN FLAGONS (*seventeenth century*)
With Hammer-head thumbpieces.

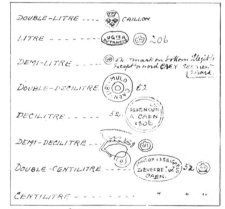

Fig. 139a —MARKS FROM A SET OF NORMAN CYLINDRICAL MEASURES

Fig. 140 — MILK FLAGON FROM LYONS

Fig. 142 — SOUTHERN FRENCH CRUET. Height 9 inches.

Fig. 141 — TOULOUSE FLAGON

from Toulouse, and in the Verster collection at The Hague. It is of the eighteenth century. The narrow neck may be grasped by one hand, and either the spout applied directly to the lips, or a jet may be poured from some height into the open mouth of the drinker, as one sees it done in the south of France.

We must here revert to Figures 107 and 108,* both of them from the collection of Gerhard Tellander of Hilversum, to say a few words about the

Fig. 143 — Tureen (*8¾ inches in diameter*) and Candlesticks (*8½ inches in height*), (*Louis XVI period*).
By Bergmann of Strasbourg.

most elegant and desirable patterns France has created in the way of flagons. The type belongs to the Champagne and is called *cimare.*† They were used for the carrying and presentation of wine in the course of reception ceremonies. These flagons are full of noble Gothic feeling, especially expressed in the quaint stirrup handles. The popularity of these cimares persisted from the sixteenth to the eighteenth century; but, owing to their highly decorative qualities, most specimens have already found a fixed place in public or private collections.

Of tableware, we would — amongst innumerable beautiful patterns, and in addition to the cruet (*Fig. 142*) already dis-

*See ANTIQUES, Vol XIII, p. 130.

†Similar vessels in Switzerland were called *cimaises.* H. H. C.

cussed — mention the soup tureens of Strasbourg, an example of which will be found in Figure 143 between the candlesticks of Louis XVI type. All these pieces are the work of the famous Bergmann of Strasbourg, who lived towards the end of the eighteenth century. They are from the Museum of Applied Arts in that city. Similar tureens were also made by Borst, and at Colmar, with engraved decorations in the form of garlands of flowers. Lyons has also produced like pieces which mostly bear the touch of the pewterer Auster.

It is a remarkable fact that these tureens and candlesticks date from a period when good pewter was already nearly extinct in France. Such are the last efforts of an old and noble trade, which in France can boast of a glorious and venerable tradition.

Pewter of the most common description continued to be made and used at the beginning of the nineteenth century. It is still found in rural districts, monasteries, and hospitals; but it is being driven from these last refuges by the spirit of modernity, and must shortly disappear from amongst the domestic objects of daily use.*

*French types illustrated or discussed in previous articles, will be found in Figures 28–30, 36, 37, and 66. Vol XI, pp. 195–196; p. 384. H. H. C.

Fig. 148a — A German Pewter Collection

Some of the world's choicest pewter, chiefly guild and Renaissance examples, mostly from Germany. Many of these, so far as space has permitted, are fully described in the pages which follow. The picture will serve to bridge over the lacunæ in the series. The object in the bottom right-hand corner — which is not very distinct in the photograph — is the interior of the old guild chest of the Altenberg pewterers, dated *1661*.
Part of the Fritz Bertram collection at Chemnitz. The photograph taken specially for these notes by personal courtesy of Herr Bertram.

European Continental Pewter*

Part IX

The Pewter of Germany

By Howard Herschel Cotterell, F. R. Hist. S.

IT may not be said of Germany, as of Switzerland, that her pewter types are not indigenous to the country, for a number of well-known types would seem to have had their origin here, and, further, to have provided inspiration for the pewterers of surrounding countries. As has already been seen, the Ball thumbpiece is of purely German conception; the curious Stitzen spout (*Fig. 54*), it seems certain, was also of German extraction; and Hanseatic flagons, illustrated in Figures 20, 25, 57, and 58,† have no counterpart elsewhere; the German handle became a thing apart in the very dignity to

which it was raised, a dignity which added to, rather than detracted from, the beauty of the *tout ensemble.* The Cologne flagons, shown in Figure 72* (and subsequently in 169), are national creations, though betraying Dutch and French characteristics; and the celebrated examples of decorated pewter, the so-called *Edelzinn* (noble pewter), exercised a world-wide influence and brought fame to Germany's Nuremberg craftsmen.

This statement is by no means intended to detract in any way from the splendid work and the extensive influence of French pewterers whose *orfèvrerie d'étain* (goldsmith's work in pewter) was second to none, as we have already seen.

*See Antiques, Vol. XI, p. 385.

Fig. 148 (left) — Monastic
Flagon (*fourteenth century*)

Fig. 149 (below) — Spouted
Flagon (*fourteenth or fifteenth century*)

Fig. 150 (right) — Hanseatic
Flagon (*c. 1500*)

If Germany had only the work of her Nuremberg and Silesian pewterers upon which to base her reputation, her claim to rank with the highest in the pewter world would find abundant justification. That, however, is to put forward but a small part of her claim, whose real foundation is the high artistic ideals which *must* have inspired her craftsmen.

Probably no country other than Germany has more readily or more unconsciously yielded to the various artistic waves which have, from time to time, swept across Europe. Gothic, then the more sober Renaissance, and, following that, the more highly decorated Renaissance — all have left their indelible impress. Later came the Baroque-Rococo movement, during which the pewterer had ever before him the fear of the annihilation of his trade through the growing popularity of porcelain, delft, glass, copper, brass, and what-not, each, in its turn, a usurper to be met and countered by some fresh and striking pewter achievement. And so the competitive pace quickened until it became too rapid; technique under such a strain attained swift climax; the impossible was fearlessly attempted; solidity, adaptability, durability, even, at times, good taste, were sacrificed on the altars of scintillating brilliance. But the end was in sight; all this was but the

last dizzy pirouette before collapse!

It was a valiant, if a losing, battle. The great urge forward had been started in the first decade of the eighteenth century by one Sebald Rupprecht of Augsburg, whose work was unequaled for the silvery whiteness of its metal.* This silvery metal, *Zinn auf Silberart* — styled variously, *étain sonnant, métal argentin,* and the like—was attained in Germany, by what is known as the *Heisguss* (hot-cast) method, as opposed to the *Kaltguss* (cold-cast), which latter was used for lead alloys, and gave little sharpness of detail.

This *Heisguss* casting was effected at a high temperature, in pre-heated metal molds, which were cooled quickly, beginning at the lowest point, by application of wet rags. During this process the pouring was continued, to make up for the considerable shrinkage of the metal. This new metal, which has a pronounced, rustling *cri*, is very sonorous and takes on a beautiful and lasting polish.

Rupprecht died in 1755, but he left behind him, to carry on the warfare, a whole school of famous pewterers who developed and elaborated

*Rupprecht's touch is illustrated in Figure 7, Vol. XI, p. 35, of Antiques.

Fig. 150a — Hanseatic Flagon (*sixteenth century*)

Fig. 151 *(left)* —
SILESIAN
FLAGON
*(fifteenth
century)*

Fig. 152 *(right)* —
SILESIAN
FLAGON
(c. 1500)

Fig. 153 *(below)*
SILESIAN OR
BRESLAU
TYPE OF
FLAGON
(1500)

the Rococo style throughout the greater part of the eighteenth century. The inventors of the process gave to it the name of *Zinn auf Silberart*, which means pewter in imitation of silver, as indeed it was, for it aimed at matching, as opposed to copying, the work of the silversmiths.

EARLIEST GERMAN PEWTER

As with other countries, there is, of course, no record of the period when pewter was first made in Germany; but, as early as 1299, the trade is mentioned in a manuscript in the archives of Lübeck; and in 1324 there are records of its being well established in such places as Augsburg and Nuremberg. But the writing of the history of the industry is not contemplated in these notes, any more than to indicate, by these few remarks, that the industry was of very ancient foundation.

Quite opposed to the custom obtaining in England, where, except by special permission from the guilds — which it was by no means easy to obtain — apprentices were forbidden to leave their own towns, continental apprentices, toward the end of their term, were encouraged to make extensive tours. As part of their training, it was by no means an uncommon thing for quite young men to make journeys of a two or three years' period, and, during them, to visit such widely scattered countries as Poland, Russia, Finland, Scandinavia, Holland, France, and Switzerland. Oftentimes these traveled apprentices never returned to their own guilds, but set up an independent business or obtained permanent employment in some more or less distant place. By such means, ideas were disseminated and the styles of one country became blended with another. And this, too, accounts for some of the freak types which one comes across from time to time.*

DESCRIPTION OF ILLUSTRATIONS

For ease of reference, and to make these notes of the maximum service, I have arranged the accompanying illustrations in more or less chronological sequence; under the head first of *vessels for liquids,* followed by *plates and dishes.* Thereafter appear some few photographs of items which do not exactly come within either of these classifications. Many of the items illustrated now appear for the first time in any work on this subject; and I desire to record my thanks to all those who have so freely placed their treasures at my disposal, with a very special word to Fritz Bertram of Chemnitz, whose fine collection represents the world's best in pewter. One of his rare Saxon tankards appears as this month's Frontispiece.

FIGURE 148

Figure 148 shows, side by side, the disjointed lid from one flagon and a complete example of the same type, the latter being some seven and one-half inches in height. These well may be two of the oldest pieces of German pewter in the world. They were found during excavations on the site formerly occupied by an ancient monastery in the old university town of Göttingen.

The lids of these most interesting relics are engraved, in Gothic characters: one with the device, F. VI; the other with F. VIII. These are the shortened designations of two of the monks, *Frater Sixtus* and *Frater Octavus;* and there exists no doubt that they

Fig. 155 — FRENCH EWER (*sixteenth century*)

were appurtenances to the cells of the respective *Fratres,* or Brethren.

Another very interesting feature of these vessels is that, in place of the relief ornament which usually decorates the backs of the handles on this type of primitive flagon (*Figs. 39, 150* and *151*), the words *Amor vincit omnia* are cast. They refer, of course, to the Christian belief that love is the greatest force in the world.† The thumbpiece, quite small in proportion to the size of the vessel, is of a rudimentary Hammer-head type,

*German pieces which have been used to illustrate the previous articles in this series will be found in Figures 20–26, 31–33, 39, 41, 57, 58, 70, and 72; Vol. XI, pp. 195–199, 382–385.

†Chaucer in his Prologue to the *Canterbury Tales,* it will be remembered, describes a bracelet worn by the comely Prioress, Madame Eglentyne. Its medallion bore this same inscription. *Ed.*

date, even to the Gothic tilt of the escutcheon, which appears on each side of the body, and the long lower terminal of the handle, fixed flat against the back. This piece is in the Bertram collection and possibly exemplifies the earliest type of spouted flagon.

FIGURES 150 AND 150a

The photographs, courteously supplied by the authorities of the Museum für Kunst und Kulturgeschichte at Lübeck (*Figs. 150 and 150a*), illustrate two more of these early treasures. Figure 150 is of the Hanseatic type, probably made at Lübeck, *c.* 1500. The base of this piece is exceptionally broad, being seven and three-quarters as against an *extreme* height of seven inches; the bottom is flush with the table, and so, since it is hollow from the inside, this would make it practically impossible for the contents to be accidentally spilled. The very slightly domed

*See ANTIQUES, Vol. XI, page 195.

and seems quite subservient to the unusually prominent central knop to the lid (see also *Figs. 39,* centre, and *150a*). This knop is crowned with the device of the double rose, in relief, so that one is tempted to speculate whether this had already become a quality mark, or denoted metal of English origin. Or, yet again, is here discoverable the origin of the world-wide association between *p. wter* and the *rose?* Such an association must have originated somewhere.

The date of these wonderful relics cannot be later than the fourteenth century; it may, quite as easily, be the thirteenth century or even earlier.

I should like to deal more fully with the salient points of this and other early German types; but I must reserve such discussion for a future chapter on primitive examples with distinctly *ceramic** feeling, here calling attention merely to their general massive construction and the truncated cone shape of their bases. I am indebted to the authorities of the Staedtische Altertumssammlung, Göttingen, for generously supplying this most interesting photograph.

FIGURE 149

Figure 149 shows a venerable and battered veteran, some ten inches in height, nothing being known either of its nationality or of the place where it was found, the fact that it is in German possession being, so far as I can see, its only claim to be included here. But, it *must* be shown somewhere, as one of the earliest pewter pieces in existence. It may well be of Rhenish origin, dating from the fourteenth or early fifteenth century, for every line declaims its early

Fig. 154 — SILESIAN GUILD FLAGON (*1608*)

Fig. 156 — REGENSBURG GUILD FLAGON (*1583*)

lid is seated flat on the lip of the vessel; the wedge-shaped piece on the lid is very high and massive; and the thumbpiece is of the Lens type. Compare this with the pieces illustrated in Figure 39, which, though found on the Island of Fünen, are likewise considered to be of Hanseatic origin.

Figure 150a also depicts a very ancient type, though probably a trifle later than the last. It is nine inches in height, and has many interesting features; the lid, with its massive knop, displays, as suggested by H. C. Gallois of The Hague Museum, all the characteristics of old Chinese pottery lids, making the handle and dimunitive thumbpiece appear as "afterthoughts." Indeed, apart from these two latter features, the piece as seen in the illustration would pass quite easily for pottery.

FIGURE 151

Figure 151 offers a fine example from the Bertram collection. Some ten inches in height, this flagon is probably of the fifteenth century. The piece is remarkable for its purity of form as also for its thumbpiece, which displays a crude, but quite unmistakable representation of a fleur-de-lis, a device which also appears in the very clear maker's mark, on the top of the handle, immediately below the hinge, and which Herr Bertram ascribes to an unknown maker of Neisse, Silesia. Covered with a wonderful patina, this must be considered one of the world's chief pewter treasures.

FIGURE 152

Another fine example of primitive pewter from the Bertram collection, will be seen in Figure 152. Ten inches in height, it was found in a well at Sagan, Silesia, and may be considered as Silesian work, *c.* 1500. Its Twin Hoof thumbpiece is extremely interesting, and its general characteristics bespeak an early date.

FIGURE 153

A fine ten-inch Gothic flagon in the Rijksmuseum, Amsterdam, is illustrated in Figure 153, by courtesy of the authorities of that institution. The date of this piece is *c.* 1500. The early Erect thumbpiece and gargoyle-like handle terminal are worthy of note; as also are the sloping-sided lid and the polyhedrous construction of the body, the various compartments of which display some fairly representative engraving of the period — wrought in clear, easy lines, with a sure hand, never in what is known as "wriggled work."

It would, I think, be safe to say that there is not a score of this type of vessel in the world, though of that number several are of much larger size than the one illustrated here. They represent one of the most coveted types of all pewter vessels, one of the best having realized, in 1909, the enormous sum — for a piece of pewter — of £1650, or upwards of $8,000!

FIGURE 154

A type which succeeded this latter, in the form of a very beautiful guild flagon from the Bertram collection, is illustrated in Figure 154. This fine piece, which stands some twenty-two and one-half inches high and is dated *1608*, is unusual in many ways, for it has lions' masks with rings for medallions, a feature usually found only on guild cups (as will be shown in Figures 175 and 176); further,

Fig. 157 — NUREMBERG TANKARD (*sixteenth century*)

two copper bands encircle the body, and a third runs down the outside of the handle; the fine decorated Erect thumbpiece is also worthy of note; but perhaps the most unusual feature of all, in a specimen of this size and character, is the omission of a tap for drawing off the liquid which it contained. When full, the weight of this enormous flagon must have offered a drawback to its too frequent use. This flagon was made at Greifenberg, Silesia, and is richly decorated and engraved.

FIGURE 155

Another of the world's greatest treasures in pewter, one which must be literally worth its weight in gold, is shown in the fine nine and one-half inch ewer from the Bertram collection, which appears in Figure 155. This is a genuine specimen of the work of that most celebrated French pewterer, François Briot (*1550–1615*). Its twin thumbpiece, besides its general characteristics, bespeaks the nationality of its maker. This is, of course, a French piece, but Briot's influence on German *Edelzinn* shall be my excuse for illustrating it in this place. It is, further, a pleasure to show such a piece to one's readers for the first time.

FIGURE 156

Figure 156 illustrates a twenty-two inch shoemakers' guild flagon from Regensburg, Bavaria, dated *1583*, with well engraved military figures in the costumes of the period. This piece — as well as that of Figure 157 — is in the Bertram collection, and shows a fine Erect thumbpiece, with an overlapping lid, from which the center ornament has evidently been broken away.

FIGURE 157

Another glorious example of pewter work — *Edelzinn* at its best — appears in Figure 157, in the form of an eight and one-quarter inch tankard with spreading base, supported on three scrolled feet with maiden-head masks, the body and lid being decorated with bands of exquisite low-relief work. It is the work of Jacob Koch II of Nuremberg (*1572–1619*), and is famous as one of the most beautiful pieces of Renaissance pewter in the world. The fine sweep of handle and base, the hammering of the otherwise plain body, and the general excellence of the design make of it a thing apart.

FIGURE 158, THE FRONTISPIECE

A fine example of Saxon *Edelzinn* is illustrated in the Frontispiece. It will be noted that here we have a higher and bolder relief, and altogether a more vigorous handling than characterizes the more refined Nuremberg work. The nature of this particular piece demonstrates fairly clearly what a high standard was, at that time, expected before mastership was recognized and the privilege of freedom of the guild obtained.

This tankard is seven inches in height, the work of Paul Günther of Chemnitz, who became a master in 1595. The episode depicted on the central band is the story of the Prodigal Son. It will be noted that the lid is of the flush variety: that is, there is no projection of its edges over the sides of the vessel.

(To be continued)

European Continental Pewter*

Part X

The Pewter of Germany

By HOWARD HERSCHEL COTTERELL, F. R. Hist. S., *and* ROBERT M. VETTER

Note.—The able coöperation which I have received from Robert M. Vetter of Amsterdam in compiling these articles (which I have endeavored amply to acknowledge in these pages, from time to time) has been of such a nature and such measure that I have tried — without success until now — to obtain his consent to allowing his name to appear with my own, as co-author of the series. But — and I now record it with pleasure — he has at last abandoned that attitude, and has consented that this and future articles shall appear under both our names, as joint authors. — *H. H. C.*

IN the last article I dealt with the more ornate of the German vessels for holding liquids. In the present one we reach the period of plainer styles, when

Fig. 159 — MARIENBURG GUILD FLAGON (*1650*)
Height, 17½". The descriptions of this and other pieces, as well as the names of those who have courteously permitted the publishing of their rare possessions, will be found in the text. The dimensions are, in the main, approximate.
For photographs of items from Mr. Vetter's collection ANTIQUES is indebted to the skill and generosity of P. J. Ducro of Amsterdam.

beautiful flagon introduces this series, in Figure 159. The exquisite scaly engraving of the body and its other delightfully restrained decoration fully warrant its selection to open this second installment of *The Pewter of Germany*. It was made in the year 1650 by E. John of Marienburg, for the bootmakers' guild of that town, and is now in the collection of Fritz Bertram of Chemnitz.

Of about the same date, but of a very different character, is the spouted flagon, or *Schenkkanne*, shown in Figure 160, which is reproduced by courtesy of the authorities of the Museum für Kunst und Kulturgeschichte, Lübeck. This flagon comes from the Holy Ghost Hospital, Lübeck, in which town it was made by Harmen Godt, in 1654. The influence of the North is seen on this piece, in the Dutch type Erect

Edelzinn, or its best period, had run its course.

An extremely

thumbpiece. The waves of the French and Italian styles hardly touched this region. The flagon bears the arms of two burgomasters, and

Fig. 160 — LÜBECK SCHENKKANNE (*1654*) Height, 16½".

Fig. 161 — SILESIAN TANKARD (*seventeenth century*). Height, 10¼".

its spout, which has no cover, is of the same hexagonal section as those on the Frans Hals and Swiss flagons already illustrated in Part III.*

The funnel-like widening of the mouth of this flagon is indeed an evolution of the seventeenth century. The necessity for this may find explanation in one of Jan Steen's paintings, wherein these large spouted vessels are depicted as being replenished from larger earthenware or glass jars, either on the sideboard or on the floor. As the evening wore along, and the fillers of these flagons became less steady in their gait and aim, the wider mouth was welcomed as affording a lesser chance of pouring the contents on the floor!

*See ANTIQUES, Vol. XI, pp. 382, 383.

Fig. 162 — NORTH GERMAN ROERKEN (*seventeenth century*)
Respective heights, 8″ and 8¾″.

Another type, from the Bertram collection, is given in Figure 161, in the form of a beer tankard made by Georg Krische of Breslau, Silesia (*1609–1674*). This piece is interesting in that it displays the adherence of the Silesian pewterers to the polyhedrous method of construction, a purely Gothic idea, at a period when Gothic was as dead as the dodo.

The engraving of the panels with figures of apostles and saints is also a Silesian feature, but if these be compared with the ones shown in Figure 153,* and other similar early ex-

*See ANTIQUES, Vol. XIV, p. 139.

Fig. 163 — NUREMBERG TANKARD
Height, 6½″.

Fig. 165 (*left*) — SCHWEIDNITZ GUILD FLAGON (*1699*)
Height, 26½″.

Fig. 166 (*right*) — NORTH GERMAN GUILD FLAGON (*1745*)

Figs. 167 and 167a — Nuremberg Tankard (1717) with Detail of its Hinge
Height of Tankard, 10″.

Fig. 168 — South German Ewer and Basin (*eighteenth century*)

Fig. 164 (*left*) — Regensburg Flagon (*1688*)
Height, 9″.

amples, the decline which artistic taste had undergone within two centuries will be at once apparent. Mr. Vetter remarks that the undulated edges of the cover and base suggest to him the starched ruffs of the period.

In Figure 162 are shown two fine examples of seventeenth-century North German flagons from Bremen, known as *Roerken*. Both these pieces are in the Vetter collection, the one with the Ball thumbpiece bearing the date *1666*. The other, with Erect thumbpiece, has the date *1667*. They were formerly the property of a weavers' guild and are extremely heavy and massive, and the well wrought bases with bulging, spun-out sides, and the general proportions of these flagons are very pleasing.

Figure 163 offers an *Edelzinn* tankard, which is a recent and very fine addition to the Vetter collection. Though the piece is dated *1677* in the mark, its *actual* date is 1686, which is engraved

upon it. The mark is that of an unknown German pewterer, but the tankard bears, in relief, the initials, *C. E.*, of the well-known Nuremberg master Caspar Enderlein. The piece was actually made by one of his successors, at a time when the taste for such pieces was rapidly declining in favor of the more passionate Baroque of the Louis XIV style. The central knop has been broken away from the lid, but the wonderful black patina, the untouched condition, the date, and the association make this flagon a very desirable possession.

A beautifully proportioned Bavarian flagon from Regensburg, dated *1688*, is illustrated in Figure 164. This finely engraved piece is in the Museum Carolino-Augusteum at Salzburg, and is reproduced here by permission of the Museum authorities. The engraving on it,

Fig. 169 — Cologne Flagons

which is very pleasing and well distributed, is Austrian, and was probably done in Salzburg.

The curiously elaborated, but easily recognized, Erect motive of the thumbpiece and handle finial of the flagon illustrated in Figure 165 give to it quite a character of its own. Now in the Bertram collection, this flagon was made in 1699 by David Schmidt of Schweidnitz, for the bakers' guild at Brauna, Saxony. It has a brass tap and is engraved with names and figures, which cover practically the whole of the body.

Leaving the seventeenth century, Figure 166 shows a fine guild flagon, dated *1745*, from the Davis collection. Here it will be noticed that

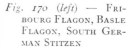

Fig. 170 (left) — FRI-BOURG FLAGON, BASLE FLAGON, SOUTH GER-MAN STITZEN

Fig. 171 (centre of page) — WEST GERMAN EWER AND BASIN (*eighteenth century*) Height of ewer, 8½"; diameter of basin, 12½".

the double-domed lid appears, a feature much in favor in northern Germany (*Figs. 160 and 162*). Further, there is no tapering of the body, either upwards or downwards, but a pure cylindrical shape, a characteristic also obtaining in Figure 167, which illustrates another of the "frilled" beer-mugs — this one, from the collection of Doctor Karl Ruhmann of Vienna, bearing the date *1717*. It is the work of a Nuremberg pewterer, and, in the smaller picture (*Fig. 167a*) will be seen the detail of the hinge, whereon, by a series of in-

Fig. 172 — BAYREUTH FLAGON (*dated 1830*) Height, 10".

Fig. 176 — NUREMBERG PORRINGER (*sixteenth century*)

Fig. 174 — GÖRLITZ GUILD CUP (*seventeenth century*). Height, 16¾".

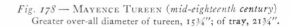

Fig. 177 — Dresden Tureen (*c. 1740*)
Greater diameter, over all, 14″.

Fig. 177a (centre) — Mark of I. G. Iahn

Fig. 178 — Mayence Tureen (*mid-eighteenth century*)
Greater over-all diameter of tureen, 15¾″; of tray, 21¾″.

dentations, a diapered effect is achieved, which is quite a German feature, though the small shield-shaped finial of the handle is un-usual on a South German piece.

The pleasingly conceived baptis-mal ewer and basin illustrated in Figure 168 are probably from Würtemberg or Baden. These pieces are from the Hirsbrunner collection, and the curiously double-hooked handle is worthy of note. With its well set Ball, it forms a fitting balance to the heavy stitzen lip.

From the collection of Mrs. L. Payne of Amstelveen, I am able to illustrate, in Figure 169, three fine examples of the Cologne flagons already referred to in Figure 72.* A wonderfully well set up trio, which must give infinite pleasure to their fortunate possessor.

Figure 170 shows three pieces from the collection of Professor Calame of Winterthur. On the right is a South German stitzen of a very pure type, compared with a Fribourg flagon (*left*) and a Basle type (*centre*), which latter compare with Figure 168. The gradual evolution from the purely "ceramic," or primitive idea, ex-pressed in the Fribourg example, to the Renaissance feeling in the other two, is very clearly marked.

A massively constructed ewer and basin, of Baroque design, with clearly defined Renaissance lean-

*See ANTIQUES, Vol. XI, p. 385.

Fig. 173 — Regensburg Council Flagon (*dated 1660*). Height, 23″.

ings, is shown in Figure 171, from the Ruhmann collection. This set hails from West Germany, and is probably of the mid-eighteenth century.

Figure 172 brings us to a point of more than passing interest, for it affords us a characteristic ex-ample of the decoration known as *Biedermeier*. Dated *1830*, this pleasing piece is from Bayreuth, Bavaria, and combines the deco-ration of the period with a type of vessel of much earlier date.

Mr. Vetter especially enjoins me to emphasize the *real* meaning of the frequently misapplied term *Biedermeier;* he writes as follows:

Biedermeier = Homely Empire or Bourgeois Empire. The word signifies a jovial, honest, though politically-narrow-minded person, sym-bolizing the ideas of the middle classes in Ger-many, Austria, and Switzerland, about 1800.

It is not the name of a designer, such as Chip-pendale, Hepplewhite, or Sheraton, as some people seem to imply when speaking of examples as being in the "style created by the well-known Biedermeier"! This is sheer nonsense and you should set it right for your readers, for Bieder-meier had just as much reality as Mr. Pickwick, John Bull, or Jacques Bonhomme; indeed this French word *Bonhomme, i.e.*, good man, is very nearly akin to Biedermeier.*

We must turn now to another kind of guild flagon — one that, in reality, is very far removed from the types which we have just been

*In fact the German word *bieder* means, *worthy* or *honest*. *Meier*, or *Meyer*, is the most usual of German names — as usual as Smith is, or was, in America. Literally, therefore, the *Biedermeier Period* is equivalent to the *Worthy Smith Period*. The connotations should require no elucidation. — *Ed.*

considering, and which will, perhaps, be best explained by turning to the one illustrated in Figure 173, which pictures a specimen from the Bertram collection. These tall slender vessels would seem to form a connecting link between flagons proper and the guild cups, which are the subject of the two following pictures. The flagon in Figure 173 is of the type called *Ratskanne*, or council flagon. It was made in the seventeenth century for the town of Regensburg, Bavaria. In an escutcheon on the front of the bulbous portion appears the date *1660*, with the device of the crossed keys. As a type, this piece is of particular interest to our subject, in that its design is similar to those which one so often comes across in pewterers' touches and control marks. It is typically German.

Figures 174 and 175 show two of the guild cups referred to above. They differ from the flagons principally in that they have no handles and that the lids are, therefore, not hinged, but loose. Apart from this, both types are raised on feet of varying heights and shapes, and both have bodies which widen out and narrow alternately, according to the whim of the individual pewterer. Figure 174 shows an example from the Ruhmann collection, made by Elias Schossbeck, at Görlitz, Silesia, in the seventeenth century; and Figure 175, a magnificent cup from the Bertram collection. This piece is from a shoemakers' guild in Silesia, or southern Germany. It is supported on three bronze feet in the form of sheep; a bronze figure of a knight, with banner, surmounts the cover, whilst the body is surrounded by several brass hoops. This wonderful piece, regarded as the finest existing specimen of Renaissance guild pewter, dates from about 1550. It well reflects the

Fig. 175 — Silesian or South German Guild Cup (*c. 1550*)
Height, 30″.

wealth and importance of the German guilds when at the height of their power in the sixteenth century.

Although a date *1729* appears upon it, the piece was certainly not made in the eighteenth century; for its importance, its style, and the nature of its engraving all point an unerring finger to a period of manufacture prior to 1600. The date *1729* may be taken as referring, in all probability, to some event in the life of the guild, or to some restoration of the piece itself.

Figure 176 shows the interior of an unique sixteenth-century porringer, decorated on the inside of the bowl with low-relief, arabesque ornament. It is Nuremberg work, and from the Tyrolese castle of Brixlegg. Arabesque decoration on the *interior* of porringers is very rarely met. The centre of the bowl displays a fine, early, merchant's mark.

In Figures 177 and 178 are illustrated two fine examples of German Rococo tureens from the Vetter collection. The former is a Dresden piece, with perpendicular folds (*c. 1740*), and bears the mark of I. G. Iahn of that city, which, as it has never been illustrated, I am showing here in Figure 177*a*.

Figure 178 shows the scroll and wave type of Rococo, and bears the mark *Sebastian Ferber, Fein Englisch Block Zin, Mainz* (Mayence). To find the two pieces in combination, each bearing the same baronial monogram, is extremely rare.

These two pieces are of a type eagerly sought by Continental collectors. So keen, indeed, is the search for them that a supply is being created, and the forgers are very busily engaged in turning them out in quantities sufficiently large to "fill all reasonable demands!"

(*To be continued*)

European Continental Pewter*

Part XI

The Pewter of Germany

By HOWARD HERSCHEL COTTERELL, F. R. Hist. S., *and* ROBERT M. VETTER

IN the two previous articles attention has been directed to a consideration only of those vessels which were designed for holding liquids. We now turn to the second part of the story.

To open the series, I have selected a piece which is so beautiful and so rare as to demand some isolation from its fellows. This wonderful little plate (*Fig. 179*), which is shown here at almost full size, is in the Vetter collection. This is the first time that it has appeared in any work on old pewter. It was made by Pankraz Coller of Nuremberg (*1616–1644*), and is a fine example of pure Renaissance pewter. The inscrip-

Fig. 179 — NUREMBERG PLATE (*early seventeenth century*)
Diameter, 4⅛". Description of this and other pieces, together with the names of those who have courteously permitted the publication of rarities from their collections, will be found in the text. The dimensions are, in the main, approximate.
For photographs of items from Mr. Vetter's collection, ANTIQUES is indebted to the skill and generosity of P. J. Ducro of Amsterdam.

tion over the central figure reads *H. V. Droia*, which is the old German rendering for Hector of Troy. The tiny mark may be seen on the rim, toward the lower edge.

Following this, in Figure 180, is another equally rare and interesting piece from the Bertram collection. It is the work of Georg Huebner of Löwenberg, Silesia (*c. 1530*), and is one of the oldest and finest Gothic dishes in existence, the beads and bosses being repoussé, *not* cast. Too small, we are afraid, to be deciphered in the reproduction, a merchant's mark appears as the device on one of the very tiny touches.

Figure 181 pictures a plate in the centre medallion of which a nude figure is seated, pensively regarding the fast-running sand

Fig. 180 (*left*) — LÖWEN-
BERG DISH (*c. 1530*)
Diameter, 22¾".

Fig. 181 (*right*) — NUREM-
BERG PLATE (*1600*)
Diameter, 9¾".

Fig. 182 — Nuremberg Plates (*sixteenth and seventeenth centuries*)

Fig. 182a (right) — Border Detail and Mark of Central Plate in the Upper Row

in an hourglass. Around it appears the inscription, *Hodie mihi cras tibi*, which means roughly, *This day is mine, to-morrow is thine.* Around this picture, on the rim of the plate, are eight cartouches, in which appear allegorical figures representing, alternately, the elements and the seasons. The date of this plate is 1600 and it is particularly interesting in that, although it bears the mark of Brassó, Kronstadt, its Nuremberg origin

is established by such authorities as Demiani, Hintze, and others. Moreover, it betrays all the characteristics of Nuremberg work. I am indebted to the authorities of the Hungarian Museum of Arts and Crafts, Budapest, for this illustration.

Fig. 183 — Nuremberg Plate (*seventeenth century*)
First plate in upper row of Figure 182. Diameter, 6½".

Fig. 184 (left) — Nuremberg Dish (*sixteenth century*)
Diameter, 11".

Fig. 185 (right) — Nuremberg Dish (*early seventeenth century*)
Diameter, 13½".

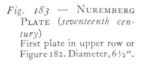

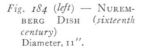

Fig. 186 (left) — NU-REMBERG DISH (*late sixteenth century*) Diameter, 7¼″.

Fig. 187 (right) — NU-REMBERG DISH (*late sixteenth century*) Diameter, 11¼″.

Figure 182 shows seven *Edel-zinn* plates of the sixteenth and seventeenth centuries, from the Vetter collection — all from Nuremberg. The pewterers and the mold makers of these plates are as follows, reading from left to right in the order shown:

No.	Pewterer's name	Mold maker's name
1.	Hans Spatz, Jr., *1630–1670*	Paulus Öham, Sr., *1604–1634*
2.	Nicholas Horcheimer, *1561–1583*	
3.	Hans Spatz, Jr., *1630–1670*	G. H
4.	Georg Schmanss, *1628–1633*	G. S.
5.	Paulus Öham, Jr., *1634–1671*	S. M.
6.	Sigmund Wadel, *1690–1719*	Paulus Öham, Jr., *1634–1671*
7.	Paulus Öham, Jr., *1634–1671*	M. S.

Fig. 189 — NUREMBERG PLATE (*seventeenth century*) Diameter, 8½″.

Note. The *marks* of the makers of the molds for these plates were cast-in, in relief, at the time when the plates were cast. The pewterer's mark was subsequently struck-in, in the ordinary way, and sometimes defaced the mold maker's mark.

Reference to Figure 183 will show the mold maker's mark detrited in the upper panel of the rim, and the maker's mark struck on the panel on the right-hand side of rim.

In Figure 182a appears an enlarged photograph of part of the rim of the plate in the centre of the upper row of Figure 182. This will serve the double purpose of showing more clearly the beautiful decoration and also the difficulty of discovering these diminutive early marks. In this instance, the mark is struck immediately

Fig. 188 (left) — NU-REMBERG PLATE (*sixteenth century*) Diameter, 9¼″.

Fig. 190 (right) — JEW-ISH SEDER PLATE (*eighteenth century*) Diameter, 14½″.

Fig. 194 — FRANKFORT BÉNITIER, DISH, AND EWER (*eighteenth century*)
Height of bénitier, 3½″; extreme width of dish, 16½″; height of ewer, 8½″.

above the arrow, as is indicated by the sketch affixed to the illustration.

Figure 183 gives a larger illustration of number one of Figure 182. This will afford a better idea of the general characteristics of these Nuremberg plates, which were sharply cast. And this sharpness must still be evident in the deeper parts, even if the tops be worn. Further, they should be light in weight, with broad, distinct, and more or less regular turning marks on the backs; for, although these pieces were made before the advent of the automatic lathe, the old workmen knew their jobs!

Two exceptionally fine examples of the celebrated Nuremberg flat-relief work are shown in Figures 184 and 185, from the Ruhmann collection.

These flat-relief pieces are supposed to have been cast from molds into which the designs had previously been etched. Figure 184 illustrates a piece made by Albrecht Preisensin (*1564–1598*), the central picture representing Fama, the seven figures around the rim typifying Luna, Mars, Sol, Saturn, Venus, Jupiter, and Mercury. Figure 185 is by Hans Spatz, Sr. (*1600–1640*), the centre panel depicting the Resurrection, with the twelve Apostles around the rim.

Two more magnificent examples are illustrated in Figures 186 and 187, both from the Bertram collection, and quite different from any of those already shown. Both are Nuremberg work, the

Fig. 192 (*below*) — NUREMBERG DISH WITH DECORATIVE RIM (*eighteenth century*)
Extreme width, 15″.

Fig. 191 (*left*) — AUGSBURG DISH (*c. 1720*)
Extreme width, 18″.

Fig. 193 (*below*) — FRANKFORT DISH (*eighteenth century*)
Extreme width, 13½″.

Fig. 195 — FRANKFORT PEWTER (*eighteenth-century Rococo*)
Diameter of salver, 11″; height of candlesticks, 6″.

first being by Wolf Stoy (*1564–1605*), and the second, by Hans Zatzer (*1560–1618*). The central bosses in both examples are spun up from the flat.

Figure 188, from the Ruhmann collection, shows another exceptionally fine plate, of a type similar to that in Figure 179; but it is more than double the size of Mr. Vetter's piece. It bears the mark of an unknown Nuremberg maker.

Yet another of Herr Bertram's treasures is given in Figure 189, in the form of a plate, the rim of which is covered with naturalistic flowers in low relief, made by Gotthold Mergenthaler of Nuremberg (*1661–1683*).

Figure 190 illustrates a very beautifully engraved, eighteenth-century Jewish Seder plate, used at the festival of the Passover. The figures around the plate typify the Aramaic song *Had Gadya (One Kid)*, which is recited at the conclusion of the Seder service. These plates were used to hold the three unleavened cakes prescribed for the ceremony of the Seder. This is another of Doctor Ruhmann's pieces.

In Figure 191 is shown a very beautiful *Silberart* dish, made by that famous Augsburg pewterer Sebald Rupprecht, whose mark was illustrated in Part I, Figure 7* of this series, and of whose methods of *Heisguss* casting,†

---

*See ANTIQUES, Volume XI, p. 35.
†See ANTIQUES, Volume XIV, p. 138.

Fig. 194a — NUREMBERG DISH (*eighteenth century*)
Extreme width, 11½″.

mention has already been made on an earlier page. This piece is in the Vetter collection and the owner informs me that, although he never cleans it, the dish retains its bright silvery surface after two centuries of life.

Figures 192 and 193 illustrate two decorated oval dishes from the Ruhmann collection. The former, by Georg Nicolaus Stark of Nuremberg, shows a prettily decorated wavy edge; the latter piece is by Johann Anzelm Fester of Frankfort. The second was, in all probability, the basin to a helmet ewer, or *aiguière en casque*, similar to that illustrated here in Figure 194, which shows another oval Rococo dish, with its companion ewer standing on its right. This set is of Frankfort make, as also is the small bénitier on the left. The triangular salver, or urn tray (*Fig. 194a*), is a very fine example of scrollwork, marked *Englisch Zinn, John. Geo. Marx, in Nuremberg* (*1745–1781*). This class of fine quality Rococo pewter is difficult to come across today, though imitations by the cartload may readily be purchased in any large centre. These pieces are all in the Vetter collection. Figure 195 gives a further group of this fine quality, early eighteenth-century, twisted Rococo work, from the same collection, all of Frankfort make.

(To be continued)

European Continental Pewter*

Part XII

The Pewter of Germany

By Howard Herschel Cotterell, F. R. Hist. S., *and* Robert M. Vetter

GUILD trophies are items of great rarity, and I am glad to be able to illustrate two genuine examples in Figures 196 and 197, the former from the Vetter, and the latter from the Bertram collection. The *fish* example was, probably, once the property of a guild of fishermen, and is dated *1698*. It bears the mark of an Augsburg pewterer, and is unique. The mouth is closed by a screw stopper in the form of a smaller fish. Every part, quite original, is beaten up from the flat sheet metal, *not cast*, and neatly soldered together. The piece illustrated in Figure 197 shows the

Fig. 196 — Augsburg Guild Trophy (*dated 1698*). Length, 26".

emblem of a masons' guild in Straubing, Bavaria, and was made by J. Pruckner (*c. 1780*).

The candlesticks illustrated in Figure 198 are considered masterpieces of the Renaissance pewterer's art, and represent another of Herr Bertram's treasures. They are the work of Matthias Bachmann of Memmingen (*1588*). They are cast from an etched mold. The date and also the initials of the maker, *M. B.*, are cast in. This flatter style of relief was in vogue before Briot and Enderlein asserted their great influence and introduced the more distinct type of relief work.

A typical Baroque altar candlestick (*c. 1720*) appears in Figure 199, from the Creassey collection; and, in Figures 200 and 201, two

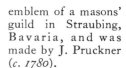

Fig. 197 (*center of page*) — BAVARIAN GUILD WREATH (*c. 1780*) Diameter of wreath, 16".

Fig. 199 (*left*) — ALTAR CANDLESTICK (*c. 1720*)

Fig. 200 (*left*) — FIGURE CANDLESTICK (*late eighteenth century*)

Fig. 201 (*right*) — FIGURE CANDLESTICK (*late eighteenth century*). Height, 9".

Fig. 202 (left) —OIL TIME LAMP *(seventeenth-eighteenth century)*

Figs. 204, 205 (above), and 203 (right) — ORDINARY PEWTER OIL LAMPS

examples of late eighteenth-century figure candlesticks. The former, from the Hirsbrunner collection, shows the type known as the "miner's" candlestick; and the latter, reproduced by the kind permission of the Hungarian Museum of Arts and Crafts at Budapest, is in the form of a Hungarian Hussar. Although this latter shows

a Hungarian figure, its form leads to the belief that it was made in Saxony for export to Hungary.

Figure 202 shows an example, from the collection of Doctor Young of Manchester, of the type of oil time lamp which was in use in the northern and other parts of Germany during the seventeenth and eight-

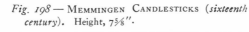

Fig. 198 — MEMMINGEN CANDLESTICKS (*sixteenth century*). Height, 7⅝".

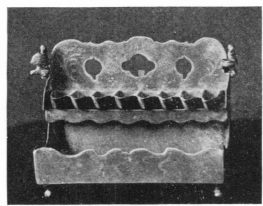

Fig. 206 — JEWISH LAMP (*mid-eighteenth century*)

Fig. 207 (left) — JEWISH LAMP (*mid-eighteenth century*)

Fig. 208 (right) — ALTAR VASE IN PEWTER (*late seventeenth century*)

eenth centuries. Figures 203 and 204
show the ordinary kinds of oil lamps,
hanging and standing patterns, which,
for countless years, have been used in
remote mountainous districts. Even
now, I do not think their use is entirely
discontinued.

The hanging example could be suspended from any convenient projection
by its hook, or the straight spike might
be driven into the wall. The hanging
lamp of Figure 203 is in the Verster
collection: Figure 204 was once in my
own possession. Contemporaneous with
these, the type illustrated in Figure
205, and known in Holland as *Snot-
Neus*, was popular in many districts,
and is more on the lines of the old oil
cruses. It is a quaintly pleasing type,
from the Denijs collection.

Figures 206 and 207 show lamps connected with Jewish ritual, both dating
from about the middle of the eighteenth
century. The former, from the Verster
collection, is what is known as a
Kanouka lamp, and was used in the
Hebrew Feast of Lights, which lasts
eight days. In its upper right-hand

corner is a small auxiliary lamp
called *Sjammos* (servant), which
burns throughout the whole of
the eight days, and from which
one of the others is lighted daily
in turn. It is of Frankfort make.
Figure 207 shows a fine example
of a synagogue lamp, from the
collection of E. W. Turner of
Herne Bay.

Figure 208 illustrates a very
beautiful and rare late seventeenth-century altar vase from
the Verster collection.

Figure 209 offers some spoon
racks and holders from the

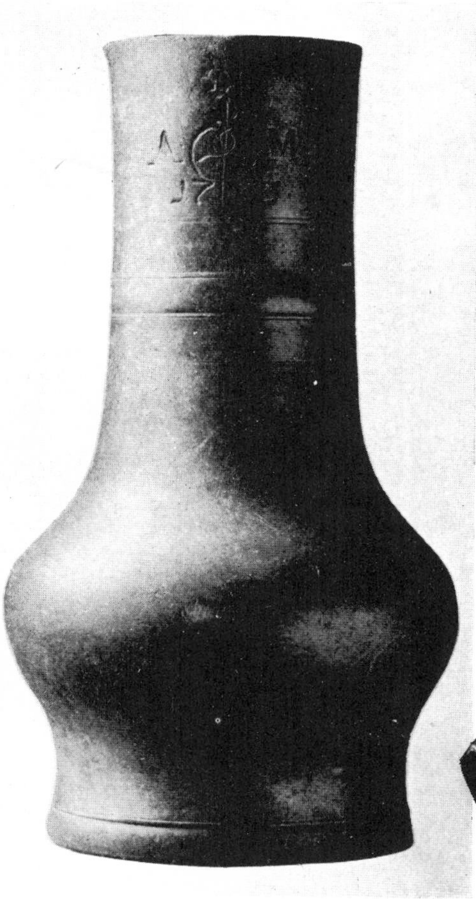

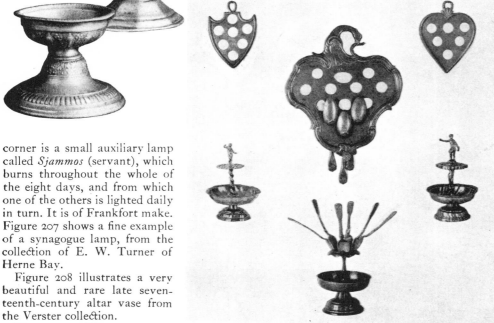

Fig. 211 — BAVARIAN MEASURE (*dated 1773*)
Height, 9¾".
Fig. 210 (*left*) — GERMAN SALTS (*eighteenth
century*)

Fig. 209 — GERMAN AND AUSTRIAN SPOON RACKS AND HOLDERS
(*eighteenth century*)

Vetter collection. The two smaller
heart, or shield, shaped examples are
by I. B. Finck of Frankfort, and the
larger Rococo rack by Sebastian Ferber
of Mayence. The sugar and spoon stand
in the centre, at the bottom, is a Nuremberg piece; and those on either side,
though similar to German examples,
are Austrian.

Figure 210 illustrates three German
salts. The two lower ones, from the
Yeates collection, are of the early
eighteenth century; and the upper one,
two and one-half inches high, of Louis
XVI design, is in the collection of
C. Rueb of Amsterdam.

Let us round off this German series
with the restful picture of a Bavarian
measure (*Fig. 211*) from Doctor Ruhmann's collection. This charming piece,
the work of A. C. Roos of Lindau,
though dated *1773*, is not one whit less
interesting than its brethren of the
primitive era, to which, apart from its
date and mark, it might quite easily
belong.

With such a piece in mind, one feels

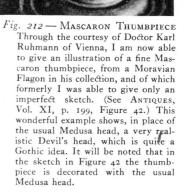

Fig. 212 — MASCARON THUMBPIECE
Through the courtesy of Doctor Karl
Ruhmann of Vienna, I am now able
to give an illustration of a fine Mascaron thumbpiece, from a Moravian
Flagon in his collection, and of which
formerly I was able to give only an
imperfect sketch. (See ANTIQUES,
Vol. XI, p. 199, Figure 42.) This
wonderful example shows, in place of
the usual Medusa head, a very real-
istic Devil's head, which is quite a
Gothic idea. It will be noted that in
the sketch in Figure 42 the thumbpiece is decorated with the usual
Medusa head.

less disturbed at having to omit
so much, and at giving so inade-
quate an interpretation of the
pewter story of Germany.

(*To be continued*)

European Continental Pewter*

Part XIII

The Pewter of Holland

By Howard Herschel Cotterell, F. R. Hist. S., *and* Robert M. Vetter

"The Hollanders were always an original and leading people." — Charles Reade, *The Cloister and the Hearth.*

To facilitate understanding of our remarks, we open the present chapter with a sketch map of the Netherlands (*Fig. 213*), whereon are marked the chief centres referred to. In Figure 214 are shown some of the local arms, so many of which appear in Dutch touches that familiarity with them may often provide the clue to the provenance of individual examples of old Dutch pewter. In evidence of this, one may note the Haarlem arms — the sword with five stars — on many of the touches later to be shown on the Haarlem touchplate.

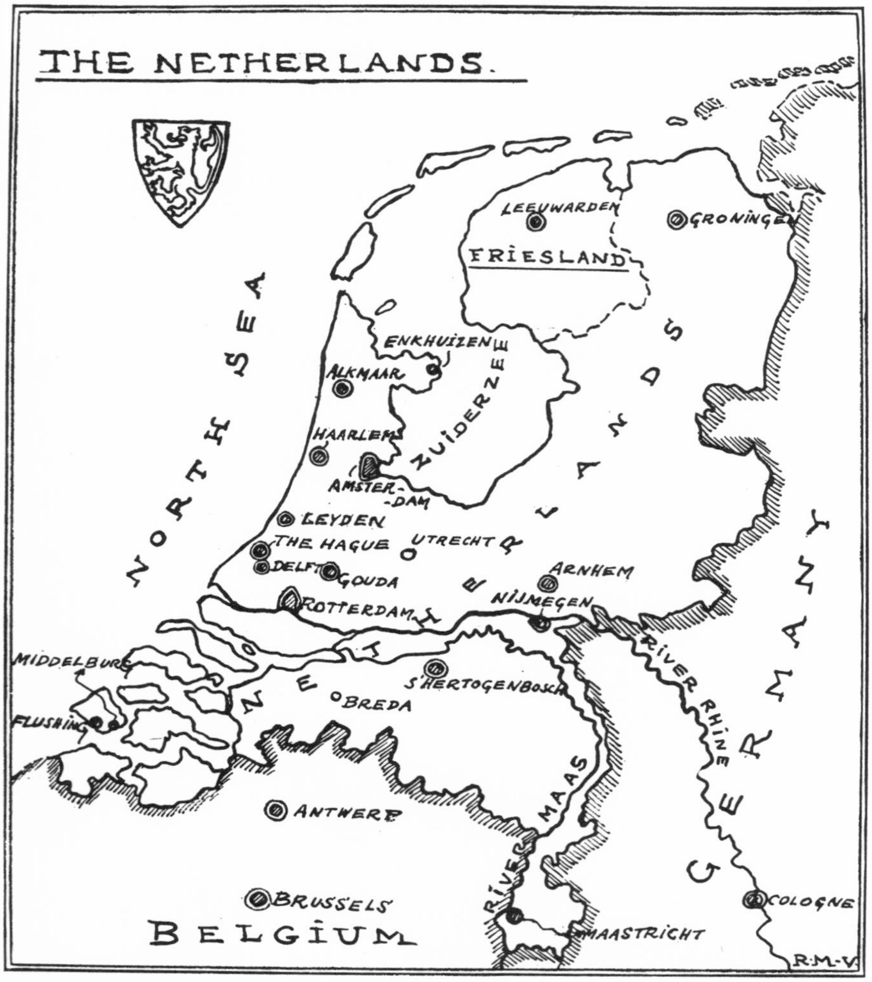

Fig. 213 — Map of the Netherlands
Showing the chief centres of early pewtermaking.

The almost entire absence of any documentary or historical foundation whereon to build our notes has made the compiling of the present chapter extraordinarily difficult. Up to the present,† literature on the subject is practically non-existent, for the importance attached to Dutch painting and the graphic arts has drawn the attention of critics and historians from the more humble, but nevertheless enormously important, arts and crafts of the country.

Dutch pewter of the best periods should, because of its soberness and practical solidity, appeal particularly to the taste of English and American collectors, for it is the one type of Continental pewter which shows the greatest affinity of idea with English productions. Even its metal, which is mostly hard and ringing, very strongly resembles that used by British pewterers.

We have, however, some cause for rejoicing in the fact that, though the story of Dutch pewter has not been written, it has been painted by those marvelous artists of the fifteenth, sixteenth, and seventeenth centuries, who are the glory of the Golden Age of the Netherlands. Jan Steen nearly always showed a piece of pewter in his pictures; and others, like the Hedas, made a pewter flagon the very centre of their compositions. And always these utensils are depicted with such truth of detail, color, and proportion that they surpass — as far as artistic value and reliability are concerned — the best photographs ever made of pewter objects.

In these paintings we have a nearly continuous representation of pewter evolution, which, to a considerable extent, compensates for the scarcity of surviving specimens and documentary information. The first pictorial

*For previous article, see Antiques for May, 1929.

†H. C. Gallois of the Hague gave some attention to Dutch pewter in his *Catalogue of the Hague Pewter Exhibition*, 1925. We understand, further, that he is now engaged in compiling a book on the subject. A. J. G. Verster, in his *Oud Tin*, Maastricht, 1924 and 1928, offers many useful hints, though his work is not confined to Dutch examples. Karl Azijnman has published valuable documentary evidence in his treatise on Dutch guild flagons and tankards at the Nijmegan Museum and has likewise contributed an essay on Jewish ritual pewter to *Oude Kunst* (August, 1918). To these writers, and to many other kindly helpers, we extend our hearty thanks for information generously supplied.

evidence of this kind which we discover occurs in a primitive painting supposedly of circa 1430. This displays a fairly large, pear-shaped flagon of vigorous but simple outline, raised on a foot. As we see from the sketch of Figure 215, the lid is highly domed, with a short crest. The lower terminal of the curved handle is not set flat against the body, but is bent outward from it. In this respect it differs from most of the surviving early pewter flagons. Unfortunately the thumbpiece is not clearly shown in the painting.

In a depiction of the Last Supper (*c. 1480*), St. Peter holds a drinking flagon, likewise pear-shaped, with a somewhat unfamiliar straight lip. Also in this picture appear a salt with hinged lid, surmounted by a conical crest of Gothic character, and — most important of all — a charger, or large dish, with a fairly broad rim, giving evidence of the existence of this broad-rimmed type even prior to 1500. On the rim of this charger, a clearly distinguishable crown was probably meant for a touch. No plates appear, either of pewter or of treen,* but before each apostle a slice of bread seems to take their place.

On a large picture of seven panels, dated *1504*, two pewter flagons are in evidence. One is similar to the flagon first described, but is of more slender proportion, lacks the crest on the lid, and shows a clearly painted Twin-acorn thumbpiece. The second has a flat lid with strengthening bar and Twin-acorn thumbpiece such as one finds on French, Swiss, Flemish, and Channel Island examples.

A flagon with curved spout appears on a panel attributed to 1520. This piece supports the hypothesis that the

* Woodenware, from the same root as *tree.*

DUTCH ARMS

THE NETHERLANDS

AMSTERDAM GRONINGEN HAARLEM

LEYDEN THE HAGUE

ROTTERDAM

Fig. 214 — VARIOUS ARMS OF HOLLAND
Familiarity with these arms will often supply a clue to the provenance of old Dutch pewter.

Fig. 215 — DUTCH FLAGON (*c. 1430*)
From a painting in the Ryksmuseum, Amsterdam

curved spout is earlier than the straight type.

A painting by Cornelis Anthoniszoon, of a Shooting Club dinner (*Fig. 216*), dated *1533*, provides us a representation of a straight-spouted flagon. It is the oldest picture we have so far discovered which shows this type. We reproduce this, not so much as a good example of Dutch painting of its period, but for its truthful depiction of the customs and table appointments of the time. Even at this date we find the table covered with a cloth. It will be observed that the spouted flagon is very similar to the Frans Hals or Jan Steen decanting flagon (*Figs. 218 and 219*) of the seventeenth century. Its straight spout of cylindrical section is ornamented with curious parallel rings, and the small flap, covering its outlet, has its own thumbpiece (Dutch *Klauw, i.e.*, claw, or thumbpiece), which, like that on the cover of the body, is of the Erect type. Again, in this picture, grasped in the hand of the marksman on the right, is a small drinking flagon with Twin-acorn thumbpiece; while on the table rests a dish of the broad-rimmed type. The plates, as evidenced by their color and graining, are of treen, not pewter.

Our next illustration (*Fig. 217*), also of a Shooting Club dinner, painted by Dirk Barentsen, and dated *1562*, is really built around a pewter flagon, in whose rounded side a deep dent is carefully reproduced.

The spouted flagon of the pure Frans Hals or Jan Steen type, plays an important rôle in contemporary still life representations, of which we give two fine examples in Figures 218 and 219. Figure 218 is from a painting by Willem Klaasz Heda of Haarlem (*1594–1678*). The second (*Fig. 219*), by Johann Torrentius (*1589–1640*),

Fig. 216 — A SHOOTING CLUB DINNER (*1533*)
From the painting by Cornelis Anthoniszoon. Sixteenth-century Dutch table fitments in metal, glass, and wood.
Courtesy of the Ryksmuseum, Amsterdam

brings out the truly monumental outline of this flagon type; and in the same picture appears a pewter lid attached to a German stoneware flagon.

The use of these Frans Hals or Jan Steen flagons (by which names they have come to be known) as decanters, has already been alluded to. In a small genre painting by Anthonie Palamadesz (*1600–1673*), in the Ryksmuseum at Amsterdam (*Fig. 220*), we see the servant boy at the side table, filling a glass with a long jet from the pew-

Fig. 217 — A SHOOTING CLUB GROUP (*1562*)
Detail from the painting by Dirk Barentsen (*1534–1592*).
Courtesy of the Ryksmuseum, Amsterdam

ter spout. On the floor stands the large stoneware *Crûche* in which the wine was brought from the cellar and from which the decanting flagon was replenished from time to time. It is interesting to note the progress in table manners portrayed by these successive paintings; for, whereas in Figure 216 the guests helped themselves from the flagon on the table, this picture of some hundred years later reveals the employment of a *garçon* for filling the glasses of the revelers. Other can-

Fig. 218 — STILL LIFE (*c. 1630*)
Detail from the painting by Willem Klaasz Heda (*1594–c. 1678*). Showing a spouted flagon and pewter plates of the period. The large glass is of the Römer type.
Courtesy of the Ghent Museum of Fine Arts

Fig. 219 — STILL LIFE (*early seventeenth century*)
Showing a magnificent Dutch spouted flagon of the period, and a pewter-topped flagon of German stoneware. From the painting by Johann Torrentius (*1589–1640*).
Courtesy of the Ryksmuseum, Amsterdam

vases bear witness to this later touch of elegance.

Less frequently do we encounter representations of the Rembrandt type of flagon.* With the exception of one pen-and-ink drawing, where something resembling it is shown, we know of no picture by the great master (Rembrandt) wherein the type appears. Jan Steen depicts

* See ANTIQUES, Vol. XI, No. 5, Frontispiece (*Fig. 55*) and p. 382.

Fig. 220 — A SOCIAL GATHERING (*seventeenth century*)
By Anthonie Palamadesz (*1600–1673*). Note the linen-covered side table and the servant pouring wine from a pewter flagon, whose source of supply is the stoneware jug in the foreground.
Courtesy of the Ryksmuseum, Amsterdam

it beside the spouted type, which was also a favorite with Frans Hals. Hence, the designation of this form as the "Rembrandt" type seems to have less justification than the term the Frans Hals, or Jan Steen.

There are, of course, several other types, equally important and some of more venerable age, examples of which we must next consider.
(*To be continued*)

Editor's Note.—No little difficulty arises in reconciling the spelling of foreign proper names with any standard English practice. In the present article the names of the various painters cited by Mr. Vetter are given as they appear in Bryan's *Dictionary of Painters and Engravers*. Their accompanying dates are derived from the same source, though, in certain instances, they differ by a year or two from the chronology given in the official museum catalogues.

NORTH-HUNGARIAN PEWTER GUILD FLAGON (*dated 1524*)
Formerly the property of the Bootmakers of Kassa (Kaschau) in North Hungary.
The engraved panels depict sundry male and female saints. The Bootmakers'
symbol occurs on the applied shield. *Height:* about 24 inches. A discussion
of the flagon will be found in the article on Austro-Hungarian pewter, which is
published in this number.
From the Hungarian National Museum, Budapest

Other Articles

A Note on the Pewter of the Channel Islands

By HOWARD HERSCHEL COTTERELL, F. R. Hist. S.

AS the Channel Islands were attached politically to Great Britain yet by ties of language and geographical position had strong French sympathies, it will at once be surmised that the influences of both countries either worked together or vied with each other over a period of many centuries. What one may almost describe as this "dual allegiance" has found expres-

Fig. 144 — CHANNEL ISLANDS' MEASURES OF THE JERSEY TYPE

Fig. 146 — KNOWN ENGLISH MARKS FOUND ON CHANNEL ISLANDS' MEASURES

sion in the better known of the pewter vessels in use on the islands.

Of plates and the general run of articles, both English and French types were in use; but there are one or two types of measures which seem peculiar to the islands, and which therefore demand special comment here. It cannot be shown that their use extended either to the mainland of France or the British Isles. They have come to be known as the *Jersey* and *Guernsey* types,

though instances are on record of both being used in either place. They are illustrated here in Figure 144 (Jersey) and Figure 145 (Guernsey).

The former type has been found in at least six sizes, and the latter in three; but, though I have no note of the smaller sizes in the Guernsey type, it would seem natural to think that such existed originally.

As will be seen, the chief differences between them lie in the more definite foot of the Guernsey type, the addition of bands to the body, and the more gradual tapering from the body to the lip, which, in the larger sizes of the Jersey type, is almost sudden.

The sizes noted of the set range from seven and one half to twenty-five centimeters. The unusual feature of these vessels, however, lies in the fact that, more often than not, this distinctly Continental type of Twin Acorn thumbpiece, with flat heart-shaped lid, is found in conjunction with the marks of known English pewterers, or the *G. R.* Crowned of British Government Inspectors.

No single instance of the use of this type of vessel in England has come to my notice, and yet they were not made in France, though purely French in all their characteristics! Are we then to class them as French or as English?

Fig. 145 — CHANNEL ISLANDS' MEASURES OF THE GUERNSEY TYPE

The answer would seem to be best given by placing them in a class apart, and regarding them — as indeed they are — as a link between the pewter of two great countries.

It would seem but natural to suppose that in the early days the islanders, with their French sympathies, bought their wares from the mainland of Normandy, probably from the pewterers of Caen; and that, in later years, a few enterprising London

pewterers made a bid for the island trade, adapting their ideas and patterns to coincide with the local requirements of the people. Hence the impasse in which we find ourselves today — French characteristics with London marks.

The London makers whose marks have been found upon these types are: John de St. Croix, who used the well-known *I.D.S.X.* mark (*Fig. 146 a*), and who was at work from 1729 onwards; A. Carter, *c.* 1750 (*Fig. 146 b*); James Tisoe, 1733 to 1771 (*Fig. 146 c*); and

Joseph Wingod, 1721 to 1776 (*Fig. 146 d*). The mark of John de St. Croix, on which his initials *I.D.S.X. appear* within a *divided* circle, is found only on the hinge pins of the lid.

In Figure 147 I give an illustration of three lids. Upon the two right-hand ones appears the mark of Carter and on the left-hand one, the mark of Wingod. In the place of *London*, one often finds the word *Guernsey* stamped on these lids, in a pointed ended label.

Attention must be drawn to the reversed *N* in the word London, both in my sketch and in Figure 147 (left). It is quite a common occurrence on Channel Island pewter, also on some specimens from English provincial towns.

(*To be continued*)

Fig. 147 — LIDS FROM CHANNEL ISLANDS' MEASURES SHOWING ENGLISH MARKS

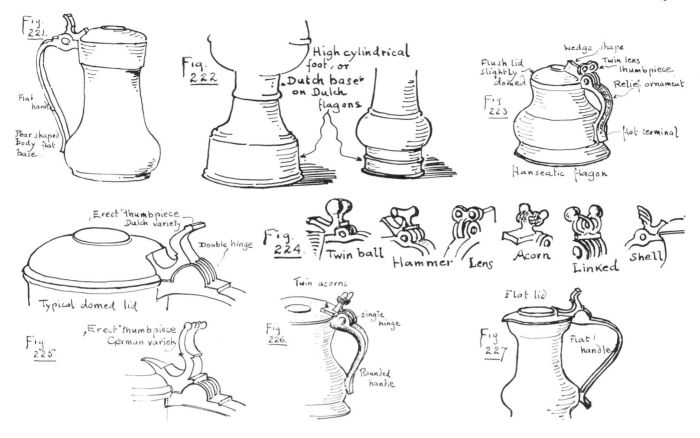

Identifying Dutch Flagons

A Chapter of European Continental Pewter

By Howard Herschel Cotterell, F. R. Hist. S., *and* Robert M. Vetter

I N THE seventeenth century, the Golden Age of the Netherlands, during which the nation attained its naval, commercial, and political supremacy, accompanied by an unprecedented blossoming of the arts and crafts, wine and beer seem to have flowed freely, and their consumption to have called for an output of hollow-ware vessels dedicated to the quenching of thirst.

FLAGON TYPES

As the pewter flagon thus became an indispensable piece of domestic gear, a list of its various types seems essential:

a, The *Decanting Flagon (Schenkkan)*, with or without a tubular spout, for use either on the board or at a side table in replenishing empty glasses.

b, The *Drinking Flagon (Drinkkan)*, plainer and less capacious than the former; sometimes with a long, curved spout which would seem to have been used for sucking purposes.

c, The *Council* or *Town Flagon (Raadskan* or *Stadskan)*, sometimes of Gargantuan proportions, used either as a show piece or as a *cimaise (cimare)*, though not exactly in the same manner as in France and Switzerland, where it served for presenting the city's "welcome" drink to some important visitor. In Holland this town flagon was used for carrying wine to the visitor's retinue, a custom which was in the nature of a lawful tribute, and which prevailed until a substitute was found in the form of money, a

shift which relieved the city fathers of much trouble (Gallois, in his *Catalogue of the Hague Pewter Exhibition*).

d, The *Church Flagon*, for carrying wine to the altar, in Protestant communities.

e, The *Guild Flagon*. Here we must distinguish between the large size and the small: the former were clearly designed for decanting, and the smaller for direct imbibing. We have not encountered guild flagons with spouts; and the types and shapes were strictly standardized. The bulbous or pear-shaped body is the form almost exclusively preferred.

The age and provenance of a Dutch flagon may be ascertained only from its general proportions and its details of foot, thumbpiece, lid, handle, and so on. In these respects the Dutch pewterers displayed a fine independence of their eastern neighbors. The all-pervasive *Stitzen* shape, so dear to the German heart, and adopted by Austria, Switzerland, Russia, and Scandinavia, was turned down by the Dutch craftsmen. A very rare, and seemingly unpopular form, shown in Figure 228, occurs sporadically. This example is of the late seventeenth century; and a comparison with the well-known *Stitzen* shapes makes evident the fact that it is not of the same family.

This is equally true of the cylindrical tankard shape, of which the few existing Dutch examples are short and of early date, and must be viewed as forerunners rather than

Fig. 228 — VERY RARE CONICAL FLAGON
Crude Dutch Erect thumbpiece, domed lid, and simple, straightforward lip. The handle evidently is a later replacement of a lost original. *Height: 8 inches.*
From the Verster collection

formerly used and are still quite common in Holland, but the shape can hardly be classed as indigenous.

THE DUTCH BASE

Frequently the Dutch pear-shaped body rests nearly flat on the horizontal (*Fig. 221*), thus appearing as a very substantial, if somewhat

imitators of the German cylindrical forms. The well-known Continental imitations of eighteenth-century English Georgian tankards were never produced on Dutch soil. Cylindrical wine and spirit measures, similar to those shown in Figure 29, ANTIQUES, Vol. XI, p. 196, were

lumpish, flagon. But, in many instances, the body is raised on a short, almost cylindrical base — a feature which occurs so frequently and so early in Dutch examples that we have called it the "Dutch" base, though it is by no means proved to be of purely Dutch origin (*Fig. 222*).

Figs. 229 and 230—
DRINKING FLAGON AND LID MARKS (*c. 1500*)
The latter show the arms of the town of Gouda at the left; Gothic initial of pewterer at the right. Twin-acorn thumbpiece. *Height of flagon: 7 inches.*
From the Vetter collection

Fig. 231 (*left*) — FLAGON OR MEASURE (*second half, sixteenth century*)
Marked with arms of s'Hertogenbosch (Northern Brabant). A forerunner of the "Rembrandt" flagon. *Height: 6 inches.*
From the Tellander collection

Fig. 232 — DRINKING FLAGON (*sixteenth century*)
Marked with the *crossed keys* of Leyden. The patina of long burial shows even in the reproduction. Twin-acorn thumbpiece; single hinge. *Height: 8 inches.*
From the Verster collection

Fig. 233 — DRINKING FLAGON (*sixteenth century*)
Leyden mark. Twin-ball thumbpiece. *Height: 7 inches.*
From the Stedelyk Museum de Lakenhal, Leyden. Photograph by courtesy of the Director, Doctor J. C. van Overvoorde

Fig. 234 — MUSTARD POT
Dutch Hammer thumbpiece, a type which occurs on pewter lids for stoneware vessels. Its curious forward tilt is characteristic, but its employment is not so frequent as that of other forms.

Very early examples of Dutch flagons, such as are excavated, from time to time, during building operations, show the typical short conical base of the Hanseatic flagon, with which they also share the following characteristics: interior medallions, handle with relief ornamentation and finial set flat against the body, thumbpiece of a Twin design and wedge-shaped attachment on lid, lid flush and very slightly domed, vertical junction of the body sections, general heavy and substantial build, and so on (*Fig. 223*). The hypothesis of Dutch pewter experts that this well defined type of Hanseatic flagon originated in the Netherlands has, thus far, been neither proved nor refuted.

Dutch council flagons of the sixteenth and seventeenth centuries are frequently raised on a foot, similar to important German and Swiss examples; but the Dutch foot is a kind of base-on-base, which — artistically speaking — seems so much out of place that one is forced to suspect some other than a decorative meaning.

DUTCH THUMBPIECES

Of the thumbpieces on Dutch flagons, we call attention to the following, which, though they have been illustrated and described in previous articles of this series, are summarized in the drawings of Figures 224 and 225.

Early types (1300–1600). Twin Lens, Twin Acorn, Twin Ball, Linked, and

Fig. 235 — FLAGONS OF THE "ILLUSTRIOUS BROTHERHOOD OF OUR LADY" (*sixteenth century*) Twin-ball thumbpieces. *From s'Hertogenbosch*

Figs. 236 and 237 — LIDS FROM THE FLAGONS ABOVE AND BELOW

Dutch Hammer (we know no better appellation), which appears almost exclusively on the lids of stoneware pots of c. 1600.

Seventeenth-century types. The Dutch Erect thumbpiece (*Fig. 225*), which also lasted well into the eighteenth century.

Latter half of eighteenth century. The Shell. In further proof of their freedom from German influence, we state that the Single-ball thumbpiece, so common in Central Europe, found no acceptance with the Dutch pewterers.

DUTCH HANDLES

Only on the very early specimens were the backs of handles ornamented with relief designs, which hardly varied in that respect from the Hanseatic types.

We have already pointed out that the Dutch handle was not treated with the same *élan* as was the German. Exceptions to this rule may be found in the handles on some of the colossal town flagons of the seventeenth century, which, at times, are fancifully shaped in the forms of snakes, fish, and so on; but the everyday Dutch handle is very plain. In early examples it is of semicircular or triangular section, with the flat side outwards; but, in later specimens, it becomes a flat bar, or strap, of nearly even width. Intricate terminals, such as scrolls and shields, are absent from this type, which rules supreme until *c.* 1750 (*Figs. 226 and 227*).

Fig. 238 — FLAGONS OF THE "ILLUSTRIOUS BROTHERHOOD OF OUR LADY" Erect thumbpieces. Later than the flagons of Figure 235.

Fig. 239 — GUILD FLAGON (*1693*)
Crested. Formerly belonging to a grocers' guild in Maastricht.
Height: 10 inches.
From the Azijnman collection

During the period of decline — in the eighteenth century — Dutch handles resemble more the Baroque type of handles on Stuart and late Georgian tankards, and are cast hollow. This hollow-cast handle is nearly always associated with the Shell type of thumbpiece.

DUTCH HINGES

The hinges are strong, mostly flush-sided, single on the earlier, and double on the later specimens. Yet there is no absolute line of demarcation between the two; for one finds the single hinge on eighteenth-century specimens, though some collectors consider that 1600 marks the adoption of the double hinge (*Figs. 226 and 227*). However, this distinction can apply only to Holland — if at all.

DUTCH LIDS

Lids are, for the most part, of the domed type and flush, with a little flat, circular eminence in the centre (*Fig. 225*). So popular and so old is this type of lid in Holland that one is almost inclined to christen it the "Amsterdam" lid, as opposed to the previously described "Breslau" lid, which, though originated about the same time, never occurs on Dutch pewter.

Then we have flat lids, either heart-shaped or round, found on flagons emanating from the southern provinces (Limburg) (*Fig. 227*).

DUTCH LIPS

Early lips other than the triangular type (that is, pointed in front to fit the heart-shaped lid) are rare, and of the simple kind shown in Figure 228. In the eighteenth century, however, they became more frequent.

* * *

The collecting of early-type Dutch flagons, and those of the seventeenth and early eighteenth centuries, affords a never-ceasing interest. The noble and sturdy shapes of these vessels rejoice all admirers of practical and expressive design. The action of the Dutch climate, which is damp and clammy, has covered many surviving pieces with tinpest, and a sombre patina; while others, excavated from the ground, are colored an inky black with bronze spots, quite unlike anything usually found in other regions. All this adds to the interest of their singular position among pewter flagons; for, both in form and in metal, they are quite unlike their German, Swiss, and Austrian brothers.

The truest joys which the advanced collector may experience are discovered in those early pieces which, now and

again, are rescued from the marshy soil or the ever-shifting river beds of Holland. As pointed out in previous chapters, similar finds are occasionally made in the wells of North Germany and in Silesia. Burial is the only means by which such ancient pieces have been preserved, for above ground all seem to have perished. They bear evidence to the fact that the pewterer's art was at its height during the late Middle Ages, when quality and dignity, correct treatment of the material, and solidity of construction were at their best. The æsthetic effect of these venerable pieces lies in the general stability and harmony of their

Fig. 240 — GUILD FLAGON (*dated 177₂*)
From a bootmakers' guild.
From the Verster collection

lines and the restraint of their purely ornamental features.

All these characteristics are evident in the flagon of Figure 229. Would that modern designers might take such examples as models of that dignified utility for which they seem to strive in vain! This flagon is wonderfully preserved and must have been virtually new at the time when it became submerged, for the original turning marks are still visible beneath a deep brown, softly-shining, bronzelike patina.

Through the scarcity of similar specimens, no definite date may be established for such pieces; but *c.* 1500 will certainly be a safe and not too optimistic guess. The shape is entirely free from the influences of the Renaissance movement, which either had not yet reached the district where this little flagon was fashioned, or had failed to sway the obstinate pewterer who made it.

In the same category belongs the flagon from the Verster collection (ANTIQUES, Vol. XI, p. 200, Fig. 45), which hails, according to its touch, from s'Hertogenbosch. It is, however, of somewhat later date, for it is not of equally simple design. All these pieces belong to the Hanseatic family of late Mediæval pewter flagons, of which those shown in ANTIQUES, Vol. XI, p. 198, Fig. 39 are also members.

The Renaissance has already cast its spell over the flagon of Figure 231. One is wont to associate the word "graceful" with elongated proportion, yet no one will deny its application to this delightful little squat flagon, or measure. Of very primitive features it retains only the Twin-acorn thumbpiece fixed to a high, wedge-shaped lid attachment, the slope of the base, and the vertical soldering. (The vessel is built up of two similar halves soldered together in the vertical plane, a method followed until about 1600.) The finial of the handle has now turned *outwards* from the body and is not stuck flat against it, as in the very early examples. The piece has been so well preserved beneath the ground that the lathe marks are still visible.

Another piece full of the charm of early pewter is illustrated in Figure 232. The form of this piece suggests a tumbler-shaped beaker with swollen lower portion, the same as in the German *Roerken*, only the feeling here is a very different one; indeed, the contrast between Dutch and German pewter forms could not be better demonstrated than by a comparison of these two types (ANTIQUES, Vol. XIV, p. 428, Fig. 162).

Figure 233 also pictures a Leyden flagon of the sixteenth century, or earlier. We illustrate it to show the Twin-ball thumbpiece, which seems a very early type, of Dutch origin. This flagon also was found during excavations.

In order to exhibit a form of thumbpiece which we have called the Dutch Hammer, we reproduce, in Figure 234, a small lidded vessel, probably a mustard pot. This type of thumbpiece occurs also on pewter lids for stoneware vessels and is always poised with this curious forward tilt

Figs. 241 and 242 — DUTCH AND SCOTCH FLAGONS COMPARED
Figure 241 is a Dutch "Rembrandt" example, from the Ducro collection; Figure 242, a Scotch pot-bellied measure. There is an obvious stylistic relationship between them.

(well known on the English "bud" type of baluster measure); whereas the hinge itself stands backward, away from the body, and the underside of the handle bulges outwards under the hinge and pin. It is curious that this combination is always found, with no seeming desire to correct it. Why did it happen in this entirely unorthodox fashion? Such questions are frequently prompted when one is contemplating early pewter types.

Here we must give a short consideration to one of the most remarkable pewter relics in the world: the famous eighteen flagons of the *Illustre Lieve Vrouwe Broederschap* at s'Hertogenbosch. This Illustrious Brotherhood of Our Lady is a sort of semireligious order, or club, still in existence, its membership composed of equal numbers of Catholics and Protestants. It was founded in the sixteenth century to create and maintain good fellowship between members of both denominations. Karl Azijnman of s'Hertogenbosch, in his paper on these interesting and important vessels, says that, in 1615, thirty-four of them were scrapped in order to provide funds to carry on, and that fifteen of the old ones remained, to which three would seem to have been added during the seventeenth century. Some are engraved with the arms and names of their owners, one of whom was the famous William the Silent (*1533–1584*), leader of Protestant Netherlands. In Figures 235 and 238, we illustrate some of these famous flagons; in Figure

236, the lid of the one belonging to William I; and, in Figure 237, a similar example.

The feebler outlines of the flagons with the Erect thumbpiece point to a later date than the more vigorous form with the Twin Balls. Otherwise, all the flagons have much in common with that shown in Figure 231.

The seventeenth century brought the fully developed "Rembrandt" flagon, of which we have already illustrated the purest and most classical shape in the famous Amsterdam guild flagon in the Vetter collection (ANTIQUES, Vol. XI, No. 5, Frontispiece, and p. 382).

Less vigorous but perhaps even more typical is the far more frequent crested type of guild flagon represented in Figures 239 and 240. Two further examples exactly similar to that of Figure 239 are in the possession of E. Scheidius of Arnhem. One is inclined to attribute the more ornate piece shown in Figure 240 to the eighteenth century, but the *type* is of seventeenth-century origin and emanates from Nijmegen, a city where the guild life would seem to have been very intensive, and where occur similar flagons, but of larger capacity, and raised on a foot. Mr. Azijnman has made a special study of this type of flagon and has brought to light many interesting details concerning it.

It would be entirely erroneous to surmise that the "Rembrandt" type was intended solely for guild use. It existed in numerous variations and sizes, some crude, others more elegant of outline. Thus, Figure 241 shows a fine flagon in the possession of our good friend Mr. Ducro, for whose contribution to these notes, in the form of skilful photography, we are under deep obligation.

Side by side with this, as an example of affinity in different countries, we illustrate, in Figure 242, a Scotch pot-bellied measure, *c.* 1700. That the two pieces sprang from a common stock seems obvious. Where did the type originate? We cannot say, but it may well be the result of Dutch influence on Scotch craftsmen, who used this same quasi-Dutch Erect thumbpiece on their great national pewter vessel — the Tappit-hen — and also used the small Ball on a later type of baluster measure. But by what means the influence was exercised we cannot say.

Church and Town Flagons of Holland

By Howard Herschel Cotterell, F. R. Hist. S., *and* Robert M. Vetter

CHURCH flagons mostly took the shapes shown in Figures 243 and 244. Simple and unassuming, without engraving or other ornamentation, they usually bear a kind of Mascaron thumbpiece, the head upon which is, however, always quite indistinct; though, being surrounded by rays, it may be interpreted as the head of Jesus Christ. These flagons — dating from the late seventeenth and the early eighteenth centuries — must have been more common than the "Rembrandt" type, judging by the comparative frequency with which they still appear.

Figure 245 shows one of a pair from a Leyden church, probably early eighteenth century. The thumbpiece and hinge, set back on the handle, have English characteristics, but the rest may quite safely be considered Dutch taste. Both pieces are comfortably substantial.

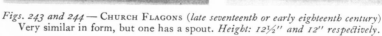

Figs. 243 and 244 — Church Flagons (*late seventeenth or early eighteenth century*)
Very similar in form, but one has a spout. *Height: 12½″ and 12″ respectively.*

and is marked with an angel, crown, and label. It seems to represent the effort of an uninspired pewterer to create something out of the ordinary. With the handle, he has certainly succeeded! It is an unique piece, dated *1789*, engraved with a pious verse, a reference to the gospel, and the names of two deacons. The thumbpiece is of the Shell type, which, about this period, was almost universal.

The period of decline produced flagons with a general flabbiness of outline. The Dutch Erect thumbpiece is replaced by the Shell, which itself becomes coarser and weaker toward the end of the eighteenth century. The metal of many of these flagons is hard and gray, very thin, and suggestive of britannia ware. It is certain that much antimony entered into its composition. The mark — generally a rose — is found either inside the lid or on the outside of the bottom; the Dutch pewterers did not place their marks on the handle, as did the German, Austrian, and Swiss pewterers.

A further authenticated example is given in Figure 246, a communion flagon from a Protestant church at Stiens, Friesland, now at the Friesian Museum at Leeuwarden, and of which the photograph was expressly taken for these pages by the Conservator of the Museum, Mr. P. C. J. A. Boeles. This piece was made by one L. Gerkens in Friesland's capital — Leeuwarden —

Figures 247 to 254*a* inclusive show varying types of Dutch flagons from the late seventeenth to the early nineteenth century. Of these the earliest are Figures 247 to 249, with Erect thumbpieces and overlapping lids. Figure 252 is by no means displeas-

Fig. 245 (left) — Church Flagon (*early eighteenth century*)
From a Leyden church. Thumbpiece and setback hinge are suggestive of English practice.

Fig. 246 (right) — Communion Flagon (*dated 1789*)
From a Protestant church at Stiens, Friesland. Made by L. Gerkens of Leeuwarden and marked with angel and crown. Shell thumbpiece, a type almost universal at this date. Now in the Museum at Leeuwarden.
Photograph made expressly by the Conservator of the Museum, Mr. P. C. J. A. Boeles

Figs. 247, 248, and 249 — DUTCH FLAGONS (*late seventeenth century*)
Erect thumbpieces and overlapping lids. Two are domed; one is flat-topped.

ing, with its partly cylindrical flasklike body. This type hails from Rotterdam. Of Figure 254, we can say little in praise. The project-

ing hinge is *separated* from the handle. The latter, which, in its turn, is of the ornate form and reminds us of the wooden ones found in coffee and teapots, is hollow cast. See Figure 254*a*. The hinge pin is of iron or brass, and the hinge itself is not so carefully wrought as those found on the older flagons.

A quite freakish church flagon (*c.*

mysteries of Rococo design than his German cousin. Although bearing an Amsterdam mark, the flagon belonged to a church in northern Brabant.

We must here pause to notice a few measures, *i.e.*, vessels used for measuring out the liquid in gin and wine shops, and thus differentiated from drinking vessels.

Figure 256, from the Tellander collection, probably of the late seventeenth century, reveals Dutch pewter at its best. It bears a Rotterdam mark.

Figs. 250 (*left*), 251 and 252 (*above*), 253 (*right*) —
DUTCH FLAGONS (*18th and early 19th centuries*)

1750), marked with four touches, one of which is the Amsterdam arms, is shown in Figure 255. The attempt to do something stylish, by crowning the piece with a pagoda lid, may cause a smile. The whole offers a singularly unhappy combination, and emphasizes the fact that the Dutch pewterer was far less versed in the

The punches near the rim are gauging marks, and on the inside is a small pin, or wart, to indicate the proper level. (A similar wart, known as a "plouck," appears in the Scottish Tappit-hens.) Many similar measures occur in the Rotterdam Museum, but in these the level is fixed by a square notch, filed into the side of the rim,

Fig. 254 (left) — DUTCH FLAGON (early nineteenth century)

Fig. 254a (below) — DETAIL DRAWING OF FIGURE 254

Fig. 255 (right) — CHURCH FLAGON (c. 1750)
Amsterdam mark. A far from happy attempt at Rococo.
From the Azijnman collection

through which superfluous liquid may simply spill over. Other measures are shown in Figures 257 and 258.

TOWN FLAGONS (*Stadskannen*)

Not always, however, did the Dutch pewterers work along the severe lines thus far indicated. The town flagons, the use of which we have described in a previous article, are grandiloquent pieces, exhibiting great technical skill on the part of their makers. Figure 259 shows one of two in the Ryksmuseum, Amsterdam. Though it is not definitely known which of the Dutch cities owned and used these flagons, as they bear neither touch nor arms, they are undoubtedly of Netherland origin, and are very similar to other flagons at Leyden (with that city's arms) and at Bolsward. They date from the

sixteenth century, and their simple and vigorous outlines win the beholder's fancy more and more with each inspection.

The change of taste after 1600 is best illustrated by comparing Figure 259 with Figure 260, which shows one of the town flagons of the city of s'Hertogenbosch, dated *1630*. In the latter, the proportions are more elegant than noble, and would be still more so if the "high," cylindrical, Dutch base were missing. After a most careful examination of this flagon at the s'Hertogenbosch Museum, we are convinced that this foot is not a later addition to the piece, but part of the original conception, intended — apparently — to give increased importance and height to the whole, which, without the missing lid, is some twenty-five inches tall. The medallion bears the

Fig. 256 (left) — DUTCH MEASURE (late seventeenth century)
Rotterdam mark. *Height: 10 inches.*
From the Tellander collection

Fig. 257 (above) — DUTCH MEASURE (early sixteenth century)
Dug up in Middleburg. Handle of triangular section, with characteristic early terminal. *Height: 7 inches. From the Verster collection*

Fig. 258 (right) — DUTCH MEASURE WITHOUT HANDLE
Supplied with lid and handle and with shortened lip, this would be a Rembrandt flagon. *Height: 5 inches.*
From the collection of Mrs. L. Payne

Fig. 259 — Town Flagon (*sixteenth century*)
Vigorous, simple, and well proportioned. *Height: 19½ inches. From the Ryksmuseum, Amsterdam*

city arms. The handle is of the fancy type, with upper terminal sweeping backward.

As already stated, the town flagon handles afford a singular contrast to the sober treatment of those on Dutch domestic pewter. Still *more* handle is given to the bizarre town flagon of Nijmegen (*Fig. 261*), which dates from *c.* 1600. In the lid we see a later addition of poor taste, and refuse to believe that the man who designed so beautiful a handle, could be guilty of creating so freakish a bonnet. In this piece, too, appears the cylindrical Dutch base, though not so exaggerated as that of the former example.

We close this series of hitherto unpublished photographs of invaluable and highly interesting vessels, by illustrating (*Fig. 262*) one of the six Amsterdam town flagons which are preserved in the Ryksmuseum. It would seem that the city fathers gave orders to their pewterer to create

something exceptional, in both size and shape, something in harmony with the world-wide reputation and prestige enjoyed by their city about 1600. The pewterer certainly responded! Quite departing from tradition, he adopted the style of the Renaissance as it was understood at the time in the Netherlands. Like the Elizabethan mode, it was in love with a turnip-like swelling in balusters, table legs, and other turnings. So here we have a tall, pewter turnip. Even the handle is of a "fancy" type, and the thumbpiece something quite new and stylish!

These flagons, which are some thirty inches in height, are engraved with the arms of Amsterdam, and considerable effort is required to lift them even when empty. The metal must have been of the finest, judging by the ravages of tin-pest, which, in several places, has eaten through the unusually thick flagon walls.

Note. — An article on the identification of Dutch flagons will be found in ANTIQUES for December, 1929.

Fig. 261 — Town Flagon (*c. 1600*)
A freakish specimen with a fine handle and an ungainly lid, perhaps of later date. *From Nijmegen*

Fig. 260 — Town Flagon (*1630*)
From s'Hertogenbosch

Figs. 263a and b — Rembrandt Flagons
Showing the low-bellied and more graceful, elongated types.
From the Tellander collection

Fig. 262 — Town Flagon (*c. 1600*)
From the Ryksmuseum, Amsterdam

Fig. 263 — FLAGON WITH CURVED
SPOUT. *From the Ryksmuseum,
Amsterdam*

Figs. 264 and 265 — JAN STEEN OR FRANS HALS FLAGONS
*The first: 7¾ inches high, from the Tellander collection; the second: 5½
inches high. From the s'Hertogenbosch Museum*

Fig. 266 — "SUCKING FLAGON"
(*fifteenth century?*) *Height: 4½".
From the Verster collection*

The "Noble Pewter" of Holland

By HOWARD HERSCHEL COTTERELL, F. R. HIST. S., *and* ROBERT M. VETTER

ONE of the most curious uses of pewter in Holland is for the external decoration of houses. In the museum at Enkhuizen, on the Zuider Zee, that unique relic of the Golden Age, are five old pewter flagons, which, though at first sight seemingly town flagons, on more detailed examination proved to contain a closely fitting core of wood. The utensils somewhat resemble those previously described in these pages (December, 1929, pp. 508–512), but the renaissance designs are curiously exaggerated, more sweeping and bulging and, in addition, the workmanship is quite crude, after the manner of a clever artist when producing a piece to be looked at from a distance, as on a stage or the front of a building. Such judgments were confirmed by the custodian of the museum, who vouchsafed the information that the flagons had been a decorative feature of the façade of an old house.

So it appears that not only the old Dutch artists but also the

Fig. 267 — SPOUTED FLAGON (*seventeenth century*)
In this development the spout is reënforced with
a strong bar. *From the Verster collection*

Dutch architects were keenly alive to the decorative qualities of pewter. We are of course aware of the use of pewter flagons as inn signs in Switzerland and elsewhere, of the occasional employment of pewter for rain-water heads and fountain spouts, but we have no knowledge of its adoption in other countries than Holland for purely decorative exterior effects. Special attention is claimed by the Dutch spouted flagon variously called, by collectors and dealers, the "Frans Hals" or "Jan Steen" flagon, the favorite object of seventeenth-century painters, and now eagerly sought by collectors.

Its use, as a decanting flagon for ceremoniously distributing wine to guests, we have already pointed out (December, 1929, p. 508). But there is yet another kind of spouted flagon, from which the contents were extracted by sucking, a process facilitated by the shape of the spout, which is circular and devoid of the small flap that closes the orifice of decanting flagons.

Fig. 268 — SPOUTED FLAGON
(*seventeenth century*)
Handle set at right angles to spout.
From the Azijnman collection

Fig. 269 — SPOUTED FLAGON
(*seventeenth century*)
Spout and handle combined.
From the Stedelyk Museum, Leyden

Fig. 270 — SPOUTED FLAGON (*eighteenth century*)
The body retains a seventeenth-century form;
handle and thumbpiece are of the subsequent
period. *From the Tellander collection*

Figs. 271 and 272 — PEWTER RELICS FROM A LATE SIXTEENTH-CENTURY DISASTER
Flagon and pepper caster. *From the Ryksmuseum*

Fig. 273 — PEWTER RELICS FROM A LATE SIXTEENTH-CENTURY DISASTER
Candlesticks that closely resemble a well-known Dutch bronze pattern.
From the Ryksmuseum

Spouted vessels (and in speaking of these we purposely omit pewter coffee and tea pots as belonging to the category of pewter imitations of silver), as every general connoisseur of antiques knows, were made not only in pewter, but in glass, china, earthenware, precious metals, brass, copper, bronze, and so on. In seeking their probable origin, one's thoughts are led through the vessels of Venice to those of Turkey and Persia and to the wine skins of nomadic tribes. Tibet and China both employed a type of sacerdotal bronze flagon, made during the Sung dynasty, and surprisingly similar to our aquamaniles of the Middle Ages, as well as to the early Swiss *Stubenkannen* (hall flagons), already considered in ANTIQUES (July, 1927, pp. 46–47).

It should be observed that vessels passing as Chinese teapots are often, in reality, flagons for ceremonial warm wine, and in that respect are closely akin to the spouted flagons here discussed. The bronze aquamanile employed during the Middle Ages for all sorts of ritual and ceremonial occasions inspired mediæval pewterers in designing their first flagon spouts. Old Dutch pictures indicate that the spouted pewter flagon as a ceremonial vessel was already established before 1500.

Figure 263 is a flagon mediæval in character. It is unmarked, but its Twin Ball thumbpiece points to Dutch origin. The English handle we have noted also on Dutch flagons. From this type evolved the Jan Steen or Frans Hals flagon illustrated in Figures 264 and 265. At the same time, the early religious and ceremonial significance of the vessel was submerged by its social utilizations.

So far as we know, the number of surviving specimens of this rare flagon type is far outnumbered by the times it appears in existing pictures, a fact that well

Fig. 274 — EWER
Highly sophisticated in form and decoration.
From the Ryksmuseum

Fig. 275 — PEWTERER'S GUILD TOKEN (*seventeenth century*)
The ewer on the obverse is similar in form to that illustrated in Figure 274.
From the Thomas Warburton collection. Manchester, England

illustrates the wholesale destruction to which pewter has ever been subjected. Some four sizes were made. Mr. Tellander's example (*Fig. 264*) — of truly classical proportions — stands seven and three fourths inches high, whilst the s'Hertogenbosch flagon measures but five and one half inches (*Fig. 265*). On this latter piece, some gauge marks, evidently of subsequent date, point to its use as a measure at a later period. The Dutch Erect thumbpiece appears on nearly all these flagons, though two in the Dordrecht Museum display the Twin Ball.

The spouted drinking flagons for sucking liquor are only about five inches high. In its mediæval shape, we picture this form in Figure 266, an early excavated flagon possibly of the fifteenth century. It has the conical base (much damaged), Twin Acorn thumbpiece, flat-domed lid, and handle of triangular section. The heart-shaped shield on the side originally supported a small spout, but this is broken away. The piece seems, therefore, to come into the *Schapenkannetje* category, of which the specimen in Figure 267 shows the seventeenth-century equivalent, with its spout supported by a strong bar without ornamentation, the whole exemplifying the simplicity of Dutch household pewter. The term *Schapenkannetje* means *lambs' flagon*, but the theory that these vessels were used for feeding lambs taxes our credulity to the breaking point. Until we have seen them so represented in some old print or painting, we cannot accept that explanation.

Figure 268 shows one of the vessels, as in Figure 266, with the handle at right angles to the spout, the more convenient way. Another variety, wherein the handle and spout are combined, is pictured in Figure 269. A curious combination of a seventeenth-century body with an eighteenth-century handle and thumbpiece is in Figure 270.

Figs. 276 and 277 — PEWTER BEAKERS WITH RELIEF DECORATION (*seventeenth century*)
Height: about 3 inches.
The first, from the Verster collection; the second, from the Vetter collection

Fig. 278 — ENGRAVED FRISIAN SNUFFBOX
(*eighteenth century*)
Diameter: about 3 ¼ inches. From the Ryksmuseum

We have investigated the question whether in Holland about the year 1600 there existed a fashion for decorated pewter like that which we have already seen prevailed in France and Germany. In the latter countries, the *orfèvrerie d'étain* (goldsmith's work in pewter) and *Edelzinn* (noble pewter) respectively were late renaissance creations singularly in contrast to representative products of older traditions. In them not only were old shapes covered with rich relief ornamentation, but the shapes themselves were revised and the form of classical vessels was imitated. During these investigations we became acquainted with what must be considered one of the most astonishing pewter finds ever recorded; and, as the date when the objects in question were deposited is exactly known, and all possibility of tampering with them is excluded, their importance cannot be overstated.

In 1596, a second attempt to reach China by a route north of Asia was made by a Dutch fleet under command of two Amsterdam captains, Jacob van Heemskerk and Willem Barentz. The expedition got no farther than Nova Zembla, where a terrible winter was spent. Barentz perished and the survivors of the adventure managed to reach Holland only after incredible sufferings. Behind them they left a litter of objects, some in very battered condition, others showing the ravages of exposure to wind and cold rather than the wear and tear of normal usage.

After almost three hundred winters of abandonment in the icy wastes of the polar regions, these relics were picked up in 1876 by a captain from Hammerfest, from whom they were acquired by a certain Mr. Gardiner of Goring (Oxfordshire). Later returned to Holland, they are now in the Amsterdam Ryksmuseum, where they bear proud witness to an heroic effort.

Amongst these relics was a lot of pewter, the principal items of which the museum authorities have very kindly photographed for us (*Figs. 271–274*).

Figure 271 shows a pewter flagon some eight inches high, of goodly girth but crude proportions, with some of the characteristics of early pieces. On the inside are struck the Amsterdam arms. This and a small, narrow-rimmed, flat, sixteenth-century plate probably represent the pewter used by the ships' crews, to whom also may have belonged the curious salt and pepper sprinkler in Figure 272. Side by side with cruder vessels, however, was pewter of the greatest refinement. Of this last, three delightful, sheer renaissance candlesticks and a ewer of the purest classical conception are shown in Figures 273 and 274.

It has been suggested by H. C. Gallois, of The Hague, that these objects may have been taken along as presents for the Chinese and that they are of French rather than Dutch origin. They are very well finished and only superficially corroded, so that we may still admire their finely gadrooned rims, and the stylish handle and mascaron finial of the ewer. In our own opinion, these ewers have nothing in common with the French work of François Briot and his disciples. On the contrary, they are full of that sober restraint that characterizes Dutch work of the Renaissance (*c. 1600*). Further, the candlesticks closely resemble a well-known Dutch bronze pattern.

Mr. Gallois may have been led to his opinion by the very rarity of *Edelzinn* in Holland, inasmuch as these ewers are probably the only examples that are known. As a matter of fact, *Edelzinn* could not, and did not, attain such popularity among the Dutch as it enjoyed among the people of other Continental countries; but

Fig. 279 — ENGRAVED PLATE (*c. 1700*)
Portraying William of Orange as King of England. *Diameter: 10 inches.*
From the "*N. N.*" collection

Fig. 280 — DISH WITH UNDECORATED RIM
Earlier than those illustrated in Figure 281.
Diameter: 15 ½ inches.
From the Tellander collection

Fig. 281 — Dishes and Plates (*c. 1600*)
Dishes with raised centres and moderately broad rims. Shallow plates with moderately broad rims. All marked with arms of the Kuyk family. Note the reeded rims. *Diameter of dishes: 15 ½ inches; of plates: 9 inches.*
From the Tellander collection

we have proof that the wave of its fashion certainly touched Holland, though it seems to have ebbed quickly away. Our evidence takes the form of a seventeenth-century Pewterers' Guild token (*Fig. 275*), supposed to have come from Vlissingen (Flushing). On one side of this pewter token (or medal) we find, in relief, a ewer, nearly identical with the Heemskerk example, and, on the reverse, a pewterer's hammer. The inscription, which is in Dutch, translates as follows:

Obverse: *Tin founders' [i.e. Pewterers'] guild.*
Reverse: *Concord gives power.*

The importance of this small object, the diameter of which is only one and seven eighths inches, can hardly be overemphasized, and we are glad to be able to reproduce it through the courtesy of its owner.

The only other specimens of relief-ornamented pewter of probable Dutch origin are certain small beakers, about three inches high. Figure 276 shows one, with a representation of a marriage ceremony, and Figure 277 portrays the story of Adam and Eve, together with allegorical designs. Although Dutch taste in picturesque decoration is betrayed in the arrangement of the figures, the cutting cannot be compared with that of contemporary French and German work.

We may thus safely draw the conclusion that the *Edelzinn* movement achieved no great popularity in Holland, a circumstance not surprising in a country where people were so rich at this time that almost everybody could afford elaborately decorated silver, for which, after all,

Edelzinn is but a substitute. Furthermore, the pewterers must have found it hopeless to attempt to compete with such famous silversmiths as Lutma, van Vianen, and many others.

Holland's fidelity to plainer pewter is like that of England, where also ornamented pewter never gained public approval.

In the same way, punched ornament was eschewed in both countries, though in Holland very fair examples of the engraver's art, showing a deep-rooted ability in design and a love of drawing, have come to our notice. Some of these engravings are, as it were, sculptured into the metal, suggesting that a relief effect was aimed at. The two barrel-carrying beer porters on Mr. Vetter's flagon (Frontispiece, May 1927) are so treated; and we give likewise an illustration (*Fig. 278*) of a very handsome Frisian snuffbox, ornamented in this manner. On the lid is engraved the word *Gratis*. To open the box, the lid is revolved by means of the central knob until the finger holes are over the actual snuff chamber. The box is simple, practical, and of pleasing design.

The state of the popular engraver's art is shown in the plate of Figure 279. This piece of very hard pewter depicts William of Orange as King of England. The arrangement of flowers may be taken as typical. Such examples were possibly used for show purposes in the same way as was *Edelzinn* in Germany. The ornamentation of pewter by lacquering we shall discuss in a later article; here we must give some attention to Dutch pewter plates and dishes.

As in England, so in Holland, pewter was preceded

Fig. 282 — Dish with Slightly Reeded Rim
Diameter: 16 inches. From the Prinsenhof, Delft

Fig. 283 — Dish and Plate (*seventeenth century*)
The plate illustrates the broad-rimmed type.
Diameter of dish: 21 inches; of plate: 12 inches.
From the Tellander collection

Fig. 284 — Alms Dish (*mid-eighteenth century*)
Showing the return to narrow rims. In the centre are the arms of the ancient town of Stavoren.
From the Azijnman collection

by treen (woodenware), and it was ousted by earthenware (delft). In following this development, paintings are again an infallible guide. Dishes were made in pewter before plates, and a painting reproduced in August, 1929 (*Fig. 216*) shows a pewter dish of good size in use with plates that are still of wood. The oldest pewter plates were square slabs of metal, sometimes with a small bead; and contemporary with these appeared deep bowls with *narrow* rims and raised centres. In the sixteenth century, plates with very flat bowls and rather narrow rims were also usual, but, by this time, dishes had fairly *wide* rims and raised centres. The characteristic of dishes and bowls of

Fig. 285 — OVAL DISH (*mid-eighteenth century*)
Again the narrow rim is shown, in this instance rigidly waved.
From the collection of Mrs. L. Payne

this period is the entire absence of a bouge at the junction of rim and well; for the well joined the rim at a very obtuse angle, and, from side to side, except for the raised centre, offered one continuous, graceful sweep. This, indeed, was equally true of dishes of this period in every country. A set of dishes and plates shown in Figure 281 illustrates the dish with raised centre and moderately broad rim, which, according to the evidence of reliable paintings, was already in vogue before 1500. It likewise shows shallow plates, also with moderately broad rims, of a type, however, that dates only from the second half of the sixteenth century. Still older are dishes without reeded edges, as in the fine example shown in Figure 280. The back of this example shows broad hammer marks. Another dish (*Fig. 282*), in so far as proportion and metal are concerned, is one of the finest to come under our observation. It was brought for our inspection and lent for photographing by the former Director of the Ryksmuseum, Jonkheer van Riemsdijk, who, some years ago, acquired it for the collection at the historical Prince's Court (Prinsenhof) at Delft. It bears three impressions of the arms of Prince Mauritz of Oranje, who died in 1625. The maker's marks are a crowned rose on the front and an angel at the

Fig. 286 — DUTCH CANDLESTICK
(*fourteenth century or earlier*)
Height: 5 inches.
From the Verster collection

back, with maker's initials I.D. The appearance of the angel mark at so early a date is noteworthy. We had this dish photographed in a perspective view in order to demonstrate what we meant above by the well meeting the rim at an obtuse angle.

During the seventeenth century, rims increased in width, and reeding was sometimes adopted. Indeed, rims were occasionally so broad that the ratio between inside and outside diameter became one to two. Hammering at the back occurs frequently at this period, but the hammer marks are broader than in English work, and not so regularly placed. The metal is hard, but lacks the lustrous silvery appearance of earlier craftsmanship, and suggests that antimony was already freely used in the seventeenth century. A dish with reeded, broad rim, together with a twelve-inch plate carrying a very wide plain rim and a splendidly engraved coat of arms (*Fig. 283*) will point our meaning. Eighteenth-century Holland pewter shows the same types as are to be found in other European countries. All, it seems, drew their inspiration from English fashions. A splendid alms dish (*Fig. 284*), which bears in the centre the arms of that most ancient town Stavoren, will be sufficient to illustrate the narrow-rimmed type with single reed. The engraved words on this dish translate: *The Church dish of the town of Stavoren, anno 1751*. The rim proved too narrow for the engraver, who had to place his design in the centre.

Plates and dishes, round and oval, with wavy edges, were also made in Holland, but these differed so little from the products of other countries that we show only one example (*Fig. 285*). The photograph shows the back of the dish, with the strengthening reed on the underside of the rim (the top being quite plain). It also reproduces the placing of imitation silver marks beneath the angel mark, and the stiff engraving of the owner's name. The rather rigid waves of the edge may be taken as characteristic of Dutch

Figs. 287 and 288 — CHURCH CANDLESTICKS (*fifteenth and early sixteenth centuries*)
Height: about 14 inches. The first pair is from the Vetter collection; the second, from the Verster collection

work. A further reference to this dish will be made when discussing the silver-imitation pewter of Holland.

Numerous and important are the various forms of candlesticks and lamps that were made in Holland. From the most crude and plain, their evolution progresses into the very elaborate and coquettish. We have already pictured,

Fig. 289 — Leyden Oil Lamp
(sixteenth century?)
From the Ryksmuseum

Fig. 290 — Typical Early Dutch Candlestick
(c. 1600) Verster collection

Fig. 291 — Pewter Beaker
(eighteenth century?)
From the Cotterell collection

in Figure 273, the collar candlesticks (*Kraagkandelaars*) left at Nova Zembla by the Heemskerk expedition, and have only to add some earlier and later types. One of the earliest of which we have cognizance is shown in Figure 286, a delightful example dug up in Holland, possibly of the fourteenth century, but probably much earlier and thus pre-Gothic. Whether it was intended for church or domestic use, we cannot say. Church candlesticks of the fifteenth century are exemplified in Figure 287. These candlesticks are of extremely robust make and show wear from frequent cleaning. Otherwise they are undamaged and as useful as they were four hundred years ago. This also may be said of the pair illustrated in Figure 288, which, however, may be a little later, from the verge of the renaissance period. A quaint oil lamp, marked with the Leyden touch and probably of the same era (*Fig. 289*), is in the Amsterdam Ryksmuseum. Its foot, and especially the sloping sides of the bowl, betray Gothic influence. It is labeled as seventeenth century; but we perceive in it a much earlier feeling.

A very simple and beautiful *Kraagkandelaar* appears in Figure 290. It is a typical early Dutch pattern, possibly from about the year 1600. Such simple pieces have a charm that is irresistible. Not so pleasing, but nevertheless interesting, is the church candlestick of Figure 292. The pricket in this example is of pewter rather than of forged iron, and the swelling and undulating contours bespeak the Dutch Renaissance of the seventeenth

Fig. 292 — Baluster Church Candlestick
(seventeenth century)
From the Verster collection

century. Eighteenth-century patterns of domestic candlesticks are numerous and for the most part very attractive, but as they slavishly follow contemporary silver patterns, we propose to discuss them in connection with silver-imitation pewter.

Goblets of the tumbler-beaker shape played an important rôle in old Holland, very large ones being used in Protestant churches for Communion purposes. A row of such goblets is shown in Figure 293. The bulbous examples are a remarkable variety of Communion beaker said to have come from a Frisian church. Frequently such beakers were engraved; but the quality of the work varies greatly. Figure 291 shows a typical example with the ever popular portraits of William and Mary.

A number of these beaker-shaped vessels, in form similar to Figure 291, but not engraved, and nearly all of Dutch origin, are to be found in use as Communion cups in many Scottish churches; for instance, at Drumlithie, Stonehaven, and Laurencekirk. But this need occasion little surprise; for have we not, in one of the best known Scottish types — the pot-bellied measures (December 1929, p. 512, *Fig. 242*) — an obvious evolution from the Jan Steen and Frans Hals flagons illustrated in Figures 264 and 265 above?

Note. Though printed as virtually independent articles, this and former discussions of European pewter in ANTIQUES really constitute a connected series, in whose preparation the authors have enjoyed the coöperation of leading foreign authorities. In both text and illustrations, the series is the most comprehensive work of its kind ever attempted; and its value to students, collectors, and dealers alike is beyond appraisal. Other articles, completing the consideration of Dutch pewter, and perhaps covering the pewter of Austria and Hungary, will be published as rapidly as space permits. — *The Editor.*

Fig. 293 — Pewter Cups or Beakers
Remarkable bulbous examples said to be Communion cups from a Frisian church.
From the collection of Mrs. L. Payne

Fig. 294 — HAARLEM TOUCHPLATE (c. 1700–1750)
Showing the touches registered by various pewterers. Actual size.
From the Frans Hals Museum, Haarlem

Fig. 295 — ROSE COMBINED WITH TOWN
ARMS
From the Azijnman collection

Fig. 296 — ROSE AND ANGEL MARKS
COMBINED
From the Tellander collection

Identifying Dutch Pewter

By Howard Herschel Cotterell, F. R. Hist. S., *and* Robert M. Vetter

SALTS

THE oldest type of salt that occurs in pictures of the fifteenth and early sixteenth centuries is exemplified in Figure 297. This fine piece bears the touch of s'Hertogenbosch and may be considered to be of the early renaissance period, probably the early sixteenth century. The knop, lid, and hinge betray Gothic influence. The first of these members serves the double purpose of raising the lid and of acting as a prop to prevent the open vessel from being overbalanced by the heavy cover. Although the relief within (*Fig. 298*) is religious in character, we cannot agree with some experts that such pieces were used as pyxes; the contrary evidence of old pictures is too strong. Moreover, the interior shows the corrosion so frequently found in old salts. The only other especially interesting salt of Dutch origin, amongst the numbers we have examined, is shown in Figure 299. We can offer no explanation for this combination but, from close inspection, we testify that the joining pieces are original, the maker's touch being on the lower one, between the two bases.

INKSTANDS

In early Holland days, pewter was the standard material for inkwells, and is still enjoying popularity. When thus employed,

Figs. 297 and 298 — Covered Salt (*early sixteenth century*)
Exterior and interior views.
From the Tellander collection

the seventeenth-century type, with lidded compartment for ink, loose sand dredger, and wafer drawer, is one of the most desirable objects for collectors. Of the many thousands of such inkstands that must have been made there are not too many survivors today; and of these the value is rapidly increasing. The fine and complete specimen, some two and a half inches high, which we illustrate in Figure 300, represents a pattern that was continued for many years, and well on into the eighteenth century.

An early eighteenth-century type is shown in Figure 301. The division between ink and sand is diagonal, and the lid has a knop in place of the Dutch Erect thumbpiece usual in older examples. A rococo version of this stand is shown in Figure 302, with the addition of a wafer drawer and scroll feet. Its form recalls the bulging Louis XV French commodes.

PORRINGERS

Porringers, in Holland, are known as *brandewijn bakjes*, literally *brandy bowls;* but this does not exclude their occasional use for porridge. One of the oldest of these vessels of which we have knowledge is illustrated in Figure 303. It has ring handles, set vertically, *not* horizontally; is dated *1556* in the touch; and is some five inches in diameter, exclusive of the handles. A remarkable feature of the piece is the standing ring on the bottom,

Fig. 299 — Double Salt, or Salt and Pepper
From the collection of Mrs. Denÿs

Fig. 300 — Inkstand with Wafer Drawer
From the Verster collection

a characteristic that appears on china only in the eighteenth century. The touch consists of the tree of s'Hertogenbosch flanked by a pewterer's hammer and the letter J. The Gothic letters on either side of the touch may be the owner's initials.

The three porringers shown in Figure 305 well represent the standard shapes of one- and two-eared types of the late seventeenth and early eighteenth centuries. Of these, many imitations exist, and too much caution cannot be urged upon collectors buying them. To this group belong also the Frisian brandy or broth bowls, of which we illustrate a fine example in Figure 304. This handsome, decorated piece is not unlike some of the seventeenth-century English posset cups.

Fig. 301 — INKSTAND (*early eighteenth century*)
From the Ryksmuseum, Amsterdam

SPOONS

Dutch pewter spoons are, in our opinion, worthy of greater attention than they have received. The number of patterns is legion, but, when arranging a selection from the Payne and Vetter collections (*Fig. 306*), we purposely omitted the less interesting eighteenth-century types. The examples shown date from about 1550 to 1700.

Spoons and other pewter pieces were often cast from molds a long time after the particular type had gone out of use; so, here again, great care is necessary before purchasing such articles.

CHURCH PEWTER

Though it would seem that Dutch church communities never underwent the financial hardships that, in less fortunate countries, led to the employment of pewter for sacramental vessels,

Fig. 303 — PORRINGER (*sixteenth century*)
From the Azijnman collection

we find that church pewter of Dutch origin is not uncommon.

We have already commented on flagons, candlesticks, and beakers, and, in Figure 307, we add an illustration of a ciborium. This fine piece, which is covered with beautiful black patina, dates from the early seventeenth century, and has the bulbous swelling of the stem so characteristic of the period. In these early ciboria, the lids are hinged.

Fig. 302 — INKSTAND (*rococo style*)
From the Azijnman collection

Of about the same date is the chalice shown in Figure 308; whereas the loose-lidded ciborium illustrated in Figure 309 is of the eighteenth century. For the base and stem of the latter piece the maker has used the die of a candlestick.

The lavabo or aquamanile shown in Figure 310 is unusual, since we recognize in it the effort of a pewterer to introduce an old bronze pattern into the pewter world. It is of sixteenth or early seventeenth-century make, but as a pewter pattern it is not a success. Numerous similar pieces in bronze have survived until the present day.

Jewish ritual is represented by the Seder dish, dated *1766*, shown in Figure 311, which was fully described in the "Connoisseur," April, 1928, and by the *Hanukka* or *Maccabea* lamp illustrated in Figure 312. It is of pleasing eighteenth-century rococo design, unusually well preserved and quite complete.

BOWLS

The pewter monteith appears in Holland during the second half of the seventeenth century. The official Dutch name is *wijnkoeler* (wine cooler). We have failed to find any representation of this type in pictures. *Wijnkoelers* are frequently portrayed, but

Fig. 304 — FRISIAN BRANDY BOWL (*seventeenth century*) *From the Verster collection*

Fig. 305 — ONE- AND TWO-EARED PORRINGERS (*seventeenth and early eighteenth centuries*)
From the A. B. Yeates collection

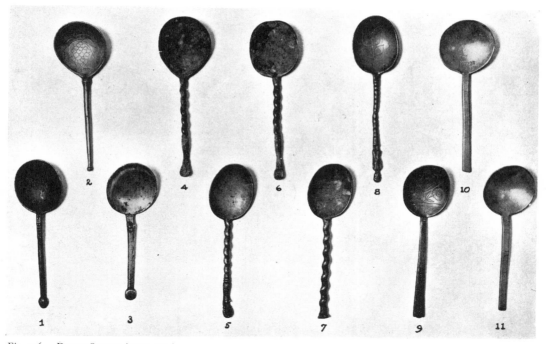

Fig. 306 — DUTCH SPOONS (*1550–1700*)
Numbers 1 and 2 are of the sixteenth century; the others of the seventeenth. Number 9 is dated *1695*; 10 and 11 show the Frisian peasant round-bowl types.
From the Payne and Vetter collections

they are always of copper or brass, and are made with plain rims.

A very graceful example, of circular form, and one of the earliest known to us (*c. 1670*), is illustrated in Figure 313. Its workmanship is of the best; but there is no touch. Another example, though of later date, and elliptical construction, is pictured in Figure 315. It is of tremendous weight, and thickly covered with scaly patina. A still later bowl of the eighteenth century (*Fig. 316*) offers a fine example of Dutch silver-imitation pewter at its best. It is unmarked. If this piece is examined carefully — and likewise the lamp of Figure 312 — it will be found

that the scrollwork on the rim is not cast in one piece with the body, but is skilfully laid on and soldered to it. This method of building up is quite characteristic of the period of decline, and was probably — like the pattern — copied from the silversmiths.

Slavish copying, without any attempt at originality, is quite characteristic of Dutch rococo pewter. It makes the type much less attractive than pieces produced in other Continental countries, where the pewterer developed new patterns such as have not been found in silver, and which, at times, show surprising inventiveness, taste, and imagination. German, Austrian, and

Fig. 307 — CIBORIUM (*early seventeenth century*)
From the Vetter collection

Fig. 308 — CHALICE (*early seventeenth century*)
From the Verster collection

Fig. 309 — CIBORIUM (*early eighteenth century*)
From the Verster collection

Fig. 310 — AQUAMANILE (*early seventeenth century*)
Unsuccessful adaptation of a bronze pattern.
From the Verster collection

Fig. 311 — JEWISH SEDER DISH (*1766*)
Diameter: 18 inches.
From the Alfred E. Green collection

Fig. 312 — JEWISH RITUAL LAMP (*mid-eighteenth century*)
Rococo design. Unusually well preserved.
From the A. J. Spijer collection

Swiss pewterers of the rococo period refused to use quasi-standardized strips of metal to build up the rims of various objects. The Dutch system, on the other hand, led to many compromises that were not always successful from the artistic point of view.

PLATES

The plates illustrated in Figure 314 are built up after this fashion. Irrespective of scale, the same sized strips are used. Furthermore, the centres are not cast and turned, but are pressed from flat sheet pewter. An early indication of mass production! The candlesticks shown with the plates are also copies of silver; but they are so well made and of such beautiful metal as to render them highly desirable possessions.

MISCELLANEOUS ITEMS

In Figure 317, we see, from left to right, the development of the Dutch tobacco box from about 1730 until 1800. We show only the three most popular of the numerous standard patterns, each one of which is but a coarser rendering of some silver form. Such boxes usually contain a leaden presser, with knop, for keeping the herb in condition.

Three-legged coffee urns, with one or three taps, were a component part of Dutch households in the eighteenth and early nineteenth centuries. They are used even now, and are still manufactured. A small stove, or lamp, *comfoor*, goes with each urn. This stove was placed on a triangular tray of pewter or brass, called a *treefje*. The *comfoor* and *treefje* are generally lost, but a good number of urns may still be found, and, by their suggestion of the peaceful and cosy Dutch home, are — and will ever be — popular with

general collectors of antiques, as well as with pewter collectors.

The example shown in Figure 318 may be taken as one of the oldest shapes, and dates from about 1700. The three legs and taps are of brass. The urn of Figure 319 is complete with *treefje* and *comfoor*; its period is about 1730. The handle is of ebony, as are also the bun feet, which protect the table top from heat conducted through the metal legs. Unfortunately the photographer has not arranged the pieces correctly; for the three feet of the urn should stand on the three corners of the tray.

We reproduce, in Figure 321, a beautiful lacquered urn with three taps, of late eighteenth-century make. This type is described as calabash-shaped, on account of its gourdlike appearance. On the urn is painted a landscape with rustic scene. The candlesticks have their original lacquer, deep red with gold. Lacquering of pewter was the rage in Holland during the eighteenth and first half of the nineteenth centuries. Needless to say, this masquerading of pewter as Peking lacquer was only a measure for giving a semblance of life to a trade that had sunk to a low ebb. Great differences in quality are observable in lacquered pieces. Quite one of the best we have seen is the tea set illustrated in Figure 320. This set comprises a teapot (*trekpot*), stove (*comfoor*), and tray (*blaadje*).

We have already seen some of the Dutch silver-imitation pewter, and our last illustration of this class (*Fig. 322*) must be a pair of so-called *kastanje vaasjes*, or chestnut vases. Did space permit, we could show many other examples, but we have already reached the Empire period (*c. 1800*), which, in Holland, marked also the approaching end of the pewter trade.

These chestnut vases exist in various shapes, mostly lacquered;

Fig. 313 — MONTEITH (*seventeenth century*)
Width including handles: 15½ inches.
From the Vetter collection

Fig. 314 — Dutch Rococo Pewter
From the Verster collection

but sometimes, divested of their original coat of varnish, they appear all the brighter for the protection they have received for so many years. It is consistent with the conservative element of the Dutch spirit that the making of pewter should have been continued up to the present day; but the use of antimony in place of lead and copper as admixtures has resulted in a kind of britannia metal, thin, gray, hard, and cold. Whereas, in other countries, the period of decline comes to a somewhat abrupt end, we see in Holland, as in Great Britain, the pewterers making brave attempts to keep abreast of the ever-changing times, giving evidences of vitality and adaptability, but, at the same time, debasing the artistic side of a once glorious craft to an incredibly low plane.

HISTORICAL ADDENDUM

It is customary to begin a treatise on the pewter of a country with a short historical introduction, with dates and information concerning guild life. In this instance, however, we have reversed the usual method by beginning with pictures and reserving our few facts until the end, for those who have found Dutch pewter sufficiently attractive to awaken the wish to know more about it.

In his searchings for the probable origin of Dutch pewter-marking customs, Karel Azijnman discovered that the *rose* as a symbol for marking Dutch pewter is first mentioned in 1544, in the guild rules of Maastricht merchants, and in other documents of Middleburg and Delft, which stipulate the rose touch in connection with a certain alloy, in 1548 and 1581 respectively. (The Nuremberg pewterers' rules, which prescribe the rose for "English tin," are dated *1578*.) Mr. Azijnman is of the opinion that the rose was used to imply English pewter, which at that time, if for Continental export, was marked with the Tudor rose.

A complete reprint of the rules of the Amsterdam Pewterers' Guild is given in the book of reference *Handvesten of Amsterdam*, which was printed in the second half of the seventeenth century, and Wagenaar's *History of Amsterdam*, dated 1766.

After a very careful examination of these sources, we have arrived at the following conclusions:

According to *Handvesten*, the oldest regulation dates from 1533. The rules speak of the master's touch as his *Crown and Letter*, which could not be altered without the consent of the guild; and it would seem that the type of crown adopted, together with a certain letter, constituted the elements of identification.

Flagons and round work were ordered to be made of an alloy containing ninety-two parts of tin and eight parts of lead, and, besides the master's initials, a *Burgoyne cross* and the town arms had to be struck. Plates, dishes, and flat work were to be made

Fig. 315 — Monteith (*seventeenth century*)
Length: 24 inches.
From the Ryksmuseum, Amsterdam

Fig. 316 — Monteith (*eighteenth century*)
Length: 16 inches.
From the Ryksmuseum, Amsterdam

of pure tin and marked with a crowned hammer.

To become a master in the guild, the passing of a certain test was a *conditio sine qua non.* This test consisted of making two molds, one for a dish and one for a *swan's neck* (a flagon with curved spout) from which to cast the respective pieces, and to finish them to the full satisfaction of the examiners. In 1575,

Fig. 317 — TOBACCO BOXES (1730–1800) *From the Verster collection*

dish, might be relieved from doing so on payment of fifteen guilders. The examination rules, here referred to, do not expressly stipulate that the test dish had to be hammered, but this may be inferred from the wording of the modification.

In 1706, it became necessary to limit the kinds of pewter objects that might be made from the inferior *keur tin*, it being expressly stated that "spouted flagons must always be made from the best kind of pewter."

swan's neck was changed to *Schenkkan*, which probably means the contemporaneously more usual, straight-spouted decanting flagon, known to us as the Jan Steen or Frans Hals flagon (*Figs. 264 and 265*, p. 211, March, 1931). This *Schenkkan* had to be made with a hollow foot!

In 1685, the regulation of the alloys to be employed is modified somewhat, and we find then in use the following alloys:

Fijn roos tin (fine rose pewter), ninety-four parts tin and six parts lead, to be marked with the rose; *keur tin* (test pewter), ninety-two parts tin and eight parts lead, which had to be marked with the town arms.

In 1688 the following grades are mentioned: *blok tin*, to be marked with an angel; *roos tin*, to be marked with a rose; *keur tin*, to be marked with the town arms.

And, in 1689, a fourth grade is mentioned: *kleine keur tin* (little test pewter), to be marked with the town arms and K K, which permitted an alloy somewhat inferior to the *keur tin*.

In 1702 is seen a lowering of the earlier ideals in the modification of the examination rules, which then permitted that a pewterer who did not succeed in beating (hammering) his test

Wagenaar, in 1766, finds in use the four grades that, for the sake of convenience, we tabulate as follows:

NAME OF ALLOY	TOUCH	ALLOY	% OF LEAD
Blok Tin	Angel, sometimes with town arms	100 parts tin	Nil
Fijn Roos Tin	Rose	94 parts tin 6 parts lead	6
Keur Tin	Town arms	92 parts tin 8 parts lead	13.5
Kleine Keur Tin	Town arms and K K	3 Ace* less than Keur tin	more than 13.5

* The Ace [Dutch *Aas*] is a very small unit of weight.

All this *sounds* very simple and clear, but we rarely find touches entirely in accordance with the above, nor do the alloys

Fig. 318 — COFFEE URN (c. 1700)
From the Korthof collection

Fig. 319 — COFFEE URN (c. 1730)
From the Ryksmuseum, Amsterdam

Fig. 320 — LACQUERED TEAPOT AND STAND (eighteenth century) From the Verster collection

employed consist of tin and lead only. A good deal of antimony seems to have been used instead of — or in addition to — lead. Only the very old Dutch pewter, say prior to 1600, shows the silvery whiteness and softness that accompany freedom from antimony.

Though not mentioned in these regulations, touchplates, for registering the individual touches of the master pewterers, have existed from earliest times; but, so far as our knowledge goes, only one of these has come down to our time. This is now deposited in the Frans

Fig. 321 — LACQUERED PEWTER (*late eighteenth century*)
From the Azijnman collection

Hals Museum at Haarlem, whose authorities have most kindly supplied us with a full-size photograph, which we reproduce in Figure 294, at the head of this article. Unfortunately there are neither dates nor names on this plate, nor any accompanying guild-roll, which would enable us to identify the various initials. However, one rejoices that the plate is now in safe keeping; for the "Rosetta stone" that will enable us to translate it at some later date may, even yet, turn up.

Such deductions as we can make from a careful analysis are as follows: *The sword and five stars*, occurring in a number of the touches, are the arms of Haarlem. Their frequent appearance proves that our touchplate was of the Haarlem guild of pewterers. General stylistic characteristics of the impressions on this touchplate indicate dates, in all probability, from about 1700 to sometime after 1750. According to the names and initials in the touches, the eighty-three impressions belonged to some fifteen different touches.

We find twenty angel marks, thirty-four crowned roses, seventeen full or abbreviated town arms, and four compound silver-imitation marks, that is, three to four small marks side by side, struck simultaneously. Of these latter, one is surmounted by the crowned x.

Some of the roses contain the letter F, which may be interpreted as *fijn roos tin*. Others contain the letter L, for which we know no interpretation other than London, a word that we know was used in Germany as a mark of quality. Some of the marks with fancy designs embody, in addition to the pewterer's initials, the words *huur tin*, or the letters H T, which mean *hire-pewter*. We know, from the regulations, that the renting of pewter for weddings and similar functions was part of the pew-

terers' trade, and that this privilege passed on each year from one guild member to another, so that each might profit in turn. Hence it is only logical to surmise that such pewter would be marked in a special way to prevent it from being stolen or from being mixed with new pewter.

As a matter of fact, we find, in this Haarlem touchplate, all the symbols mentioned in the Amsterdam regulations. We may, therefore, conclude that these rules served as a model for the other towns in old Holland.

The combination of the rose and the angel marks occurs very frequently, and we must assume that this denotes an intermediate quality, since pure tin — which had to be marked with an angel — was not easy to work, was brittle, and was very subject to tin pest. The combination of these two marks, on the back of a broad-rimmed charger, is shown in Figure 296; whereas, in Figure 295, we see the rose combined with town arms (the tree of s'Hertogenbosch). The initials in the one are G V G, and in the other G.

The number of touches we have seen on Dutch pewter is legion, but very rarely have we seen the same device more than once or twice; for the number of pewterers working in Holland was as great as their activities. Yet, strangely enough, no names have come down to us that stand out from their fellows, as was the case with French and German craftsmen.

A résumé of salient Dutch features, then, gives us: a preference for pear and bulbous shapes, probably derived from ceramic examples; a scarcity of original pewter designs in tableware, nearly all patterns of certain periods being coarser copies of contemporary silversmiths' work, that is, copies to simulate silver, not — as in Germany and France — inspired therefrom; the making of hard, gray alloys, based on antimony and having a considerable tendency to blacken, and very subject to tin pest; an almost complete absence of relief decoration; and a resistance to classical renaissance influences. At its zenith, a feeling for utility, sobriety, and solidity, for reality and realism, guided Dutch genius in its independence, and kept it true to itself, without entirely protecting it from occasional coarseness. The robust flavor of Dutch pewter appeals to many collectors — but those to whom sweetness is synonymous with beauty are not included among the number.

Fig. 322 — CHESTNUT VASES (*c. 1790*)
From the C. C. Zeverijn collection

Pewter Flagons of the Former Austro-Hungarian Empire

By Howard Herschel Cotterell, F. R. Hist. S., *and* Robert M. Vetter

THE choice of a title for this discussion was fraught with great perplexity. The periods with which it deals reveal a series of changes with which it is impossible adequately to cope, except under some widely embracing, generic title. That which we have finally selected seems to be the one most likely to be intelligible to the greatest number of our readers. With this in view, we have based our considerations on the Austro-Hungarian Empire, as it appeared at the time of the decline of the pewter industry (*c. 1815*), and of which a sketch map is appended. From this time onward pewter forms definitely degenerate and cease to make any appeal to the imagination either of the antiquary or of the collector. The items here to be discussed are, therefore, such as were produced within the confines of our map, with also Venice, which at that time belonged to Austria. But, after all, we would point out that we make *no* claim to present either an ethnographic or a political consideration of the localities with which we have to deal.

It is by no means easy to circumscribe by exact description the pewter forms fashioned within the confines of the many component districts of this ancient monarchy; for we have to deal with Old Austria — Tyrol, Styria, Salzburg, and Carniola; the middle portion, upper and lower Austria; and the northern districts with Bohemia, Moravia, Silesia, and Galicia; and, finally, Hungary.

The pewter of these localities drew much of its inspiration from Germany, while, at times, we find evidence of a French or a Dutch idea; but a certain grace and gaiety of design distinguish it from that of its northern and western neighbors. Clumsiness would seem, on the whole, to have been avoided, though sometimes at the expense of solidity.

But what distinguishing features may we look for as appearing (*a*) solely on Austro-Hungarian pieces, or (*b*) if not *solely* on such pieces, at any rate in larger measure than on those of other countries?

In Figures 3, 4, 5, 6, and 9 (ANTIQUES for January 1927, p. 35) some Austro-Hungarian marks were shown, and in Figures 42 (March 1927) and 53 (May 1927), the mascaron device, flat against the body, as a lower terminal to handles, is illustrated as typically Austrian. In some measure the same is true of the small shield-shaped terminals similar to the one pictured in Figure 50*a* (May 1927). But, in addition, there are other and lesser indications, such, for instance, as these:

Note. — This is the first in a series of articles on a notable group of early European pewter, to which, hitherto, little or no systematic study has been devoted either in America or abroad. The authors are the same distinguished connoisseurs whose discussions of Continental Pewter previously published in ANTIQUES have been eagerly accepted by students and collectors on both sides of the Atlantic. With these earlier contributions, the present series falls into a well-appointed place to round out the most comprehensive treatment of European pewter ever undertaken. Following the accompanying article, others will appear at irregular intervals during the coming year. — *The Editor.*

dishes. The hammer marks seem to take the shape rather of a squarish oval than of the more circular form.

1. Granulated punched groundwork.

2. Straight-sided stitzen.

3. Stamping the touch on the inside of stitzen lids is a Tyrolese custom.

4. The hollow-sided stitzen with overlapping lid as illustrated here in Figure 7 (*centre*).

5. The hammering of plates and dishes. The hammer marks seem to take the shape rather of a squarish oval than of the more circular form.

6. Certain types of engraving to which attention will be called as they occur in our illustrations, but a few general notes on which will be not out of place here.

Engraved Pewter

Engraving, as a means of pewter embellishment, seems to be more frequently resorted to in Austria than in other countries, and so much is this the case that one finds it, not only on the finest pieces, but likewise on the commoner objects, thus proving that, even in the households of the poorest, engraving was by way of being a necessity, a complementary part of national expression. Much commonplace ware, made of inferior metal and without marks, may be found in Austria, which is said to have been produced largely by traveling Italian pewterers who traded illegally, and, in the Tyrol, earned for themselves the *sobriquet* of *gatzelmacher*. The doings of these traveling tinkers were a source of great offence and loss to the local craftsmen, and just when guild influence was waning their machinations were most strongly felt. Hence many complaints were lodged against them and numerous steps were taken by the authorities to control the vagrants. These met with little or no success, and pewter of shameful quality was produced everywhere in the last stages of the decline. (In England and Scotland the same trouble was experienced. These traveling hawkers had no expenses. They carried on their backs their stock in trade, consisting of a few parts for repairs, and effected minor mendings and the making of the simpler forms of pewter wares at prices with which the legitimate tradesman could not compete.)

The names of Italian pewterers appear among those of the best artisans of Austria, but these were honorable guild members who had become settled in their various districts and who, themselves, looked with anything but sympathy upon the hawker-pewterers from their own fatherland.

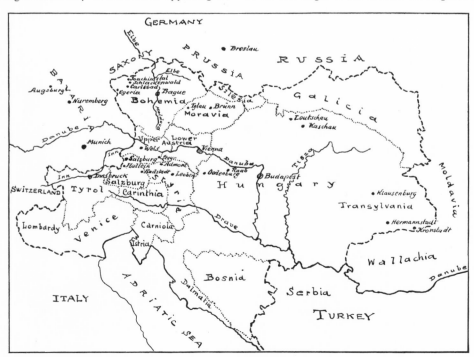

THE AUSTRO-HUNGARIAN EMPIRE IN THE NINETEENTH CENTURY

Early Pewter Centres

Bohemia and Silesia, once wholly Austrian, are regarded by many as the oldest pewter centres of Central Europe, that is to say, the ones that reached a state of artistic perfection at an early period, a state not equaled elsewhere, or at any other period.

Numerous and truly monumental examples of pewter are still to be seen in Bohemia today, in the form of huge bell-shaped baptismal fonts, enormous candlesticks, shrine lamps, and guild flagons of unparalleled capacity — survivors of what one may describe as the "gigantic pewter" age. Visitors to Prague may see such things, and marvel at them.

The country was rich, its traders were enterprising, and tin was abundantly available from the mines at Schlackenwald and Joachimstal. But the monumental pieces, locked up forever from circulation among collectors and described in numerous but scattered papers, need not detain us here. Together with quaint and mysterious monuments of architecture, they stand as witnesses to the titanic and heroic struggles of a bygone age.

Guild Ordinances

Adequately to deal with the history of the pewterers' guilds in Austria-Hungary is impossible within the space at our disposal. However, in a town of average importance, such as Salzburg, strict guild ordinances already existed in 1487 whereby it was ordained that a "hall-mark" in the shape of the town arms was to be struck by the aldermen of the guild on all pieces. These ordinances provided also for sealing the marking punch in the guild chest after use.

By the courtesy of Herr A. Walcher von Molthein of Vienna, we are happy to illustrate the later guild chest of the Salzburg pewterers (*Fig. 1*). This interesting relic, now in the possession of Baron Gutmann of Vienna, is made of deeply toned walnut and bears the mark of Lorenz Hentz (*c. 1600*). A pewter disc inside the lid displays the guild arms — a ewer, a *pitschen*, a gun, and a bell, the two latter testifying to a former association with the brass-founder's trade. Very artistically engraved pewter panels, let into the four sides, complete the decoration of this chest.

The enforcement of guild rules was very strict, and the metal remained always good. None of the poor stuff, so common in some parts of Germany, was made on Austrian soil; whiteness of metal and great resistance to allotropy (or tin pest) were — as also in Augsburg — among its characteristic features. The oldest of the pieces illustrated in this discussion date from a time when a great part of Hungary was overrun by the Turks, who have left their influence on the products of the country, as they certainly did on its costume.

Influence of Early Alien Settlers

The prolific soil and favorable climate of Hungary have, forever, been an attraction to surrounding peoples, who have entered it repeatedly either as usurping invaders or as peaceful immigrants. Among the latter were many German tribes who settled on unreclaimed soil as farmers, or in the towns as craftsmen. Among their chattels they brought in pewter and began to produce yet more, after the manner of their forefathers.

These and other incursions brought with them the various stylistic conventions of Europe to which a ready response was made. In 1500, Gothic was still the fashion; but the Renaissance movement is clearly reflected in pieces immediately preceding the year 1600. The baroque is indulged during the second half of the seventeenth century and during the early eighteenth; but attempts at rococo are less frequent in Hungary than in Germany and in Austria proper. On the other hand, much ware in that style was imported. It is wrongly labeled Hungarian.

Where German influence obtained, the original forms underwent a change on the more prolific Hungarian soil, and assumed grand and sweeping lines. The pewterer gave great attention to thumbpieces, handles, and finials, of which, indeed, he made "a whole affair," as may be seen by comparing many of the accompanying illustrations with those shown in ANTIQUES for March 1927, page 195. All other details are of a similar elaborate character, but the proportion and profiles of the vessels themselves are good and well balanced.

Pewter was plentiful in Hungary, especially in the Saxon districts of Erdély (Siebenbürgen, Eastern Hungary), where the chief pewter-producing towns from the sixteenth century until the nineteenth were: Brassó (Kronstadt), Kolosvár (Klausenbürg), and Nagy-Szében (Hermannstadt), all in the Erdély (Siebenbürgen) district. Here the town and richer peasant populations were made up of Saxon immigrants whose descendants have lived for many centuries on what was then the Turkish borderland. The town marks of these places were: Kolosvár, *a wall with crenelated towers*; Brassó, *a crown above a tree trunk with roots*; Nagy-Szében, *two swords crossed*.

Hungarian pewter is but imperfectly recognized by collectors, and

Fig. 1 — GUILD CHEST OF THE SALZBURG PEWTERERS (*c. 1600*)
From the collection of Baron Gutmann, Vienna

Fig. 2 — HOOPED STITZEN (*early sixteenth century*)
From the Museum Carolino Augusteum, Salzburg

Fig. 3 — EAST-HUNGARIAN HOOPED FLAGON (*1550–1600*)
From the Hungarian National Museum, Budapest

Fig. 4 — WEST-HUNGARIAN FLAGON (*dated 1541*)
From the Hungarian National Museum

Fig. 5 — UNIQUE GOTHIC FLAGON (*dated 1520*)
From the Hungarian National Museum, Budapest

most of that which appears in collections outside of Hungary is wrongly described either as "German" or "probably German." Hence it is high time that justice should be done to the products of a beautiful and romantic country.

High Status of Trade Guilds

That the guilds of Hungary enjoyed great reputation and respect is evident from the guild flagons that still exist. Treasured heirlooms, they speak to us of the veneration in which they were held by their peasant possessors.

Early Marks

Reference to the labeltable in ANTIQUES for January 1927 will show, under Austria and Hungary respectively, many of the devices and marks that are to be found on Austro-Hungarian pewter. Many old pieces in Hungary carry a w, which is generally interpreted as standing for Wratislava, the old Polish name for Breslau, the Silesian capital, one of the mightiest centres of the pewter industry in the fifteenth and sixteenth centuries. This gothic w, however, must not be confounded with the w of Wien (Vienna), which appears over a quartered shield enframing the date, thus: **W** This mark is found in conjunction **1 6 6 3** tions, as are also the Nuremberg with Hungarian inscripand Leipzig marks.

Herr Julius Leisch-Carolino Augusteum at Salzburg, was among the first to render us service by sending a number of excellent photographs, several of which we have used as illustrations for this chapter. With our sincere thanks for his coöperation, we begin with the picture from the Museum collection of a very interesting Gothic flagon some eleven inches in height (*Fig. 2*), which, according to the maker's mark (*two bells, with the letter* P) and the hall mark (*the arms of Salzburg*), is the work of Hans Pergheimer, who became a master pewterer in 1507.

Early "Stitzen" Form

In comparison with contemporary German work, this piece displays a certain sober restraint. It may be described as a straight-sided *stitzen* encircled by three broad bands, which strongly remind one of the hoops on certain wooden pitchers, built, like barrels, of staves and hoops. Of such wooden pieces many may still be met with in Alpine districts, and as this early form of pewter *stitzen* nearly always displays

a suggestion of bands, we may safely assume that it was evolved from those very old wooden pitchers. A stiffly pleated banderole, with a Latin inscription, and some crude leafwork complete the decoration.

The "Breslau" or Overlapping Lid

The lid is of the "overlapping" type, with a rather flat top, slightly tapering sides, and a dislike projection on the top. It is worth our while to examine this lid a little more closely, for it is a Gothic shape constantly recurring on sixteenth-century work. Furthermore, since we invariably find it on the famous Silesian-Breslau flagons, we propose to refer to it henceforth as the "Breslau" lid. It is always combined, as in the present case, with an "erect" thumbpiece, and this combination ruled the south and southeast of Europe in the sixteenth century. On the other hand, lids in the west, north, and northwest remained true to the types shown in Figures 39, 40, and 45 of ANTIQUES for March 1927. In later years, the two types became somewhat mongrelized. Nevertheless, in the regions now under discussion, there is an almost complete absence of any thumbpieces corresponding to the "twin" series: *i.e., twin-acorn, twin-pomegranate, twin-linked;* the only patterns employed being the *erect, plume, ball, cleft,* and occasionally the *shell* and a few bastard types.

This "Breslau" lid appears also, with erect thumbpiece, on the two Hungarian flagons appearing in Figures 3 and 4. Both are in the Hungarian National Museum. We are able to reproduce them through the courtesy of Herr Elémer von Varju, Director of Historical Studies there, who had the photographs specially taken for us.

Flagon Types

The flagon of Figure 3 hails from the second half of the sixteenth century, and was made at Nagy-Szében in eastern Hungary, and here again we have the hoops. That of Figure 4, dated *1541* and made at Sopron (Oedenburg) in western Hungary, shows hoops merely *hinted at* by circular, engraved bands. Both pieces may have been church flagons.

The two flagons that follow (*Frontispiece and Fig. 5*) are extremely important examples of pewter ware. They are likewise from the Hungarian National Museum. Both have the "Breslau" lid. The Frontispiece portrays the ancient guild flagon of the bootmakers of Kassa (Kaschau) in north Hungary.

Fig. 6 — FLAGON FROM JOACHIMSTAL (*early seventeenth century*). *From the Fritz Bertram collection, Chemnitz*

Fig. 7 — EAST-HUNGARIAN STITZEN (*early seventeenth century*)
From the Hungarian Museum of Applied Arts, Budapest

This magnificent piece, some twenty-four inches in height, bears the venerable date *1524*, and is one of Hungary's most treasured national possessions. Our photograph is so distinct as to require little exposition; but the rich engraving, and the wonderful state of preservation of the piece — considering its great age — are worthy of note.

Of totally different aspect, but of about the same period, is the fine flagon of Figure 5. Made at Nagy-Szében, and some twenty inches in height, it bears on its "Breslau" lid the date *1520*; on its Gothic escutcheon the emblems of a smiths' guild, with the date *1558*. The frontal iron loop handle is, it would seem, a later though ancient addition; for the weight of a filled vessel must probably have been too great for managing with the one handle. This piece may be regarded as virtually unique, its main characteristics being those of a Wallis flagon with a "Dutch" foot.

Figure 6 exhibits a piece, some

Fig. 8 — STITZEN FROM PRESSBURG
(*baroque style, 1659*)
From the Fritz Bertram collection

Fig. 9 — GUILD FLAGON FROM RAAB
(*c. 1750*). *From the Hungarian National Museum*

twenty inches in height, which, besides being exceptionally well proportioned, throws further light on the evolution of the *stitzen* shape. From the fine Fritz Bertram collection, upon which we have already been permitted freely to levy, it was formerly the properly of a bakers' guild at Joachimstal (Bohemia). Though this guild, according to the inscription on the flagon, was founded in 1535, the piece itself certainly was not made prior to 1600. The engraved *brezel* (fancy loaf) on the shield, and the round "bread-loaf" feet, symbolize the everyday activities of the guild members. The sides of the vessel have assumed the well-known inward sweep of the later *stitzen*, and the extremely narrow hoops no longer suggest the binding together of the body. The central portion is beaten into panels of a quasi-polyhedral type, reminding one strongly of the methods employed by the early Silesian pewterers. Nevertheless, the bold sweeps of the erect thumbpiece and handle, the highly domed lid, as well as the bands of punched ornament around lip and base, all convey the spirit of the late Renaissance, and thus entirely obscure the feeble traces of Gothic reminiscence.

Further developments of the *stitzen* are seen in Figures 7 and 8, the former, from the Hungarian Museum of Applied Arts, reproduced through the kindness of the General Manager, Herr Julius von Végh; the latter from the Bertram collection.

Of the *stitzen* shown in Figure 7, the smallest — in the centre — is the earliest, and bears the date *1594* in the maker's touch on the handle. We are, therefore, safe in placing it in the early years of the seventeenth century. It was made at Nagy-Szében, and is notable for the particularly graceful inward sweep of its sides. The flagon on the left is fourteen inches high, from Kolosvár, and that on the right, twelve and a half inches high, from east Hungary (Siebenbürgen). Both are of the early seventeenth century.

The florid example of Figure 8 is universally recognized as one of the noblest guild pieces of the baroque period, toward

which it illustrates the first step from the Renaissance. It was the flagon of the brassfounders of Pozsony (Pressburg), and is adorned with gilded brass hoops, and dated *1659*. Only a wealthy guild could pay for such a piece. It is the work of the pewterer Christoph Böhmer of Pressburg, and is twenty-two and a half inches in height. Formerly it had a faucet, or tap, in front; but this is missing, and the hole in the triangular ornament at the front of the base has been filled. The squat, *stitzen* body seems almost suffocated under its mass of florid ornamentation, while the thumbpiece and handle terminal strike one as a masterpiece of constructional contortionism.

The flagon from the Hungarian National Museum illustrated in Figure 9 was the more modest possession of a small brushmakers' guild at Györ (Raab), in west Hungary. On its shield is depicted an arm supporting an old-fashioned whisk broom. The piece dates from the middle of the eighteenth century. Similar pieces, without the lion and shield, were given as wedding and jubilee gifts by one member of a guild to another, or to the master of a craft by his workmen. Such friendly tokens, usually with two or more names engraved upon them and often some trade emblem, serve to remind us of the good feeling which then existed between master and servant and between fellow members of the guilds, and of the prevalent fondness for the good Hungarian wine! These vessels are more often than not erroneously ascribed in European collections, because so little is known about Hungarian pewter.

We conclude this notice of Austro-Hungarian flagons with an example (*Fig. 10*), kindly photographed for us by Doctor Karl Ruhmann of Vienna, whose generosity we have also laid under heavy contribution. Doctor Ruhmann took the photograph especially for us at the Niederösterreichisches Landesmuseum in Vienna.

Of the early seventeenth century, this superb lavabo set is interesting; first, because of its absolute authenticity — it was found built into a wall of a farm at Poisdorf, near Vienna — and second, because of its completeness and elegance. Probably it was hidden away from the approaching Turks, who invaded that region in the seventeenth century.

The beautifully simple basin has a raised centre, upon which stands the ewer, of compressed baluster form. We know of only one similar example. Such an outfit, we may be sure, was, even in its day, a very desirable possession.

Having thus reviewed some of the flagons produced by Austro-Hungarian craftsmen in pewter, we now come to their more decorative wares, wares, that is, which correspond in motive with the *Edelzinn* of the German craftsmen and the *Orfèvrerie d'Étain* of the French pewterers of the late sixteenth and early seventeenth centuries. Examples showing relief work, repoussé, hammer work, and various kinds of engraving will subsequently be discussed.

Fig. 10 — LAVABO SET (*early seventeenth century*)
From the Niederösterreichisches Landesmuseum, Vienna

The Fine Pewter of Austria-Hungary

By HOWARD HERSCHEL COTTERELL, F. R. HIST. S., *and* ROBERT M. VETTER

Figs. *1, 1a* — EWER AND BASIN OF
EDELZINN (*c. 1550*)
By Heimeran Wildner of Egeria,
in northwestern Bohemia. *Flagon
height*, 14¾ inches; *diameter of
basin*, 18 inches

IN A previous issue of AN-
TIQUES (September 1933) we
reviewed some of the flagons
produced by Austro-Hunga-
rian craftsmen. We now come to a
consideration of their more decora-
tive wares, which correspond in intent with the *Edelzinn* (noble pewter)
of the German pewterers and the *Orfèvrerie d'Étain* of their French
contemporaries of the late sixteenth and early seventeenth centuries.

Relief Pewter

The realms of this ancient Empire lay open to the dumping of the
surplus productions of German — and especially Nuremberg — pewterers. Consequently one could, until quite recently, pick up good examples
of the latter's well-known *Edelzinn* in Austria and Hungary. This
process of dumping hurt the market for local producers of fine wares,
but nevertheless very successful efforts were made, examples of which

still exist. First, we may
note the figures of apostles,
in high relief on some of the
inverted bell-shaped bap-
tismal fonts already re-
ferred to, the advent of
which preceded by some
two hundred years the
German *Edelzinn* move-
ment. Of contemporary
ware we illustrate, in Figures 1 and 1*a*, a ewer and
basin from the Bertram
collection, which possess
all the characteristics of
Edelzinn. The maker of
these pieces was certainly
influenced by the *œuvre* of
Briot and Enderlein,
though failing quite to attain the suavity of contour
achieved especially by
Briot in his masterpieces.
But Heimeran Wildner
judged the possibilities of

pewter perhaps more soberly and more justly than did these classic
masters. He certainly possessed sound decorative feeling, and his general detail and structure, though of a more rough and ready sort and
somewhat sketchy, combine perhaps better with the nature of the
material — and thus produce a sounder *pewter* effect — than the too
refined and academic designs of Briot and Enderlein.

Blending Engraving with Repoussé

The addition should be noted, of some characteristic wavy engraving and a circle of repoussé
bosses, as a sort of *trait d'union* between the plain
and the relief surfaces. A further example of this
trait d'union is found in Figure 2, from the Ruhmann collection. It was made by Heimeran Wildner, Junior, of Egeria, at the end of the sixteenth
or beginning of the seventeenth century.

Moravian "Edelzinn"

In Moravia a school of pewterers successfully
attempted to emulate the German *Edelzinn*. With
their centre at Iglau — the town mark of which is
a hedgehog — they produced some very beautiful
types, all in high relief, examples of which, though
rare, still survive. Among these are specimens of
the so-called *Europa* plate (*Fig. 3*) from the Ruhmann collection. This school seems always to have
given to its products some personal or national
touch, by adding lenticular bosses and some engraving, thus demonstrating the fact that no soul-
less repetition was aimed at — as in the case of
some Nuremberg work — but the creation of a personal achievement.

Relief Work on Handles

A further phase of the *Edelzinn* fashion, we may regard the relief
decoration, already mentioned, on the backs of Hungarian handles.
A fine example, again from the Ruhmann collection, is shown in Figure
4. This custom may be regarded as a very early one, for we know already of relief work on the backs of the handles of several of the early
North German flagons. The same feature also occurs on Roman examples. This piece is also remarkable for the characteristic circles of
punched ornament around the lid, lip, and base. This type of handle

Fig. *2* — DISH (*late sixteenth or early seventeenth century*)
By Heimeran Wildner, Jr. *Diameter*, 13½ inches

Fig. *3* — SO-CALLED "EUROPA" PLATE (*c. 1620*)
Moravian work. *Diameter*, 18½ inches

continued in use in Eastern Hungary until the end of the century.

As has been pointed out in our French chapters, in later years relief work becomes a subservient factor of decoration and at the same time increasingly meaningless. Such is the case of the Austrian Church candlestick in Figure 5. This piece was recovered from the Austrian war-metal requisition of 1916, when many a fine piece of pewter was melted down and converted into ammunition during the Great War.

Figure 6 shows a porringer of the second half of the eighteenth century, from Doctor Ruhmann's collection. Very few porringers were made in Austria, and this somewhat crude example was made at Innsbruck, Tyrol. A Bishop's head is represented on the centre panel, which follows the tradition of *Edelzinn* quite closely; but the irregular Rococo ears, cast in relief, are, in contrast with the body, quite Tyrolese in character.

Fig. 6 — Austrian Porringer (*after 1750*)
Diameter, 8 ¼ inches; *overall,* 13 ¼ inches

Hammer Beating of Dishes

We have referred above to repoussé bosses as a form of ornamentation, but such hammer-work must not be confounded with the beating or hammering of plain plates and dishes, whereby the depressions made by the pewterer's hammer, appear in circles. This latter process had the effect of strengthening the metal, whereas the main idea of the repoussé bosses was decorative. Surface hammer-beating would seem to have been widely and skilfully applied by sixteenth- and early seventeenth-century Hungarian pewterers. Many examples of this technique are still preserved in the Hungarian National Museum. Three of them, found in excavations at Vojszka, Comitat Bács-Bodrog, South Hungary, will

Fig. 4 — Hungarian Flagon (*c. 1650*)
Observe relief work on the handle, and circles of punched ornament around lid, lip, and base

Fig. 5 — Austrian Church Candlestick (*c. 1700*)
Relief work subservient.
Height, 23 ¾ inches

serve to illustrate varieties of the type with their clear examples of the "three-touch" system of marking.

Figure 7 has the most unusual feature of an inner fillet, at the junction of the rim with the bouge, and is of the wide-rimmed type. Figure 8 is of the narrow-rimmed type. Figure 9 gives an exceptionally clear illustration of the hammer depressions, and Figure 10 is a plate of the same type and period, without the hammer marks but with an uncommon inner molding in the well. Figure 9 gives an impression of the Wratislava (Breslau) Gothic *W* mark, *circa* 1500, whereas the other three bear the *O* mark of Sopron (Oedenburg) and are of the same period.

Styles of Engraving

Earlier in this discussion, mention is made of the popularity of engraving in Austria-Hungary. Perhaps nowhere else in Europe was it more universally employed. This engraving may be identified in three more or less distinct grades, to be described as "academic," "popular," and "peasant" styles. Between these it is not possible, of course, to lay down hard and fast lines of demarcation, but examples will illustrate our meaning.

Figure 11 shows a narrow-rimmed dish, dated *1596* in the engraving. This illustrates the academic style, wherein the work is done by a sure and vigorous hand by means of the burin and without resorting to wrigglework. The distribution is perfect. Only a highly trained engraver and draughtsman, well versed in the conventional academics of his time, could have done it. The piece is in the Museum Carolino Augusteum at Salzburg, a town where much of this class of work was done.

Figure 12, from the Hungarian National

Figs. 7, 8 — Hungarian Hammered Plates (*c. 1500*)
From Oedenburg

Fig. 9 — HUNGARIAN HAMMERED PLATE
(c. 1500)
From Breslau. Showing the hammer depressions very clearly

Fig. 10 — HUNGARIAN PLATE, UNHAMMERED
(c. 1500)
From Oedenburg. Diameters of this and preceding plates range from 15 to 18 inches

who may have received this beautiful gift on her wedding day.

"Methkrugs" and Nutmeg Mugs

Turning from plates and dishes, we give three examples from the Museum Carolino Augusteum. Figure 14 illustrates a late seventeenth-century tankard, known in Austria as a "Methkrug," being used for mead, a drink made by fermenting bees' honey and formerly very popular in Austria. Similar tankards, raised on three feet and provided with various devices for holding nutmeg and spices, were used

Museum, gives us an example of the popular style. It is a so-called wedding plate, dated *1679*, and bears the mark of Löcse (Leutschau), Northern Hungary. The engraving is beautifully done, though by no means academic, the lines being slightly wriggled and not so easy-flowing as in the preceding example; but the expression of the central scene is charmingly naïve and appeals to popular feeling.

To illustrate the peasant style we have chosen Figure 13, dated *1709*, from Doctor Ruhmann's collection and made by the Iglau (Moravian) pewterer Jonas Ziegler. One is immediately reminded of the peasant paintings on woodwork, of woolwork, and of the ceramics of the Slav peasants of that region. The wrigglework is coarse, and the broad tulips and other flowers would seem to have been designed to delight the heart of some rural bride,

Fig. 11 — AUSTRO-HUNGARIAN DISH (1596)
No wrigglework. "Academic style." *Diameter,* 16 inches

which, to this day, is always accomplished by using a hot infusion of wood ashes, as a solvent, with a handful of *pewter grass* (Equisetum Hyemale) as an abrasive. Anyone who has these ingredients at hand may convince himself of their marvelous action upon the metal.

Dealers have a penchant for talking of *silver-tin* and *silver-pewter,* implying that some silver has entered into the composition of the metal; but metallurgists know how badly these two metals unite, giving a brittle substance unsuitable for any purpose. That romantic notion, therefore, must be exploded.

"Pitschen"

In Figure 15 the reader will recognize one of the most frequently recurring types of Continental pewter, though specimens so beautifully engraved are very rare.

for hot beer, the legs serving to keep the hot surface from marking the table. This piece was made in Radstadt, a small town in the Salzburg district. With its clear Renaissance moldings and the graceful sweep of its sides, it bears strong resemblance to contemporary Augsburg work. The metal in it is whiter than silver.

"Silberzinn"

This dazzling whiteness which occurs frequently in the pewter of Austrian Alpine regions accounts for its designation as *Silberzinn,* or silver-tin. Besides freedom from lead, this whiteness owes much to the method of cleaning,

Fig. 12 — ENGRAVED WEDDING PLATE (1679)
From north Hungary. Some wrigglework. "Popular style"

Fig. 13 — ENGRAVED DISH (1709)
From Moravia. "Peasant style" with wrigglework

Fig. 14 — Austrian Tankard (*late 1600's*)
Known as a *methkrug*. Made near Salzburg. *Height*, 7 inches

These articles are known locally as *pitschen* (corruption of the French *pichet*), and were used for carrying and holding wine, honey, oil, syrup, and so on. The prismatic shape tends to prevent accidental unscrewing when the vessel is carried against the side. It was likewise an easy pattern to make, especially as the screw and screw cap might be bought ready made from the pewter merchants of Nuremberg, where the manufacture of pewter screw threads was carried on as a specialty. The piece illustrated is a fine example

by Hans Lehrl of Salzburg; but many are of very poor metal, and it would seem that, in the end, the peasants crudely fashioned their own from sheet metal.

In the article on German pewter, reference was made to guild emblems, and how eagerly they were sought by Continental collectors, so much so that at Munich and Nuremberg shops are full of reproductions without value to the collector. The emblems of Figure 16, however, became the property of the Museum Carolino Augusteum, long before the era of the falsifier and almost before old pewter had begun to receive appreciation even from collectors. The set represents a caskmaker's mallet and caulking chisel, both hollow and closed by screw caps. Probably the mallet held wine and the chisel some more potent liquor. They are dated *1746*, and the Salzburg mark bears the date *1741*. The engraving is done in free lines, without wriggle, by a trained engraver.

Figure 17 illustrates a square *pitschen* from the Ruhmann collection. The handle is missing from the cover. On two sides the engraving shows the Austrian double eagle, and on the third and fourth respectively *Die Erden* (Earth) — a girl planting flowers — and *Das Wasser* (Water) — a girl washing her hands. The *pitschen* illustrated in Figure 18 is also

Fig. 15 — Pitschen (*1680*)
Used for a variety of liquids

Fig. 16 — Guild Emblems (*c. 1740*)
Caskmaker's mallet and caulking chisel, from Salzburg

from Doctor Ruhmann's collection.

A Styrian beer mug, also from the Ruhmann collection, is illustrated in Figure 19. Its engraving depicts the Annunciation. With it we conclude the series of examples of the Austro-Hungarian pewter engraver's art. Plainer types and Rococo forms will be discussed in a later article.

Fig. 17 — Groz Pitschen (*seventeenth century*)
Height, 11 ½ inches

Fig. 18 — Pitschen (*early eighteenth century*)
From Graz.
Height, 10 inches

Fig. 19 — Styrian Beer Mug (*eighteenth century*)
The engraving portrays the Annunciation

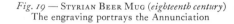

The Fine Pewter of Austria-Hungary

By Howard Herschel Cotterell, F. R. Hist. S., *and* Robert M. Vetter

IN THE November 1934 number of ANTIQUES we discussed the decorative, engraved wares of the Austro-Hungarian pewter craftsmen. Examples illustrated were mainly of the sixteenth and seventeenth centuries. We now turn to the plainer types, produced from the close of the seventeenth century through the 1700's.

"Grained" Work

A further and, so far as our knowledge goes, exclusively Austrian method of surface decoration is shown in Figures 1 and 2. Here the surface is roughened with a punch, giving it a grained effect. Figure 1 shows a curiously lobed *Pitschen* which has been treated in this way. A still finer example — likewise from Doctor Ruhmann's collection — is pictured in Figure 2. This piece, dated *1717*, is six and three-fourths inches high, and was formerly the property of the linen weavers at Admont, Styria. It is fitted with a highly baroque handle and "cleft" thumbpiece,

Figs. 1 and 2 (above, left and centre)— "Grained" and Lobed "Pitschen" and "Grained" Tankard (eighteenth century)

Fig. 3 (above, right) — Measure (eighteenth century)

Figs. 4 and 5 (left and right) — "Pitschen" (eighteenth century)

the measure shown in Figure 3. Again from the Ruhmann collection, this piece will, in view of earlier references, at once suggest to the serious student, though in a somewhat distorted fashion, the Dutch "Rembrandt" flagon (see *Fig. 55, Part III* of this series; Frontispiece, ANTIQUES, May 1927). Thus we see how the tentacles of a so-called local type may extend far beyond the confines of their own particular sphere. The fixed thumb-piece of the French *erect* type, and the hooked handle, are also elements in construction rather alien to Austrian ideas and, did one not recognize as Austrian the assay marks on the lip, and had one not encountered the same type of measure more than once on Austrian soil, and thus been convinced of its local origin, one would have been compelled to omit it from this chapter as a freakish exception.

In Figures 4 through 11 and Figure 13 we give illustrations

Fig. 6 — BARREL-SHAPED TANKARD
Popular in northern Austria during the eighteenth and early nineteenth centuries, and varying in quality and capacity. *Height, 8 inches*

Fig. 7 — STANDARD TYROLESE "STITZEN" (*18th century*)
Usually marked inside the lid. Occurs in heights from 2½ inches up; here, 11½ inches. Small size locally known as *Frackerl*. Note mascaron handle finial

features culled from contemporary silversmith's work. Doctor Ruhmann's fine photograph well reproduces this grained surface.

Plainer Types of Austrian Pewter

To Western readers the pieces hitherto illustrated may savor of the overelaborate. That wholly undecorated pieces of noble and refined simplicity may also be discovered in Austria is evidenced by

of some of the plainer and more frequently recurring types of Austrian pewter vessels, mostly from the Ruhmann collection. Accompanying captions afford adequate descriptions.

Scarcity of Viennese Pewter

M. Riff, in his notes on French pewter in this series, pointed out the reasons for the almost entire disappearance of *Parisian* pewter, and we can do nothing more than reiterate his remarks as to the

Fig. 8 (*above*) — MARK FROM TYROLESE "STITZEN"
Showing customary method of marking pieces such as that of Figure 7

Fig. 9 (*left*) — AUSTRIAN "STITZEN" (*seventeenth century*)
Overlapping lid. Of the early spreading base, lipless type, preceding the lipped variety. From Wels, in upper Austria

Fig. 10 (*right*) — "STITZEN" (*c. 1880*)
By Christof Götzl, of Egeria (Bohemia). Typical of the locality and more frequent than attractive

disappearance of pewter made in the old Austrian capital.

Vienna, a highly important centre of the pewter industry, was distinguished for the high quality and elegance of its productions. A few of these we are able to place before our readers, though the guild flagon shown in Figure 12 hardly deserves enthusiastic commendation. This piece is in the Vienna Municipal Museum and was photographed for us especially by Doctor Ruhmann. It belonged to the Trunkmakers' Guild, the members of which had their names and birthplaces engraved upon the sides of its almost cylindrical body.

This quaint piece is dated *1740*. Perhaps more humorous than elegant are the gargoylelike lip and the exceptional knop which serves as a thumbpiece.

Fig. 11 — PEAR-SHAPED FLAGON (*c. 1800*)
Typical of Brünn, the capital of Moravia

Fig. 12 — VIENNESE GUILD FLAGON (*1740*)
Originally the property of the Trunkmakers' Guild

"*Imperial*" Beakers

The beaker illustrated in Figure 14, from Doctor Ruhmann's collection, is one of a series which yearly, from the reign of the great empress Maria Theresa (*1740–1780*) until the last of the Hapsburgs abdicated in 1918, were personally presented by the emperors and empresses, with a money gift, to the twelve oldest men and the twelve oldest women in the city of Vienna. Thus, twenty-four of these beakers were annually brought into use. They were always alike, in shape, finish, and decoration, and many were made by pewterers of the Stoll family, who seem to have held the appointment to supply

them to the court. The one illustrated is dated *1837*. Examples are found in many collections, sometimes with the dates fraudulently altered, anticipating in some cases the date when the custom originated!

The dainty elegance, however, of Viennese pewter may best be seen in the lobed dish illustrated in Figure 15 from the Vetter collection. Dating from about the year *1700*, this piece is made of the very best metal, meticulously finished and equipped with finely cut handles.

In a subsequent, and concluding, article we will consider baroque, or rococo, forms of Austro-Hungarian pewter.

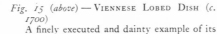

Fig. 15 (above) — VIENNESE LOBED DISH (*c. 1700*)
A finely executed and dainty example of its type. *Length*, 18 inches

Fig. 13 (left) — SPOUTED FLAGON (*c. 1700*)
Occasionally but infrequently met in the Tyrolese Mountains. Type consists of a lipless *Stitzen* with long spout, hexagonal or round in section, steadied by a bridge-piece as in Bernese and other Swiss spouted flagons

Fig. 14 (right) — VIENNESE "IMPERIAL" BEAKER (*1837*)
Memorial of an old Austrian imperial custom. *Height*, 5 ½ inches

Index